EUROPEAN CINEMAS IN THE TELEVISION AGE

Dorota Ostrowska and Graham Roberts

Contributions by

Gunhild Agger
Valeria Camporesi
Luisa Cigognetti
Will Lehman
Magrit Grieb
Malgorzata Radkiewicz
Pierre Sorlin
Heather Wallis

EDINBURGH UNIVERSITY PRESS

© in this edition Edinburgh University Press, 2007
© in the individual contributions is retained by the authors

Edinburgh University Press Ltd
22 George Square, Edinburgh

Typeset in Sabon and Gill Sans by
Servis Filmsetting Ltd, Manchester, and
printed and bound in Great Britain by
Cromwell Press Ltd, Trowbridge, Wilts

A CIP record for this book is available from the British Library

ISBN 978 0 7486 2308 2 (hardback)
ISBN 978 0 7486 2309 9 (paperback)

The right of the contributors to be identified as authors of this work has been
asserted in accordance with the Copyright, Designs and Patents Act 1988.

CONTENTS

PREFACE

The existing scholarship about European cinemas focuses on the questions dictated by textual formal analysis and its ideological implications. The structures of film production, financing and distribution have little bearing on the predominant understanding of the European cinemas. *European Cinemas in the Television Age* is a radical attempt to develop the understanding of the production structures of European cinemas from the perspective of their relationship to national and transnational television industries and thus to create a new direction for the debate about European cinemas. In every European country television has transformed economic, technological and aesthetic terms in which the process of cinema production had been conducted. Television's growing popularity drastically reshaped cinema's audiences and forced governments to introduce policies to regulate the interaction between cinema and television in the changing and dynamic audio-visual environment. The recognition of the impact of television upon European cinemas offers a more authentic and richer picture of cinemas in Europe in which popular and commercial production not only co-exists and cross-breeds with the art house one but virtually makes the latter possible through subsidising, distributing and exhibiting.

The central objective of this book is to demonstrate the ways in which the range of changes and innovations brought about by television (a complex and multifaceted phenomenon) allows us to open the debate about cinema in new directions and possibly to redefine the existing concept of cinema from the perspective of television.

The nature of film production in Europe is national. The involvement of television with cinema also takes place on the national level. For this reason we have preserved the focus on the individual countries in the central chapters of the book. We are most grateful to a number of national experts who have contributed parts or whole chapters to this part of our project (whilst noting that any general thematic points drawn from an overview of the national cases are of course our own). A Europe-wide survey has allowed us to investigate some broad categories in which television's impact on cinema can be considered in terms of four key categories: economics, practice, technology and aesthetics. The examination of the impact of television has allowed us to address a number of key concepts in European cinema(s) in new and more realistic ways.

In spite of the efforts of such scholars as Ginette Vincendeau and Susan Hayward 'national cinema' is still mostly understood in terms of art film.

Historically, art cinema has dominated critical construction of the European film. A study of national cinema in Europe from the perspective of the impact of television takes into account genre cinema/popular cinema and not only art cinema. Complex ways of financing films which are provided by private television companies, which like Canal Plus could be a French station investing in various European countries, not only widens the range of films made but also complicates the issue of defining a film product in strictly national terms

Auteur/individual film-makers are associated with the creation of European art cinema. Critics like Vincendeau argue for the recognition of popular auteurs (she quotes Almodovar and Tavernier in this category) who are both cross-over and mainstream film-makers. TV has played an important role in financing these film-makers' films. Hence, the exploration of the concept of auteur in the context of television allows us to investigate the notion of popular auteurs and to understand authorship in the industrial, social and cultural context as opposed to being just an expression of an individual genius.

Film texts are the primary source of the current definition of cinema. By focusing on the role of TV we have been able to examine the industrial/financial complex in which these film texts are produced. As a result, the understanding of cinema expands. In particular we have been able to come to terms with a number of key questions including: How does television transform/modify the concept of national cinema? What is the impact of television on the concept of film auteur? How does television change the nature of the film text?

Throughout the work on this volume we have been inspired, puzzled and (admittedly) sometimes distracted by the accelerating changes in production, distribution and consumption of images. We are, as Graeme Harper has put it, experiencing: 'the new Cinema of Complexity' (Harper 2005: 90). This cinema of the DVD and download world has potentialities for experimentation and a do-it-yourself ethos. There are possibilities for the democratisation of production via digital film-making even for an increased role for the viewer in arranging and manipulating the narrative (or otherwise) of 'films'. It is impossible to ignore such phenomena whilst thinking through the issues involved in our project. Nonetheless – even as we enter what might be a 'post-television age' – we felt it worthwhile to look back over a half century of relationship between the two audio-visual mass media. Not least we have a need to build on previous experience for a fast-changing complex present and future. For, as *Screen International* has editorialised, the future (of cinema) has nothing to do with technology – this is just a means of transport' (*Screen International*, 19 May 2006: 2). The art of cinema has proven again and again its extraordinary resilience while facing all various changes and revolutions. We should remain hopeful for 'cinema has clearly proven itself to be an invention with the future' (*Screen International*, 19 May 2006: 2).

Graham Roberts and Dorota Ostrowska

Summer 2006

ACKNOWLEDGEMENTS

Thanks to:

All of the contributors (as authors, researchers and interviewees) to individual national studies contained in this volume.

All our friends at the Institute of Communications Studies, University of Leeds, who saw us through all the stages of this project, in particular Stephen Hay, Simon Popple, John Edmonds, Isobel Rich, Cristina Archetti, Myria Georgiou, Vibha Metha and Robin Brown.

Everybody at EUP – and in particular Sarah Edwards for uncomplaining responses to requests for 'just a little more time . . . something really interesting has come up . . .'

John Orr for his ongoing interest in this project.

Dorota Ostrowska –
I would like to thank my parents, Irena and Jan Ostrowscy, and my brother, Wojciech, who have always been there for me, following the progress on the book and supporting me in their own unique ways. I would like to thank the Louis Le Prince Centre for the financial support, which allowed me to conduct interviews in Denmark and undertake research in Paris and in Warsaw.

I would like to thank Stephen Hay for helping us to arrange a range of interviews in France, which proved to be invaluable for the completion of this book.

I would like to make special thanks to Søren Falgaard who was helping me with researching the Danish chapter. I also would like to thank the staff of the Danish Film Institute, Filmoteka Narodowa and Archiwum Telewizji Polskiej TVP SA in Warsaw.

I would like to thank Heather Wallis for stimulating discussions about filmmaking and scriptwriting, for her ongoing support and care, and for opening widely the doors of her home and welcoming me so generously on so many occasions. I would like to thank Charlotte and Sammy who grew up together with the project for just being there and most of all I would like to thank Graham for giving me a chance to work on this book with him, for taking my hand and leading me through all the stages of the process. He was holding me when I was falling.

Graham Roberts –
All of the above of course – minus myself and adding Dorota Ostrowska who

has the invaluable knack of letting you think you are helping her when it is invariably t'other way round. I have received moral and intellectual support from a number of colleagues at Leeds and beyond including Lucia Nagib, Paul Cooke, Graeme Harper, Rob Stone and Owen Evans. I would also like to publicly express my thanks to friends, neighbours and family (including Shirley Roberts, all the Days and the good people of the Back Lane) – you have no idea how much I need you to keep on keeping on. Most of all to Heather Wallis – good enough a friend to tell me when I may not be getting it *quite* right.

CONTRIBUTORS

In addition to the authors the following scholars have contributed national chapters to this volume:

Gunhild Agger, Associate Professor of Communications at Aalborg University, a member of the 'Aesthetics of Television' Research Program, and co-editor with Jens F. Jensen of *The Aesthetics of Television* (Aalborg University Press, 1999).

Valeria Camporesi, Universidad Autónoma de Madrid, author of *Mass Culture and the Defence of National Tradition* (European Press Academic Publishing, 2002).

Luisa Cigognetti, Institute PARI, Bologna and Pierre Sorlin, Emeritus Professor of sociology of the audiovisual media, University of Paris III, author of *European Cinemas, European Societies* (1991) and *Italian National Cinema* (1996).

Margit Grieb, Assistant Professor of German, University of South Florida, author of *Transformation of the (Silver) Screen: Film after New Media* (forthcoming) and Will Lehman, Associate Professor, University of Florida.

Małgorzata Radkiewicz, Assistant Professor at the Institute of Media and Audio-Visual Arts at Jagiellonian University, Kraków.

Heather Wallis, Teaching Fellow in Cinema, Institute of Communications Studies, Leeds co-author (with Graham Roberts) of *Introducing Film* and *Key Film Texts* (Arnold, 2001 and 2002).

This book is dedicated to

Dorota's mother, father and brother and Graham's mother

As well as Charlotte Sam and all the children of the age of complexity

Oh brave new world that has such things in it ...

1. INTRODUCTION: A CULTURAL ECOLOGY OF FILM AND TELEVISION IN EUROPE

As Groucho Marx once put it: 'I find television very educating. Every time somebody turns on the set I go into the other room and read a book' or to (misquote) another famous Marx . . . 'A spectre is haunting European cinema(s) – the spectre of Television.'

Perhaps television has been haunting cinema from day one. There exists a brochure by the Portuguese Professor Adriano de Paiva entitled *La téléscopie électrique basée sur l'emploi du sélénium* published in Porto in 1880. Laurent Semat deposited a 'brevet' (FR 321.876) for 'un téléphote' (un appareil permettant la transmission à distance des images animées) in June 1902 (the 'brevet' was published 22 January 1903[1] i.e. less than a year after Méliès' *Le Voyage dans la lune* and before Edwin S. Porter had launched 'American' cinema with *The Great Train Robbery*.

James Monaco makes a succinct distinction between the audio-visual media by reference to the 1960s work of Samuel Beckett – a play called *Play*, a film called *Film* and *Eh Joe* (a television play):

> For Beckett, the stage play is deep focus mise en scene, not controlled montage. . . . *Play* emphasizes the interaction between and among characters and the relative freedom of the observer to mould the experience . . . *Film*, on the other hand, emphasizes . . . the drama between subject and artist, and the observer's relative lack of involvement in the process. *Eh Joe* . . . cannily emphasizes the unusual psychological intimacy of this medium'. (Monaco 1981: 349–51)

A key element of this book is to chart the similarities and differences – even convergences – between the media in a period roughly bracketed by the end of World War II in Europe and the present day (where we begin to take cognisance of at least the possibility of a post-cinema and post-TV world). Within our study there are interesting parallels but major differences with Hollywood's relationship with US network TV so well documented and analysed in Tino Balio's collection *Hollywood in the Age of Television*. Part 1 of that volume is entitled 'Responding to Network Television'. The use of the word 'responding' (Balio 1990) is apposite. Seen from cinema's point of view the relationship to TV has largely been responsive (even reactive). Whilst there is general acceptance that cinema cannot live without 'them' (TV), there is nonetheless a clear position (at least within 'film studies') that 'they' are leaching away whatever cultural power cinema did have. There is clearly a qualitative connection here to European cinema's relationship to Hollywood. That particular relationship remains largely a subtext in this volume for two reasons. First, the story has been told elsewhere (and brilliantly by Puttnam and Elsaesser from very different perspectives). Second, because the 'battle' against Hollywood was over in any real sense before the historical remit of this book:

> By the mid-1920s, the sway of America's cultural industries was so powerful that some Europeans questioned whether old-world states still exercised sovereignty over their citizens' leisure. In England, 'the bulk of picture goers are Americanized to an extent that makes them regard the British film as a foreign film,' commented a *London Daily Express* writer in 1927. (de Grazia 1989: 54)

Overarching the period of the 'TV age' hung a question as to whether cinema had much of a resonance at all. Thus Monaco could write – confidently – of the: 'END OF CINEMA':

> By 1980 it was clear that it was no longer possible to make a distinct separation between what we call film and what we know as video, or television. These various forms of audiovisual narrative have been seen as separate – even antagonistic – for more than thirty years. Now, they must be regarded as parts of the same continuum . . . (Monaco 1981: 302)

In technological terms this media convergence is ever more the case. However Monaco continues in a vein which today seems vaguely anachronistic and certainly Anglophone-centric: 'Despite its well publicised economic gains in the seventies, commercial fiction film-making has grown ever closer to the television industry. In fact a balanced view of film and television now should describe the former as a subcategory of the latter' (Monaco 1981: 302–3). In fact one of the aims of this book is to highlight a rather more complex relationship between two mediums, closely related in technological and functional terms, which may at times look conflictual even subjugational (economically or aesthetically) but is actually much more a matter of shifting forces and tensions.

POLITICAL ECONOMY

The present volume began with one of its authors formulating a project with a very similar title – but rather different, more 'Monaco-ian' hypothesis – that wished to focus on what could be termed the 'political economy' of the relationship of film and TV in Europe in the second half of the twentieth century. It was very much a project seeking to explore the relationships between political and economic institutions and processes. It took as a given that resources were scarce and which 'laws' operated to regulate the distribution of those resources. Thus the story of 'European cinemas in the TV age' was to draw on the study of economics, policy and political science in terms of how (cultural) institutions operate within their commercial environment. Much of the thinking (conscious or not) behind the original project drew on the belief that central to a study of the cinema–TV relationship was a sense of 'dependency' (with reference to the work of Andre Gunder Frank or Immanuel Wallerstien). With this assumption came an a priori position that cinema had become peripheral to 'audio-visual' production, distribution and consumption and that TV was happy to keep it that way. This 'political economy' *weltanschung* would allow for a study of 'European cinemas in the TV age' to concentrate on the economics (or at least economically driven shaping factors) of institutions within and external to the audio-visual industries and the identification of forces of domination within the field. As Susan Hayward (in apocalyptic mood) puts it: 'Placed at such a disadvantage, cinema has had to adapt its own film-making practices which has meant, in great measure, being a post-aesthetic Abel to an image-conscious Cain' (Hayward 1993: 295).

Unfortunately for the original project – though rather fortunately for our study – we (by now two authors) found that the facts did not fit the model. It is not that concepts of (Gramscian) hegemony or Bourdieusian 'habitus' and 'field' (particulary as developed in pieces collected in *The Logic of Practice* (1990) and *The Field of Cultural Production* (1993)) have been abandoned. Indeed investigations of internal and external power relations and professional 'habitus' are central to most of this volume and expressed overtly in the UK and 'production' chapters. However what became clear from a holistic reading of the national chapters was that the relationship between the audio-visual media had to be seen in a rather more complex, even organic light. Valeria Camporesi – in the chapter on Spain – grapples with the nature of an 'intersection'. Our German contributors point to the complex nature of 'an astonishing mêlée of cooperation and antagonism'. In Italy it was noted that the cinema business as a whole was supported through crisis after crisis by RAI (whilst the state broadcaster also allowed artists and craftspeople to continue to function and develop). Valeria Camporesi identifies how 'interchanges between the two media did work as a creative driving force'. In every chapter of this volume we find what Camporesi describes as 'the filmmakers, who would come back and forth from television to cinema, or reverse, asserting themselves as good professionals in the two media . . .' In Germany Margit Grieb and Will Lehman found it 'difficult to trace this interplay as either productive or hostile to either medium's development, it can certainly be characterized as a formative relationship'. It was the German chapter which highlighted the concept of 'amphibious film' and thus introduced organic even biological terminology to our discourse. Instead of 'forces' and 'fields of power' we began to think through a more (cultural) ecology analysis.

Cultural Ecology

'Cultural ecology', as developed by Julian Steward in his *Theory of Culture Change: the Methodology of Multilinear Evolution* (1955), is the study of 'ecology' (the study of the living organisms and how they are affected by interactions between themselves and their environment – literally the study of the household) but factoring in the actions, reactions and interactions of humankind and social groupings. In particular 'cultural ecology' stresses the study of adaptive processes i.e. the key factor in the relationship central to this book. Thus 'cultural ecology' is a good fit for a study of two so closely related 'organisms' as TV and cinema, particularly as they are so closely linked in terms of technological and cultural parentage and are inextricably linked in terms of material dependency and at the same time compete for resources and audience. Because 'cultural ecology' can work so fruitfully with and develop upon political economy we can keep in view artistic-cultural issues whilst developing a model of the social and political forces at work in the audio-visual environment. Such an approach also allows us to continue to utilise more traditionally arts and social sciences approaches (including even textual and formal analysis – as we do in our 'cinematic forms' chapter) whilst holding in view the bigger picture of the field we are discussing.

Within this 'ecology' our national chapters have thrown up relationships that are more or less ambiguous, mutually beneficial and continuing in their complexity and potential. Thus we can portray 'British cinema under the spell of TV (Meet Mr Lucifer)' in which UK cinema is fast turning into TV and at the same time note that in Denmark it was the liberty of experiments in (children's) TV that had been so formative for the future film-makers of Dogme. Thus TV acted as a vehicle for the renewal of the art of cinema. Breaking away from a unidirectional flow model in Germany the 'Screen Wars' have actually produced an interplay 'characterized as a formative relationship'. And in Spain 'bipolar visions' are actually 'unified realities'.

Several of our national chapters have pointed (however guardedly) to potential future success. Thus in Spain 'the blurring of borders between the two media might be an interesting development for the good . . .' and in Italy (where cinema and television are characterised as both collaborators and threat): 'Both media are under a serious threat, collaboration would help them face the danger.' This need to look forward is illustrated particularly keenly in our French chapter where it is noted that: 'This culture is rapidly becoming history' and thus it is debatable what can be considered 'cinema' at all.

Problems of definition and (e)valuation have occurred in our national and thematic chapters to a point where we are forced to the conclusion that we have not yet learned how to think clearly about the result of media convergence and are only now beginning to take faltering steps in how to discuss and make sense of such an age. As we enter a post-TV or even post-cinema age we can gain from a historical overview of the period that has gone before. In particular we must be careful not to fall into earlier critical discourses in which new media, such as television, have been treated as 'unwanted growth'. Rather we must continue to carefully observe the evolution of the audio-visual ecology, not least so as not to do it irreparable harm.

NOTE

1. http://histv2.free.fr/cadrehistory

2. BRITAIN: MEET MR LUCIFER: BRITISH CINEMA UNDER THE SPELL OF TV

Graham Roberts and Heather Wallis

On 22 August 1932 the British Broadcasting Corporation began low-definition television broadcasts using Baird mechanical equipment while encouraging Electrical and Musical Industries (EMI) to develop electric TV. British broadcast TV had a stuttering start with less than 300 sets using the Baird or Marconi-EMI system. Until 1937 TV reception was only available in London area. The medium was struggling without a reason for audiences to watch. That reason was supplied by an event of national interest – the Coronation of King George VI in May 1937. However, the new medium's faltering steps towards a national profile were dealt a blow on 1 September 1939 when, with war two days away, all TV transmissions were stopped. In the war years there was no broadcast TV in the British Isles. There were no resources for development and the existing equipment if operational could be targeted by night bombers. Nonetheless a television committee had been set up by the National Government as early as 1943.

The 1943 Commons Select Committee report stated baldly if somewhat optimistically: 'television has come to stay'. The Committee also gave a strong steer that after the war the BBC should continue to control it and that the coverage should be extended to six 'most populous areas'. TV returned on 7 June 1946 with coverage of the anniversary of victory parades. This was far from a national event. Television sets were comparatively expensive in contrast to the US where costs were kept relatively low due to volume of production plus higher wages. In the UK a television receiver cost seven times the average weekly wage. In any event the coverage was far from national as the BBC seemed remarkably reluctant to build transmitters. Thus in 1947 there were only 14,560 TV licences in UK. By 1948 there were 45,560 licences, a figure which only rose to 100,000 plus by 1950. Meanwhile cinema attendance was starting a steady decline from its attendance peak of 1946 (1,635 million).[1]

It is useful to note that the 1,000 million plus cinema attendance phenomenon was relatively short-lived in the UK. Attendance only hit 1,000 million in 1940 and continued steadily to rise during the war years. From the peak of 1946 attendance steadily fell by 3–4 per cent (beginning in a period well before widespread TV ownership). The 'golden age' of attendance was fuelled by audiences watching American films. This situation was a very long-term reality. Rachel Low (1949: 3) notes: 'in 1910 France provided 36% of films released in the UK and the US 28%'. Thus the British (unlike their contemporaries on the continent who had no access to Hollywood films during the war) had enthusiastically watched American films through the war years. Naturally the failure of British films to significantly penetrate their home market continued in the post-war period.

Nonetheless some of the enthusiasm for cinema-going was predicated upon the rise to national and international prominence of a number of key figures in British cinema such as Michael Powell, David Lean and Carol Reed. At the same time the Rank Organisation began to expand into an exhibition-based empire embracing the Gaumont British Company (including the Gainsborough Studios) as well as studios at Pinewood and Denham and the Odeon cinema circuit. The Ealing Studio, under Michael Balcon, managed to succeed in attracting British audiences to culturally British material such as *Passport to Pimlico, Whisky Galore!* and *Kind Hearts and Coronets*, all made in 1949.

Thus at the turn of the decade, much as in the USA, it was far from certain that TV would rule the entertainment cosmos. The history of British television as a 'national' institution began in 1953. Twenty million viewers saw the coronation of Queen Elizabeth II and the number of sets doubled in a year. TV ceased to be a minority concern, not least because public houses and clubs were using TV to draw in customers.

In 1953 Ealing Studios made *Meet Mr Lucifer*; produced by Michael Balcon, directed by Anthony Pelissier and starring Stanley Holloway with Peggy Cummins, Barbara Murray and Jack Watling. Holloway appeared as Hollingsworth, an actor who is playing Lucifer in a repertory theatre pantomime. In between acts he disappears to the pub to rage against the 'goggle box' and its deleterious effects on theatre audiences. On his return to the theatre, while being hoisted through a trap door, Hollingsworth is knocked out. He 'meets' the real Lucifer who replaces him. Seizing his opportunity to inflict suffering on the ordinary folk of middle England Lucifer comes up with the most hellish device of all. His weapon of choice is television.

Meet Mr Lucifer's combination of contempt mixed with fear is illustrative of the British film industry's attitude to television; a reaction notably different to that seen in post-war US where 'the industry monitored developments closely and manoeuvred to get in on the ground floor of the new medium'.[2] The big difference between the US and UK film industry responses to TV is that it took many years for the British film companies to catch on to the opportunities, by which time the terms of trade could be set by the TV companies. Christine Geraghty has pointed out how 'Ironically *Meet Mr Lucifer* goes some way towards indicating what the attractions of television might be . . . the possibilities of the new medium in terms of domestic comfort and communal watching are indicated' (Geraghty 2000: 17).

Through the 1950s cinema attendance continued to decline although that decline actually slowed in 1953–4. It is possible to define a rather more dramatic 'break' in 1954–7 (6 to 7 per cent p.a.). The year 1957 can be seen as symbolic due to a slip in ticket sales below 1,000 million. British cinema continued to produce films particularly in a 'tradition of quality' manner though now aimed more firmly at an international market (often as co-productions). Films such as *Moby Dick* (1956) and *The Bridge on the River Kwai* (1957) judiciously mixed British and American themes and stars.

On a more prosaic level *Carry On Sergeant* (1958) started the long running film series and *The Quatermass Experiment* (1955) launched the Hammer horror 'studio'. British-based cinema was not dead. Nonetheless there is clear evidence of a steady decline in box-office share for UK films and that of a steadily shrinking box office. The long-term effect of this was even more serious as, since the initial negotiations for airing fees took place in the early 1950s, the levels of TV payments for film showings have been linked directly to box office receipts.

In November 1953 a Government White Paper recommended a new TV service with some private companies. Thus ITV was born of the Television Act July 1954 with its first broadcast (a banquet from the Guildhall in London) on 22 September 1955. The first advert shown was for Gibbs SR toothpaste ('tingling fresh') and 'What we want is Watneys.' National coverage was not completed until September 1962.

'Independent' TV (actually a cartel of commercial broadcasters) supplied rather more 'showbiz' fare than the BBC, largely because the executives in independent TV came from show-biz background not Oxbridge. ITV's top show was *Sunday Night at the London Palladium*. As a distributor of 'light entertainment' there was less emphasis on film showings than at the BBC.

The question of how ITV affected the cinema audience in the UK is moot. Did it change the audience and 'kill' British cinema?[3] Even in 1955 when the TV service covered 95 per cent of the UK only 4.5 million licences had been issued. Emmett, writing in 1956, claimed approximately 30 per cent of households had a TV licence breaking the figure down by 'class': 40 per cent of middle-class homes and 26 per cent of working class homes. (Emmett, 1956: 284). The uptake of TV in 'working class homes' was liable to be the big factor in falling cinema audiences. Thus Hand (2002: 13): 'The introduction of ITV can be said to have encouraged, rather than driven the adoption of television in lower income households.' In broad terms the introduction of ITV could be seen as a 'price cut' i.e. an extra station and more programmes rather than that the 'commercial' material was more appealing. Hand (2002: 6) points to another important cinema-affecting factor: 'the number of children in the household is an important determinant of television ownership. Emmett finds that the presence of (up to three) children in the household makes owning a television set more likely (Emmett 1956: 306).

We can (here) focus on a demographic issue. The birth of children correlates to less leisure time spent *particularly* away from the home (i.e. in 1950s terms the cinema). The decline in cinema attendance continued through the 1960s from 581 million tickets sold in 1959 to 214 million in 1969, indicating a possible correlation between the postwar baby-boom and the growth of home-bound entertainment such as TV.

The 1960s saw the launch of a most successful franchise with the first James Bond movie *Dr No* (Young, 1962). The same year saw the release of David Lean's epic *Lawrence of Arabia*, followed three years later by *Doctor Zhivago*. The early years of the decade were notable for a series of films with a realistic and hard edge influenced by Italian neo-realism, such as *A Taste of Honey* (Richardson, 1961), *A Kind of Loving* (Schlesinger, 1962), *Loneliness of the Long Distance Runner* (Richardson, 1962) and *Billy Liar* (Schlesinger, 1963) (the latter two enlivened by flashes of a more cineamatic 'nouvelle vague' feel).

John Caughie has noted that 'With a striking irony, it is precisely the kind of modest, naturalistic realism which people thought of as the mark of British art cinema . . . which became in the 1960s the mark of the prestige of British television drama' (Barr 1986: 199). Caughie also highlights that this trend of British TV (at least at its high-profile public service end) taking on the best attributes of British cinema for its own purposes was further developed and entrenched through the 1970s: 'Social realism and literary/historical adaptations: throughout the 70s the two co-existed, setting a standard, and securing for television a distinctive place within the national culture' (Barr 1986: 196–7). Thus for the cultural critic or the legendary man (or woman) on the Clapham omnibus the material for debate, discussion and social interaction was as likely to be the latest 'Play for Today' or episode of *Coronation Street* as the sports scores or *News of the World* scandal.

At the same time cinema had slipped in its artistic and cultural significance. As Margaret Dickson put it:

> 'Between the 1940s and the 1960s the role of the cinema in British society changed radically. From being a very influential mass medium, and an important business in its own right it became a minority entertainment and a sideline of the leisure industry.' (Dickson, in Curran and Porter 1983: 74)

By the 1960s there was no question that *the* leisure industry was TV.

The 1970s saw a continuing of the trend of relative decline and drift towards televisual language, while dwindling audiences could only be attracted to the crumbling theatres with such 1973 'blockbusters' as *The Sting* (Hill, USA) and *The Way We Were* (Pollack, USA). What was left of the British film production industry focused on some truly dreadful 'sit com' movies from the likes of Benny Hill, with *The Waiters* (1971). Many of these films were spin-offs of hit TV series such as *Steptoe and Son* (1972) and *Steptoe and Son Ride Again* (1973). There were no less than three 'On the Buses' films in the early 1970s.

Alongside this risible fare lay serious attempts at cinematic films from the likes of Ken Russell from *The Devils* (1971) to *Altered States* (1980) and Nicolas Roeg with *Walkabout* (1971) and *Don't Look Now* (1973). Both art-house directors needed a good deal of US money and distribution muscle from the likes of Warner Brothers to succeed internationally. British TV had funded Russell's earlier 'documentary' films but – in the form of BBC films – only caught up with Roeg in 1995 with *Two Deaths*.

Whatever the value (in terms of cinematic or narrative quality) of the British films of the 1960s and 1970s the steady decline in audiences continued into the 1980s until the all time low of 54 million in 1984. Independent British film-makers struggled to survive on small fiction development funds from arts organisations such as the BFI, the Arts Council and Greater London Arts. The amounts were small but crucially allowed film-makers to develop a relationship with the funding bodies which made progression into full production funding easier and more harmonious for both parties.

Cinema-going was revived as a leisure activity with the rise of the multiplex. However these new monster cinemas were home to *Jaws* and *Star Wars* rather than a revival of British movies exploring British themes. Such British fare increasingly had to find a home (and crucially a funding stream) via television in particular both old and new public service broadcasters.

The cosy duopoly of British TV came under concerted attack from Margaret Thatcher's Conservative governments of the 1980s. In 1981 pay per view 'satellite' programming was launched by BSB and the Home Office accepted the need for legislation on satellite broadcasting. In March 1982 Home Secretary William Whitelaw announced the first DBS licences. By the end of the year terrestrial television had its fourth channel – aptly named Channel 4.

Chariots of Fire (Hudson, UK, 1981) was released to acclaim and (quadruple) Oscar success. Colin Welland (the writer) gave his stirring (and fallacious) 'The British are coming' speech at the Academy Awards. The following year another Goldcrest production (admittedly financed with US venture capital), Richard Attenborough's *Gandhi*, took eight awards from eleven nominations. In the real world, on 16 January 1984, Sky TV arrived in the UK and soon became the dominant brand in subscription based broadcasting. Its key market driver was high profile sports events (not least a monopoly on top-flight soccer) but it also led the way in niche channels particularly for pay per view movies (initially invariably US product).

In the spring of 1984 the Conservative government announced that it was abolishing the Eady Levy. Instead British cinema was to be kept alive by the drip-feed of a hand-out of £2 million a year through a new private company, British Screen. In 1988 Goldcrest, makers of *Chariots of Fire*, went into liquidation. The industry's financial backers panicked and withdrew their venture capital. The 'star' directors (including Alan Parker and Ridley and Tony Scott) left for the greener pastures of Hollywood.

The sense off all-pervading gloom was captured in a key text of British cinema at its low point: *Take 10* by Jonathan Hacker and David Price. Their introductory chapter looks back at decades of failure and sets the tone of doubt about 'A British Culture? A British film industry?': 'A British audience, which might naturally be reluctant to watch foreign films, has always openly welcomed American cinema' sadly notes: 'This unconscious disposition'. Thus 'Cinematic education [of the British audience] has been effectively formed by Hollywood's finely crafted, glamorous entertainment. . . . Parochial comedies like *Porky's* . . . are more popular than a British equivalent like *Rita, Sue and Bob Too*' (Hacker and Price 1991: 1).

Hacker and Price – after rehearsing the usual possible 'definitions' (economic and cultural) of British cinema and the usual (cultural imperialism) reasons for its failure – tell the story of Simon Relph – Director of British Screen in 1980s – who 'asked some major advertising agencies to come up with a concept for an image to promote British cinema, not one of them could come up with anything constructive . . .' (Hacker and Price 1991: 1).

The surprising 33 per cent rise in box-office revenue in 1985 was thankfully not an example of 'dead cat bounce'. UK cinema attendances rose steadily from the 1984 nadir to reach more than 140 million by the turn of the century. It is well documented that this upturn was a direct result of the improvement in the cinema-going experience (Ballieu and Goodchild 2002: 105–8). Figures for 'British' share of this (slight) boom are increasingly difficult to identify in a 'globalised' media world.[4] However, as Ballieu and Goodchild relate: 'With rising cinema attendances, both exhibition and distribution channels came to be dominated by American interests. The trend for more multiplexes continued with greater concentration and intensification of American interests' (Ballieu and Goodchild 2002: 124).

The 1980s continued with 'increasing integration of independent cinema and public service television' (Caughie in Barr 1986: 201). By the end of the decade BBC2 and C4 were not only the true heirs of Reithian Public Service Television; the two broadcasters via BBC and Channel 4 Films were supplying what little domestic support there was left for independent British cinema. Caughie argues these 'institutional dependencies' were also fuelled by a need for (British) filmmakers' search for audience, quoting David Puttnam thus: 'I make films for people to see . . . In Britain the audience has an expressed preference to see my work on television' (Caughie in Barr 1986: 201–2).

It is not too much of a simplification to state that by the end of the 1980s British cinema was utterly dependent on British television for survival. Survive it did thanks to TV but its mode of survival was now utterly dependent on the needs of the small screen medium.[5] Whilst thankful for survival the 'film industry' was expected to on very small amounts of patronage (or interest) indeed:

> The BBC has worked with an annual budget for film production of approximately £5m through the 90s. This is tiny in film industry terms . . . BSkyB has invested small amounts in British films . . . in order to fulfil obligations for European content. . . . in 1998, Channel Four Films accounted for just one per cent of UK box-office revenues. (Miller in Murphy 2000: 41)

Independent writer-director Sue Clayton describes her experience of working with Film Four in the 1990s thus:

> In the early stages input was very relaxed and aware of the creative process; as I went through successive drafts and more partners came on board, the notes became much more pointed and specific, relating to issues around audience and marketability.[6]

Clayton perceives a difference between Film Four and the BBC in the kind of support offered to film-making:

> For the BBC the first commitment was still to the license fee payer, therefore although they released some of their dramas theatrically, this was only done after broadcast. Film Four was far more autonomous and certainly in my case did not appear to consider either the aesthetic or practical aspects of TV broadcast while developing the film – it was always a feature film which would later be shown and repeated on television. The Film Four Channel obviously increased Channel Four's branding of 'its' films, but again the branding was to do with cinema films, not TV drama which might later be distributed.[7]

Film Four had a working rule of thumb at the time that Clayton was working with them that if it made eight or ten films every year, at least four or five or these would get a theatrical release in the UK (an achievement in itself given the collapse of the art-house cinemas in the 1990s). At least one or two would do extremely well at box office. Thus profits from *Trainspotting* (Boyle, UK, 1996) and *Secrets and Lies* (Leigh, UK, 1996) would cover the costs for releasing other films which, while they might be critical successes, may for a number of reasons (e.g. lack of stars or innovatory form) have had limited box office appeal. It was a system that worked both economically and creatively. During the life of Film Four, executives went on to make about one in three of everything they developed whereas in the same period at the BBC only one in eight or ten went forward to be made. Thus at Film Four, development funding was a more sure guarantee of progress, and the relationship was that much more secure.

When Paul Webster took over from David Aukin as Head of Film Four they departed from this formula and tried to enter the larger mainstream release circuit with product such as *Charlotte Gray* (Armstrong, US/UK, 2001). It was an attempt to take on the large companies but it failed for the same reason Puttnam's similar strategy with both Goldcrest and Enigma failed. There was not enough risk-spreading, and one bad box-office result wiped out the potential to invest in a wider slate of films. A generation of film-makers who were working without the level of state support they would have had in Italy, Germany or Scandinavia, for whom Film Four had been a 'home', were left high and dry:

> The specific mode of Film Four's development, its informality, approach-ability and human scale, as well as its status internationally for attracting co-finance and distribution deals, was something of great value which was always going to be hard to replace.[8]

It is not true to say that there were no alternative investment streams. However those streams, the tax credit system, the lottery franchised companies, have proved to be more or less problematic. It is a moot point if more recent developments, including central government's increasing interest in the cultural industries in general and cinema in particular, have done much to address this situation.

In 2002 Alan Parker (from his position as increasingly frustrated Chair of the UKFC)[9] reminisced thus: 'In June 1990, Margaret Thatcher invited Richard Attenborough, David Puttnam and a number of others into Number 10 Downing Street for a seminar.' Here she made her famous 'something must be done' call to action. The result was a handout of £1 million a year to create the British Film Commission which, together with the introduction of Section 42 tax relief in 1992, aimed to provide a boost toward inward investment. This was principally for large-scale American productions in the UK.

In the mid-1990s the indefatigable Attenborough persuaded the Con-servative Government to give a share of lottery receipts to film. The scheme had a fatal flaw: All the money for film had to be sunk into production. The money was to be distributed through an unprepared Arts Council. Parker concludes (whilst begging a question): 'a mistake which was not rectified until a change of Government and the creation of the Film Council.'[10]

The 'New Labour' Government arrived in May 1997 promising 'things can only get better'. Chancellor Gordon Brown's first budget reinstated the 100 per cent first year tax write-off for British films. The Department of Culture, Media and Sport's 'Film Policy Review' (headed by producer Stewart Till) delivered 'A Bigger Picture' identifying the need for a distribution-led approach. These policy proposals were blocked by the ITV companies promising instead to invest £100 million in British films. This money never materialised. Any hope of a revival in the fortunes of British cinema appeared to now rest firmly within the sector itself and was highly dependent on any support central Government felt willing or able to give. Thus was born the UK Film Council.

The UKFC (United Kingdom Film Council) was launched in the spring of 2000. This new 'super body' (as the trade press dubbed it) had been set up by government to be 'the strategic organisation set up by the Government to create a coherent structure for the UK film industry and to develop film culture in the UK' (www.ukfilmcouncil.org.uk). The Film Council officially came into existence on 1 April 2000 and unveiled full details of its plans and strategies (Towards a Sustainable UK Film Industry) on 2 May 2000. This first phase of the Film Council's work included a package of film production initiatives backed by a total fund of $35 million (£22 million). Its first financially significant actions came six months later.

The UKFC began with grand ideas of encouraging and supporting production and – latterly – marketing of the product. This 'big bang' strategy left major doubts over whether there was going to be enough attention paid to the 'education' of the next generation of film-makers or indeed a domestic audience steadily weaned off anything outside of Hollywood product and decreasingly ambitious TV fare.

The training issue (specifically *not* education in its wider sense) was to be dealt with by the 'Film Training Fund', with a surprisingly slight £1 million a year to train both script-writers and executives and the 'First Movies' fund which earmarks £1 million for children and young people to make low-cost films. Appended to this was a wish list: 'a skilled, competitive and culturally diverse workforce', as well as the desire for a film culture 'properly reflecting the cultural diversity of the UK'.

The strategy document also called for building a more film-aware audience and improved distribution and exhibition of a broader range of films in the UK. *As if this was not* enough the industry also had to deal with the new technology issue i.e. 'exploiting the full potential of digital technologies'. Surely a £55 million p.a. budget could be spent on that alone never mind the call to increase 'access to film heritage'.

Whilst acknowledging the need to improve distribution and exhibition to a domestic audience (without a viable strategy to do so) the film council pronounced in *Towards a Sustainable Film Industry* that poor quality scripts were the central problem facing the British Film Industry (www.ukfilmcouncil.org). Lack of support and resources for script development was highlighted as a weakness of the UK film industry. This resulted in 'too many poor quality films being made' and 'finished films which are sub-standard and therefore partly or wholly rejected by the distribution sector' (www.ukfilmcouncil.org). This was the point being made so vociferously in the popular press in criticising the films funded by the early lottery funding. Thus:

after discussion with the commercial industry the UK FILM COUNCIL has concluded that the well publicised problems facing British feature films seeking theatrical distribution will not be solved by subsidising print and marketing costs with public funds. Instead, the UK Film Council believes that more effective distribution of UK films will be achieved partly through the development of consistently better scripts (aided by a Stage One initiative) and partly as a result of new film policies.[11]

As a result of this the first five years of the Film Council saw the Film Training Fund only put money and training into writing.

If the quality of screenplays is poor there are two options – train the writers to be better at their job and train the development executives to recognise good material when they see it and more importantly recognise problems with a script that is going into production. It is cheaper than trying to fix it in the editing room.[12]

Thus in the financial year 2001–2 a total of £1,443,819 was spent on Training Awards supporting the training of writers and development executives (incorporating producers, script editors, readers and other personnel involved in film development). Providers of such training were many and various from higher education, e.g. Leeds Metropolitan University (Short Courses for Development Executives: award £100,000); the National School of Film and Television (Project Development Workshops: award £13,000) to industry body the New Producers Alliance (Short Courses for Development Executives: award £16,777) and The Script Factory (Short Courses for Development Executives: award £27,000) among others. In addition new providers sprang up to take advantage of the training fund e.g. *Draft Zero Ltd* set up by Film Council consultant Phil Parker and offering Short Courses for Development Executives (award £44,104), Project Development Workshop (Film Council award £26,000) and Training the Trainers (Film Council award £5,630).[13]

Draft Zero was launched thus: 'This programme of Project Development Workshops have grown out of the highly successful MA in Screenwriting at LCP, whose graduates have gone on to work throughout the British Film and TV industry . . . '[14] The programme and the LCP MA were designed by Phil Parker whose claim to fame is as author of *The Art and Science of Screenwriting* (Exeter: Intellect, 1998), a book in which he sets out the concept of the 'creative matrix' where 'six key elements form a framework for originality'. The primary thrust of Draft Zero training was focused on training producers to recognise genre characteristics and work with writers on producing more generic product. In spite of the substantial Film Council awards and relatively high fees (£1639.13) Draft Zero is no longer operating.

A more recent example of attempts to strengthen development procedures is 'Write Directions' developed by the Script Factory and supported by the Film Council. 'Write Directions' is advertised as

> script development for directors . . . a series of 3-hour seminars on all aspects of script development, designed to give Directors and their Assistants insight into the practical processes of script development, from recognising the potential in a first draft screenplay, through negotiating redrafts with the writer, to pitching the project to financiers and producers . . . Supported by the Skillset Film Skills Fund, in an initiative to encourage cross-sector skills development.[15]

A generic session runs as follows. Angeli Macfarlane (Script Factory, UKFC consultant) puts forward to a group of directors and producers – and in this case Screen Yorkshire's New Talent Manager – the magic formula for the award winning short. She argued that short films can be 'expressive, experimental, personal *but if so keep them as home movies*. We are here to discuss linear narrative and how to make it successful'. She went on to generically categorise good short films as either (1) twist in the tale or (2) slice of life. A room full of (potential) producers and directors wrote down every single word said – each seeking the magic formula for their project – and the narrowing down of the form into two options with rigid rules attached was not questioned. Angeli Macfarlane has been on the Bafta short film jury for five years as well as executive producing short films for Pathe and Channel 4. Her arguments are convincing – but they are only one set of arguments and there is a self-fulfilling prophecy element to this, i.e. I will train you to produce a certain kind of work. When you produce it I will be one of the industry judges and will reward the work that fulfils my agenda.

Short films are important because they are a calling card or gateway through which young film-makers can start their careers. But short films (though undergoing a revival) have little commercial potential, therefore finding the money to make them is difficult. The UKFC with its remit to encourage diversity and seek out new talent has a number of short film initiatives – the Write Directions seminar described above being part of that process. Development training of the kind found on the *WRITEDIRECTIONS* programme has a significant impact on the kind of material selected by the Screen agencies who administer the UKFC 'Digital Shorts' schemes with the result that their short film schemes are acting more as gatekeepers (only allowing films fitting the pattern described above to get through) rather than a gateway.

Thus the 2003 'Digital Shorts' scheme – run by Screen Yorkshire and the UKFC – stated that they are looking for projects that: 'are innovative, cinematic and will have audience appeal'. But once scripts are accepted onto the scheme, writers do not have the right of approval of the final screenplay.

UK Film Council and Screen Yorkshire will have right of approval over all cast and crew proposals and will have final cut approval. If successful, you will participate in script development and a training programme during September. Successful teams will participate in script development sessions with industry professionals. Additional training will also be offered. Please note that attendance at all sessions is vital and is therefore compulsory. We would expect writers and directors to attend a minimum of three, half-day script development sessions when you would work with a professional script consultant/editor. (www.Screenyorkshire.co.uk)

Just in case that is not enough to hammer a project into a template: 'Screen Yorkshire also reserves the right to attach a different writer to the project if the submitted script is not of a high enough standard.'

Initially (on the surface at least) anyone was eligible to apply but the way the selection procedure worked was designed to screen out those film-makers who had not already participated in S.Y. training programmes. As Hugo Heppell, Screen Yorkshire's Head of Production, explained: 'We operate a pyramidal structure – we would be unlikely to give a digital short commission to a film-maker who had not already done some work with us.'[16] This informal screening out of the unknown has now been formalised. Thus to compete for Screen Yorkshire's £20,000 short film commission (which funds one film a year) 'directors *must* have previously made a film with Screen Yorkshire through one of our schemes or have made a film funded by UKFC FilmFour or the BBC'.[17] Thus it would appear that rather than opening up access and finding new talent there appears to be a narrowing down of access and a very hands-on role in the development of each project: a clear case of 'one size fits all'.

Development under the UKFC seems to be concerned with a small group of consultants setting a very specific agenda for the kind of material to be developed – this agenda is taken up by the regional screen agencies and *other providers (see above)* who then devise programmes with the maximum level of development or you might choose to substitute the words control or even interference over projects. Thus even at entry level encouraging innovation despite being listed as a key aim of the UKFC is limited. It is not that new 'British' voices aren't emerging, simply that it's a struggle against institutional constraints.

Lynne Ramsey has brought a visionary edge to traditional British realism. Her experience with the film *Gasman* (1997, the precursor of 1999 feature *Ratcatcher*) that UKFC now praises in their teaching materials is a paradigmatic case in point. Ramsey started as a photographer and reacted badly to cinematographers training at the NFTVS: 'as a photographer you do your own works at film school . . . I started hating the formulaic structure . . . I wanted to experiment with form and not be tied down to the quirky ending' (Elsey and Kelly 2002: 52). Ramsey goes on to note that due to her background she writes/thinks in images – which seems to have created some problems with TARTAN SHORTS (funded by Scottish screen). 'They did take the project on . . . and then they tried to change it.' Note well Ramsey's response: 'I was pretty adamant that I wasn't going to change it too much . . . I have done it this way before. It works for me' (Elsey and Kelly 2002: 53). The film-maker was proved right by her festival successes (including Cannes) but what if she had not made a couple of films before and did not have a strong personality and visual confidence? Could most entrants to the industry resist formulaic cine-matographer training and heavy handed script-doctoring?

Schemes to develop writing talent are equally hide-bound to restrictive con-ventions. In 2003 a number of regional screen agencies rolled out the *Introduction to Screenwriting* course developed by the Film Council. The rela-tionship between the Film Council and the Screen Agencies was exemplified in the course description 'developed by the film Council and facilitated by . . .' Screen Yorkshire promoted it as able to: 'provide you with the skills you need to write a successful screenplay . . . The course is designed in twenty-two linked, two-hour sessions which explore the use of character and characterisa-tion, visual style, *television writing*, genres and selling a screenplay.'

The course materials comprised of a very fat manual provided by the Film Council and written by Film Council consultant Phil Parker (of Draft Zero) that prescribed every aspect of each session including which exercises to be done and which clips to watch. A constant tension appears between the very dull and dry course material written in development language about character arcs, three act structure and inciting incidents and the tutors' and students' natural enthu-siasm to tell their stories in their way. In the twenty-two week course no feature films are recommended for viewing or discussion. Episodes of the most popular UK television 'soaps' (*Eastenders, Coronation Street*, and *Emmerdale*) were recommended and used to illustrate much of the course material from plotting to structure to characterisation, visual storytelling and dialogue. Specific ses-sions were devoted to situation comedy writing. The final careers advice and 'Next Steps' sessions advised emerging screenwriters to apply to Channel 4 (which had recently stopped commissioning) and the BBC for funding.

Film Council investment in script development has totalled $35.8 million in the past six years (Rickett 2006: 12). The consequence of the lack of results from all this writing training has been the quiet disappearance of many of the initiatives outlined above and the Film Council's recent turning of its focus on to distribution. The 'pitch culture' and more formal approach to development has resulted in the talent of many of the 'trained' writers struggling to survive the ever increasing number of stages required (initial pitches, outlines, first drafts, even revised first drafts) to be offered on spec (i.e. without payment or commitment from producers).

> The worst aspect in my view of the current system, where more work is done on spec, is the 'pitch culture' where writers and producers are encouraged to verbally and publicly pitch for the prize of a couple of thou-sand or a new mobile phone. The 'pitch culture' does not allow for serious

progression of talent and skill and more often confirms the aphorism someone made about Cannes – 'people pitching ideas they don't own to people who can't afford to buy them'.[18]

In part this is the result of a saturated market – the result of so much training as Stephen Cleary of Arista Development puts it 'at a time when production is diminishing development is expanding. We are setting up unrealistic expectations for younger writers – the chances of their film actually getting made is very low' (Rickett 2006: 13).

Ian W. MacDonald, ex-head of the Northern School of Film and Television, has asked: 'What is the task involved in screenwriting? (MacDonald 2004: 261). He proposes a 'simple answer':

> it is to produce a positive response to narrative in the mind of his reader (or listener) which will correspond to what the reader is seeking. The reader is seeking something which conforms to their understanding of the field of fiction film production and their own sense of judgement, and these incorporate everything ranging from the first moving image they ever saw to their current brief.

MacDonald in an earlier article revealed that most 'readers' (83 per cent) don't like what they read (MacDonald 2003: 242). We should note well MacDonald's phrase: 'conforms to their understanding of the field . . .'

MacDonald (265) quotes Bourdieu in correctly pointing out that this understanding is: 'something that is firmly located in current cultural requirements' (Bourdieu 1996: 190–1). Bourdieu's 'rules of art'are predicated upon the fact that '. . . finally analysis involves the genesis of the habitus of occupants of these positions' (MacDonald 2004: 214). MacDonald himself conducted a sample survey of fifty-two professional screenplay readers within the UK across winter and spring 2000–1:

> This attempted to identify a profile of readers, clarify common practice and test a number of hypotheses based around the broad question of what readers seek when evaluating screen ideas. Results show that 90% of readers are white, 62% are male and 48% are over 40; 50% claim to have had over ten years experience in reading scripts . . .' (MacDonald 2003: 242)

Pierre Bourdieu has pointed to the defining nature of: 'The habitus, an objective relationship between two objectivities, [which] enables an intelligible and necessary relation to be established between practices and a situation' (Bourdieu 1990: 101). Habitus is seen in terms of dispositions (structured structures lead practitioners to see their practice and practices as natural). It is difficult to see how this self-selecting and defining group of 'readers' could not have a set of dispositions.

MacDonald (2004: 262) asks another question 'how do you define success' and answers 'obtaining a positive reaction . . . The cues in the proposal are cultural; they have meaning in a particular social context . . . They form the professional ground on which writers and their readers walk'. This 'professional' relationship between reader and writer contains a major danger of orthodox and highly stylised ways of presenting treatments and scripts. Those 'in the field' swim in their clichés: 'a good story well told'. The early twenty-first-century development buzzword – along with 'high concept' – is 'genre.' Leaving aside the laziness of such a label,[19] 'genre' is surely a concept with a high potential for formula (if used uncritically and inaccurately as it undoubtedly is). This approach also rather mitigates against concurrent calls for 'innovation' 'edge' . . . 'originality'.

We can identify a *habitus* within those both teaching screenwriting and reading the scripts. Others have pointed out that the problem goes higher and deeper. As Erik Knudsen has put it:

> The relative lack of success for British films in the marketplace is often cited as being rooted in the lack of quality screenplays. As the primary strategic body for film in Britain, the UK Film Council subscribes to this broad analysis and has identified training as one of the key strategies for overcoming this weakness. In this article, I question this assumption and examine to what extent the decision makers, and the processes of decision-making, themselves are a problem in the development of talent and quality British films. (Knudsen 2004: 113)

The problem is increasingly deep seated within a field of power. The field is notoriously hard to break into and probably a mystery to those outside. It is those very outsiders who might still produce something interesting. Even the entrants are being institutionalised. Screenwriting is an example sitting within the UKFC 'field of power' but it is not just screenwriting. Thus in 2005:

> Skillset has developed a whole range of initiatives working directly with further and higher education as well as the media subject associations. . . . as in any relationship, there have been various issues over the years that have provoked lively debate. We are on the verge of major changes in the way Skillset and the industry engages and supports FE and HE and will be making some exciting announcements on July 5. (Curtis 2005)

In *The Guardian* article Richard Brown, chief executive of the Council for Industry in Higher Education, described Skillset as a 'trend-setting' sector skills council. 'As such it acts as corrective to education . . . Academic institutions are autonomous institutions. That's a strength but also a weakness, because it means that companies don't quite know what they are purchasing in a graduate. If sector skills councils can set national standards, the large players – the

BBC or whoever – know that . . .'. Thus it becomes specific that the 'one size' that fits all is apparently the BBC size.

The fact that this chapter is part of a book entitled *European Cinemas in the Television Age* does beg the question as to whether the TV age is actually coming to an end. Yet, at this precise moment the UK Government and the self-appointed bodies shaping its policies are using TV as focus and model for a 'film industry' just as it becomes irrelevant to the multi-media globalised environment the UK film industry must work in. Meanwhile the UK's public service broadcaster the BBC continues to drip-feed support to the film industry.

There are some exciting initiatives positioned within the BBC's online presence, for example 'The Writers' Room' and 'Film Network':

> the BBC's interactive showcase for new British filmmakers, screening three new short films in broadband quality every week, adding to a growing catalogue of great shorts. The site allows people to comment on and rate films and also provides filmmakers with tools to create online profiles and exchange tips, advice and ideas. The purpose is to expose new talent and create a platform for some great films that are rarely seen elsewhere.

Film Network launched as a six-month trial in early 2005 in collaboration with the UK Film Council's New Cinema Fund, who provided us with forty-two shorts made through their digital shorts scheme to help kick-start the site. The purpose of the trial was to work out the best way to support new film-makers and partner the industry. The trial was deemed a success and the full service launched in October 2005 in partnership with many of the industries' key organisations and showcasing a catalogue of over 150 shorts.

Meanwhile – with the demise of Channel Four Films and its 'restructuring' into Film Four Productions[20] – BBC Films continues to be the only significant and consistent broadcasting support for film-makers in the UK.

> BBC Films is the feature film-making arm of the BBC. It is firmly established at the forefront of British independent film-making and co-produces approximately eight films a year.
>
> Working in partnership with major international and UK distributors, including Miramax, PolyGram, Fox, Buena Vista, Pathé, Momentum and UIP, BBC Films aims to make strong British films with range and ambition . . . As well as cinema features, BBC Films has been responsible for some of the most groundbreaking and acclaimed BBC television dramas in recent years, working with award-winning writer-directors such as Stephen Poliakoff, Dominic Savage and Francesca Joseph.
>
> BBC Films continues its commitment to make British films and television dramas of integrity and ambition while widening its scope to include international and American coproductions.[21]

It is noteworthy that whilst eight films per year (as a maximum) are financed, 'BBC Films has been responsible for some of the most groundbreaking and acclaimed BBC television dramas in recent years'.

At the same time 'BBC Films continues its commitment to make British films and television dramas of integrity and ambition while widening its scope to include international and American coproductions.' Thus BBC films has made a sizeable commitment to Woody Allen's first British-set film *Match Point* (2005), thus continuing the tradition of UK financial support for American auteurs.[22]

Undoubtedly there is much merit in a number of productions with BBC involvement. These include *Mrs Brown* (Madden, 1997) starring Judi Dench and Billy Connolly and the Academy award-winning *Iris* (Eyre, 2001) again starring Dame Judi as well as Kate Winslet and Jim Broadbent. Stephen Daldry's *Billy Elliot* (2000) is 'BBC Films' most successful film to date, which has taken some $100 million worldwide, won three major British Academy Film Awards and was nominated for three Academy Awards'.[23] BBC films has clearly carved a niche for both heritage cinema on a small scale (compared to the acknowledged masters Merchant and Ivory) and 'quality' (i.e. small screen) drama writ slightly larger than on TV. Nonetheless the national broadcaster has also rather more bravely supported 'independent' auteurist work such as Stephen Frears' *Dirty Pretty Things* (2002), Michael Winterbottom's Berlin Golden Bear winner *In This World* (2002) and Lynne Ramsay's *Ratcatcher* (1999) and *Morvern Callar* (2002). Neither should we underestimate the role of BBC films in promoting the career of Pawel Pawlikowski (*Last Resort*, 2000 and *My Summer Of Love*, 2004).[24]

But underlying this admirable support for British auteurs is the undeniable fact that BBC films activity is a contribution to the (broadcasting) dependency factor tugging at the creative strings of British cinema. Once the next generation of film-makers have been pressed through the (broadcasting) craft agenda of Skillset/UKFC machine maybe no-one will even notice any more.

Meanwhile the BBC as a commissioning body continues to make movies on TV in the guise of 'Quality Drama'. In November 2005 came BBC2's epic £60 million new drama series *Rome* with an eleven-week run and packed with British acting talent and boasting (US centred) movie production values, filmed on the 'largest standing film set in the world' i.e. the five acres of back-lot and six sound-stages at Cinecitta. The result is the look and feel of (Cinecitta shot) *Gangs of New York* (Scorsese, USA, 2002). However, in content we have the most risible soap opera family disputes: 'A saga set during the last years of Julius Caesar's reign, centred on two Roman soldiers, Lucius Vorenus and Titus Pullo, and their families' ('Mother you don't understand me' etc.) and 'episodic' cliff-hangers. This is US soap writing (from Alexandra Cunningham of *Desperate Housewives* fame) squeezed into British TV formatting (via Adrian Hodges, doyen of BBC mini-series) mixed with John Milius bombast and faux-Hollywood production values. Of rather higher quality (at least in terms of writing) is the work of the

BBC's pet drama series writer/director Stephen Poliakoff, *Shooting the Past* (1999) and *Perfect Strangers* (2001). In 2006 Poliakoff and the BBC finally elided the differences between British film and TV by producing a single feature-length drama, *Friends and Crocodiles*. For cinema in the UK the BBC is both friend and crocodile or – to use an earlier metaphor – 'Meet Mr Lucifer'.

Included in Charles Barr's introduction to *All Our Yesterdays* is a reference to the third edition of *Cinema 1969* containing a black-bordered obituary (written in response to a viewing of Attenborough's *Oh What a Lovely War*) by Tom Nairn:

> 10 April 1969: Deceased at the Paramount, Piccadilly. London. W1 THE BRITISH CINEMA. (Barr 1986: 7)

How much worse might the reviewer felt after *Sex Lives of the Potato Men* (Humphries, UK, 2004) rather than Attenborough's perfectly acceptable movie. Cinema in the UK could find a way out of the forty years (or more) of an 'inferiority complex'[25] that has typified it in the 'Television Age', but not whilst the purse strings are held by British broadcasters and/or their formulaic values are enshrined in a Skillset/UKFC televisual agenda. As Erik Knudsen puts it:

> . . . we must look at the decision-makers. Who are these people? What do they see? While it may be possible to train screenwriters and other creative talent to work within existing patterns of creation, very much apparent in television, the outcome is likely to generate more of the same product. (Knudsen 2004: 181)

'Television has become more or less the film industry' wrote Hill and McLoone (1996: 1). Now we can say that much UK TV is cinema whilst UK cinema is fast turning into TV.

NOTES

1. www.bfi.org.uk/filmtvinfo/stats/boxoffice.html
2. See for example T. Balio (1990). The studios could not buy TV stations after the 1949 Paramount decision but became a major supplier of back catalogue (after RKO's sale to General Teleradio in 1955) and programme supplier soon after.
3. See for example Abrams (1956); Emmett (1956); Hand (2002).
4. Thus allowing the UK Film Council to claim (in its 2005 statistical yearbook) that UK productions can claim: '6.7% of the US box office' (almost all of it through co-productions and the vast majority from UK/US productions such as *Cold Mountain* UK/USA/Romania/Italy) and *Tomb Raider II* (UK/USA/Japan/Spain). Duncan Kenworthy, Chair of BAFTA and himself with a TV production background until *Four Weddings and a Funeral* (Newell, UK, 1994), at the launch of the BAFTA shortlist could claim '34% of UK box office' for 'British' films and compare the situation with the nadir of 'the low teens' (unspecified when). Kenworthy's 'British' cinema included *The Constant Gardener* (Meirelles, UK, 2005).

5. 'Television has become more or less the film industry.' Hill and McLoone, Introduction to Hill and McLoone (1996: 1). Aesthetic implications of this 'relationship' have been explored in *Big Picture, Small Screen* (M. McLoone, 'Boxed in', Hill and McLoone 1996: 76–106) and J. Hill, *British Cinema in the 1980s* ('A new relationship', Hill 1999: 53–70).
6. Interview with Heather Wallis 5/6/2006.
7. Interview with Wallis 6/6/2006.
8. Interview 6/6/2006.
9. www.screendaily.com/stroy.asp?storyid=10140
10. www.screendaily.com/stroy.asp?storyid=10140
11. www.ukfilmcouncil.org.uk/
12. Towards a Sustainable Film Industry: www.ukfilmcouncil.org.uk/
13. National audit Office http://www.nao.org.uk/publications/nao_reports/02-03/0203211.pdf
14. www.draftzero.co.uk
15. www.draftzero.co.uk
16. Interview with Heather Wallis 17/9/2004.
17. www.Screenyorkshire.co.uk Short film and feature film funding guidelines.
18. Interview with Heather Wallis 5/6/2006.
19. Although we are reminded of a comment from Ken Loach: 'I hope you have banned your students from using the word . . . it's so lazy . . . meaningless.' Interview with Graham Roberts 23/3/1999.
20. Much encouragement has been taken from new head Tessa Ross' ambition to 'act as a magnet for the best and most innovative UK talent' (www.channel4.com/film/ffproductions) e.g. 'New-look FilmFour boasts tantalizing slate' (Adam Minns in *Cannes Screen International*, 16/5/2003). Nonetheless the restructuring involved a cut in Channel 4's annual investment by two thirds to £10 million
21. http://www.bbc.co.uk/bbcfilms/
22. Evidenced by UKFC's first foray into major budget movie production with Robert Altman's *Gosford Park*.
23. http://www.bbc.co.uk/bbcfilms/
24. See Chapter 10 of this book for a detailed analysis of Pawlikowski's work in terms of the aesthetic relationship between film and TV.
25. Gilbert Adair (Night at the Pictures 1985) 'The History of British cinema is that of an inferiority complex' quoted in Barr 1986: 4.

3. FRANCE: CINEMATIC TELEVISION OR TELEVISUAL CINEMA: INA AND CANAL+

Dorota Ostrowska

The decision of the French government to launch a new public channel 'La Sept' committed to the promotion of 'film as culture' when the privatised French television channels and a newly established Canal+ were becoming the biggest film producers in France shows that it was *cinéma d'auteur* which was particularly privileged in the French audio-visual context. This type of cinema has enjoyed a continuous support of the policy-makers and that of public funders even at the time when the number of TV channels was increasing, stepping up the demand for TV fiction and drama, and when the notions of high culture were being eroded. In the new audio-visual landscape determined by the emergence of the Canal+ television-driven costume dramas and *cinéma du look* co-existed with the *cinéma d'auteur*. What made this cohabitation of those various kinds of cinema possible is of central interest in a discussion of relationships between and within the audio-visual industries.

Since the early 1970s the production of *cinéma d'auteur* was an expression of the 'mission créateur' of public television and of an effort to legitimise TV in the eyes of intellectual elites. It was in the early 1970s with the restructuring of the centralised television agency ORTF that the commitment to produce auteur films was strongest and resulted in the creation of the Institut National d'Audiovisuel (INA). The establishment of the INA was underpinned by an idea that television cannot develop its full potential unless it is involved in some kind of creative experimentation and research into the possibilities of its own medium. Paradoxically, the formal boundaries of television were to be tested by some of the most established French film-makers thus not only redefining what television was in terms of form but also bridging the worlds of cinema and television in a very interesting and productive way.[1] Arguably the *cinéma d'auteur* continued to be made in the context of the INA project by auteur film-makers themselves who were using the television as a medium of expression, as a source of funding and as a distribution platform. Even though INA was an experiment on a very limited scale in terms of production values, it was hugely important culturally facilitating traffic between the worlds of cinema and television.

In the 1980s with the advent of Canal+ French television became the main source of financing and exhibiting French cinema on the scale which was in no way comparable to that of INA. Instead of some sixty hours of fiction programmes produced jointly by INA and the public channels, there was suddenly a whole channel solely dedicated to cinema. Ultimately, it was Canal+ rather than INA which was to change what cinema was in France, the ways in which it was made and consumed, while bringing the relationship between cinéma d'auteur and television out into the open. René Prédal described the impact of television upon cinema as 'the radical transformation of the product [i.e. cinematic film] itself, of its composition, of its making and of the aesthetic choices the product entailed' (Prédal 1991: 373). Not surprisingly the new regime of financing and exhibiting films established by a television supported by viewers' subscriptions resulted in a new type of films. They were welcomed by both television and cinema spectators and thus managed to bridge the gap between the worlds of cinema and television in a quite a different way than in the times of the INA. For as Daniel Toscan du Plantier at Gaumont points out, in spite of the INA experiments involving the auteur film-makers, the distance between the two mediums had become very wide since the mid-1970s when 'there existed an almost religious difference between art, which no longer worked, and the rest of the [audio-visual] production' (Raspiengeas 2001: 214). By the 'art that no longer worked' the Gaumont CEO means the film production in the 1970s France which never managed to generate as much enthusiasm as the French production of the 1960s associated with the *Nouvelle Vague*. In other words, the *cinéma d'art et essai* seemed to have little in common with fiction broadcast on the small screen. In the 1980s it was the production of costume and heritage drama and of the *cinéma du look*, which created a new synergy between the worlds of cinema and television while providing the fodder for the critical debates about lamentable but inevitable televisualisation of cinema. Generously supported by the socialist government the costume drama was seen as both a popular and prestigious type of cinema by TV executives, politicians and numerous members of the public. In order to maintain its popularity with the audiences, heritage and costume drama had to adjust its aesthetics to the limitations and challenges of the small screen. But at the same time, it was not supposed to become a simple téléfilm, for this would mean that the drama would lose its prestige and cultural value, which came from the association with cinema guaranteed by the theatrical release of the film which was also lined up for a television broadcast shortly afterwards. The genre of heritage and costume drama was thus an attempt to strike the balance between the worlds of television and cinema reflected in the aesthetics of the genre and the way in which its cultural value was calculated.

Next to the renaissance of the heritage drama shown on both small and silver screens the 1980s saw the emergence of the *cinéma du look*. According to the critics television played a crucial role in the development of this type of film-making. In 1983, a *Cahiers du cinéma* critic, Pascal Bonitzer said:

> When people understood that cinema and disco, film and video-clip, were no longer separate domains, but the elements of an explosive cocktail (in terms of public approval, marketing and box office), cinema took a historical turn. In France Beineix represents that turn. (Powrie 2001: 15)

Susan Hayward, the author of *French National Cinema*, also identified the growing influence of television in French culture as the reason for the momentous turn taken by the French cinema in the 1980s:

> Indeed, more than any other medium, television, with its endless flow of images, has been the prime mover in the dissolution of the great divide between high and low art. Placed at such a disadvantage, cinema has had to adapt its own film-making practices which has meant, in great measure, being a post-aesthetic Abel to an image-conscious Cain. (Hayward 1993: 295)

Hayward's presentation of cinema's relationship with television is truly apocalyptic as she evokes one of the most famous murders in history. Her example reflects how threatening the critics like Hayward felt that television was to the survival and well-being of *cinéma d'auteur*, which is a kind of cinema to which the label of 'high art' could have been easily attached. Cinema was losing its prestige and status as the seventh art because it was becoming more and more difficult to distinguish between cinematic and televisual images. The increasing proliferation of televisual images and the growing consumption of such images by the young public have shifted the preferences of the cinema spectators from the aesthetics of the *Nouvelle Vague* to those associated with TV advertisement, music video and TV fiction. Hence, television has been seen as the breeding ground for the audiences of a new type exemplified by the *cinéma du look* and heritage drama. Certainly, there exist important differences between the audiences of *cinéma du look* and heritage drama. While the former is aiming at younger spectators, the latter provides more family-oriented entertainment.

The convergence of cinematic and televisual images was connected to the production practices which cinema had to embrace. Television was responsible for cinema's adapting new film-making and production practices derived from television. Hence, the changing preferences of audiences were as important as the growing alliance of cinema and television in the realm of production and distribution when it came to identifying reasons for the emergence of new types of cinematic production (*cinéma du look*, heritage and costume drama) which reflected the impact of television.

There is little doubt that television channels such as Canal+ changed profoundly the ways of cinema funding in France. The part of the story which Hayward does not emphasise is that this financial impact of television, exemplified by Canal+ and also the contribution of public broadcasters, was welcomed, appreciated and needed by the cinema practitioners. It is so because apart from the examples of cinema influenced by television aesthetics which Hayward and Bonitzer correctly identified there are various other types of cinema (le cinéma) which television funding made possible in the times running to Canal+ and when the channel came to existence. If we think about, on the one hand, *cinéma du look* or costume dramas as examples of popular, commercial and genre cinema aimed at the wider public, and, on the other hand, cinematic productions which flourished at the same time (Garrel's, Rivette's, Rohmer's), we could argue that televisual explosion of the 1980s, identified with the impact of Canal+, was nothing more than just another chapter in the very long tradition of French cinema in which commercial and popular cinema have existed as a backbone to less profitable and marginalised *cinéma d'auteur*. Paradoxically, the *cinéma d'auteur* is what international audiences identity French cinema to be while ignoring completely the wealth of genre and big budget comedies, which are distributed only in France and the francophone world, but do not reach non-French speaking audiences.

Canal+ television reshaped the audio-visual industries' relationship, creating lots of anxiety among critics in particular, but did not change this relationship in any fundamental way. Thus it preserved the traditional dynamic between the popular and art cinema in the French context. This may be why some independent French producers, such as Frédéric Bourboulon, do not see television as a threat to the films they wanted to make. His view is quite telling given that Bourboulon has been producing Bertrand Tavernier's films for the last thirty years – before, at the peak of and even after the televisual age. Bourboulon does not reproach television for encroaching onto cinema's territory but rather points to distribution difficulties which prevent Tavernier's films from being seen in cinemas if they are not successful at the box office in the first week of their release: 'there was a space for these films there, there was . . . There is now, but it is very difficult.'[2] He argues that in France today the problem is similar to that which existed in the US before the introduction of anti-trust laws whereby studio films had a guaranteed distribution within the cinema circuit belonging to the studios: 'Thus one is obliged to go with these large groups to sell our soul to the devil.'[3] However, this experienced producer notes sanguinely that: 'Films are still made, because the vitality of the French system means that there are nevertheless many films which are completed, but with small means.' Bourboulon's comments and wry tone point to the important aspect of the ways in which some cinema practitioners relate to television, which they find an irritation (at most) but definitely not an obstruction to their creativity.

In this chapter I will examine the role television had in shaping cinematic culture in France in the times of INA and after the appearance of Canal+. My contention is that television was a way of continuing a tradition of popular French cinema, such as heritage drama, while also supporting the emergence of some new types of films such as the *cinéma du look*. The impact of television was such that these dramas did embrace certain stylistic elements associated with television, in the same way that the *cinéma du look* did.

What created the greatest anxiety among the critics of cinema in France and abroad was the fear that these hybrid products, when exhibited in the cinema, would take over the place of films made by auteurs. It is a paradox because the Canal+ pact with the cinema practitioners entailed that all the films funded by this television channel will also have cinematic exhibition before being shown on TV. (Canal+ embraced this idea because it was selling itself as a 'canal du cinéma', which meant that it needed to show what TV viewers could safely identify as cinema films.) With the stigma of television attached to the costume drama and even to *cinéma du look*, Canal+ was looking out for films which could have been safely labelled as 'le cinéma'. The *Nouvelle Vague* veterans were able to provide this kind of guarantee along with the annual discoveries at the Festival de Cannes and Venice and Berlin film festivals, and the film-makers associated with the producer Alain Sardre – a maverick figure in French cinema and one of the first to be linked to Canal+. The list of films produced by Alain Sardre from the mid-1970s is extremely impressive making him into one of the key producers in France in the post-Nouvelle Vague era. It is widely acknowledged that Canal+ decided to purchase Films Alain Sardre because of its impressive film catalogue, which consisted of about 200 features including films by Claude Sautet, André Téchiné and Nicole Garcia (Delmas and Mahé 2001: 55). The specialised press, especially the prestigious magazine *Cahiers du cinéma*, also played a key role in providing the interface between the world of business, represented by Canal+ and that of art populated by auteurs, film-makers and cinéphiles. This role was acknowledged by the Canal+ CEO who argued in an interview in the *Cahiers* that 'the magazine like yours plays a pivotal role in the propagation of the phenomenon (of the Nouvelle Vague), which is something like an ideology which is very expensive and in my opinion has reached an impasse' (Jousse and Toubiana 1992: 99–100). The hybridisation of popular cinematic genres into cine-televisual ones has not led to the disappearance of the *cinéma d'auteurs*. To the contrary, the emergence of the hybrid types of film-tele-making drew a distinct line between *cinéma d'auteurs*, which is still doing quite well, and other examples of audio-visual production. As in the era of the Institut National d'Audiovisuel, through channels such as ARTE, television still offers support for *cinéma d'auteurs*. In other words popular and auteur cinema co-exist in France as they have always done, with popular cinema subsidising the survival of auteur cinema.

INA

In the early 1970s a new institution was established as the Institut National d'Audiovisuel [INA], whose role was to pursue a policy of producing experimental film made by film-makers who thus far had been working mostly in cinema. The French public television channels (the only ones in existence at that time) had to broadcast thirty hours of INA programming made with INA's resources and thirty hours of INA programming commissioned by the TV channels. In the 1970s, apart from the INA film series 'Caméra Je', FR3 was producing its own film series 'Cinéma 16' and TF1 was running 'Caméra une, première' thus offering different production and distribution outlets for experimental cinema. The motivations behind the establishment of INA and the results of this initiative were quite varied and often surprising. One of them was an effort to counter the negative image television had in the French society. Bertrand Tavernier's films from the 1970s and 1980s are an interesting way of thematising the cultural anxiety associated with television at that time.

Une semaine de vacances (*A Week's Holiday*, 1980) is a story of a school teacher who is very disenchanted with her job and the attitudes of her pupils. She wonders whether the fact they watched so much TV did not have something to do with their behaviour. The other film is *La Mort en direct* (*Death Watch*, 1980) – shot in Glasgow, in English, starring Harvey Keitel and Romy Schneider. There exists a true mixture of televisual and cinematic images in this film supported by the film's main theme. *Death Watch* is about a TV journalist played by Keitel who has a camera installed in his eye in order to transmit directly for television broadcast the images of a famous female writer who is dying and with whom Keitel's character strikes a friendship which then develops into a relationship. This is a complex film about how circuit and life television is threatening and can jeopardise privacy of an individual. The film shows television as driven by profits and rating and thus very different from cinema.[4] In the first of Tavernier's films *L'Horloger de Saint-Paul* (*The Watchmaker of St Paul*, 1974) television functions more like a radio which is transmitting information about French politics and it is watched not privately but in a public venue (café). Hence, it is a source of information for the public, who is trying to form its political opinions, without becoming the centre of attention for people debating politics or a major factor shaping their political choices. This is different from his film *L'Appât* (*The Bait*, 1995), where videotape watching becomes an incentive or an inspiration for a series of brutal and appalling crimes committed by juvenile offenders. We can say that in Tavernier's films, especially the ones from the 1970s and the 1980s, television is thematised in terms of a growing social threat which the film-maker sets out to document and analyse.

The INA project could be seen as an effort to legitimise TV in the French cultural context by offering film-making opportunities for established and elite film-makers often associated with the *Nouvelle Vague*. Thanks to INA, television could develop an aesthetic dimension of the medium and thus (re)legitimise itself in the eyes of the French intellectual elites in quite a similar way that cinema became culturally legitimised in its own times.[5] The purpose of INA was to gather people who were particularly interested in working for television and in developing an 'auteur TV'. Among film-makers who were invited to work for INA there were Raul Ruiz, Andre Téchiné, Philippe Garrel, Eric Rohmer, Jacques Rivette, Jean-Marie Straub and Danièle Huillet.

Television was perceived as a child, which needs to be educated and formed in order to contain the threats which it carried in itself if it was to be left unsupervised. At the moment of the establishment of INA, television did not have large funds. More importantly it was not yet the hydra with many heads – television channels – which needed to be fed constantly with audio-visual diet. Hence, the INA experiment belongs to a particular moment in the history of television – the time when there was no natural exchange yet between the two worlds – that of television and cinema. In fact, they kept quite distinct. The INA's involvement with the world of cinema was part of the public service of television, but it had very weak commercial underpinnings. The cinema against which television was measured and with which television was comparing itself was the *cinéma d'art et essai* whose concept was developed through marginalisation of some important aspects of popular cinema, especially that of the *tradition de qualité*. This comparison of television to *cinéma d'auteurs* complicated the reception of television and television determined films (such as costume dramas and *cinéma du look*) and negatively affected the understanding and appreciation of the televisual aesthetics. One of the reasons why INA could have been such a purist project seemed to be associated with the fact that the motivations of its founders were not commercial but primarily aesthetic and formal. At the same time, it is interesting to examine the ways in which film-makers perceived INA as an opportunity for new channels of distribution and for reaching new audiences for their films. They were not interested in television as such or in their aesthetics. They had a much more pragmatic attitude towards it which was based on the realisation that television could become a vehicle for continuing their experimentation with the cinematic forms they were most interested in. Television was also seen as a new distribution platform for the *cinéma d'auteurs*.

The reasons why some film-makers were attracted to working for television was not linked to their particular commitment to the medium of television or the desire to develop it. Rather, their motivations had to do purely with their identity as film-makers, committed to cinema. Raul Ruiz agreed to accept the INA commissions because the work in television gave him an opportunity to be continuously involved in film-making. Presumably, as a freelance film-maker he realised that the opportunities to be employed on film projects were difficult to find and rather rare. Andre Téchiné found a way of making films on television liberating because he was able to work without any pressure of box office successes or concerns about the reaction of the critics while still being able to reach a wider audience with his films (Forbes 1984: 3). Ruiz also appreciated the potential of the television medium which he did not perceive as much different from cinema. He pointed out that 'everything there has been in the way of experimentation in the cinema in the last few years, including Straub, even Duras, could be found on television, except that it was very clumsy, in general, very bad, but there it was' (Forbes 1984: 3). Rohmer went as far as to say that he saw in many television films an impact of *Nouvelle Vague* aesthetics. He also described the experience of seeing his own film, *Le Genou de Claire* (*Claire's Knee*, 1970), on television as a rediscovery of his own films. Watching it on television emphasised the aspects of the films which he described as 'the sensuousness, the bloom, the tactile aspect' (Forbes 1984: 4). This brings Rohmer to a very surprising conclusion that some of auteur films actually work better on a small screen than on a big screen:

> (. . .) those films, 'talkative films', *auteur* films, if they are well scheduled, sometimes come over better on TV than in the cinema. Television does not play on the sensational, I don't see it as the enemy of *auteur* cinema. On the contrary, it could be its ally . . . (Forbes 1984: 4)

Echoing Rohmer's view Rivette admits that he made his thirteen-hour-long *Out One* (1971) with full awareness that the film will not be suitable for any extensive cinema distribution because of its non-standard length. Instead, he said he had been thinking about some sort of a television series or parallel distribution on TV and in cinema (Forbes 1984: 5).

It may come as a surprise that auteurs classify their own films as more suited for television than for cinema distribution. But film-makers unlike many critics or academics have to learn how to function and survive in a changing economic and cultural environment. It also may be that the film-makers' definition of experimentation and the direction that this experimentation takes often do not coincide with the opinions of the critics. The development of new media and technology, such as television for example, is not dictated by the tastes of critics or artists, rather it is driven by diverse forces of which the desire for profit is one of the most fundamental. Occasionally, the passion for the medium could be expressed in the film's reaching some new artistic heights. Film-makers want to continue making films and have to find the ways of re-adjusting or re-fitting into this changing world. Film-makers learn how to make television or other technological changes work for them. The testimonies of the film-makers involved with the INA show how open-minded they were towards new audiovisual technologies. It is very interesting to see how positive the alliance of television and cinema has been in the times of INA. For instance, Rivette seems to see the INA initiative as the moment when television actually accepts its responsibility to help find distribution for films which struggle commercially or simply lose in the competition with popular movies (Forbes 1984: 5). TV is seen as a lifeline of cinema rather than the proverbial Cain.

During the period of the INA film-makers saw television as an alternative distribution to cinema distribution and a way of breaking the monopoly of theatres. It was another market, which was seen as much more free and liberal than the traditional cinema market. Auteur film-makers who were invited to participate in the INA project were also very well aware of the place the cinema they were interested in occupied within the French cinematic production. They realised that the audience for their type of cinema was naturally very small:

> in France there's an audience for the cinema, an audience that isn't 'popular' in the old sense but is a smaller audience, if not cultivated then at least better informed, an audience that wants fairly specific things and which is in itself differentiated. (Forbes 1984: 5)

Rohmer's assumption seems to be that with the help of television, as a new distribution platform, the needs of this specific audience could have been met much easier. At the same time, television could help to bring new members to this highly specialised audience. Straub believed that the audience his films could reach on TV was not only larger but also much more diverse: 'on TV you find a socially mixed audience and not just people who go to arthouses' (Forbes 1984: 5). This homogenisation of the public interested in *cinéma d'auteur* was a very serious and fully justified concern. In 1990 the families of state employees and various professionals (teachers, academics, lawyers) constituted 39.1 per cent of the cinema-going public and paid for 51.8 per cent of the tickets sold. This privileged audience would further increase if the students' contribution was added in (Farchy 1992: 62). Hence, thanks to TV the *cinéma d'auteur* in its experimental and most challenging form was reaching out to new audiences.

Rohmer also pointed out two trends within the contemporary television production; one of them was drawing on the *Nouvelle Vague* tradition and the other one was gesturing more towards pre-*Nouvelle-Vague* 'quality' (Forbes 1984: 4). This is a very interesting argument, which encapsulates in itself two visions of cinema which can also be identified in television. The obvious reason why some of the television film-making seems to emulate the *Nouvelle Vague* is that the *Nouvelle Vague* itself, in its own times, was inspired by then budding television. The direct recording and film-making which was so very important for the realisation of the New Wave aesthetics was inspired by documentary film-making and TV reportage. It was beautifully and humorously thematised in Jacques Rozier's *Adieu Philippine* (1962) where the main character works as a television technician and his various girlfriends all aspire to work in television advertising the way girls from Godard's films, like Nana in *Vivre sa vie* (*It's My Life*, 1962), all want to be in the pictures. In other words, even in the minds of the *Nouvelle Vague* film-makers, who were working at the very beginning of television, there existed affinities – culturally and stylistically – between the two mediums. At the same time the negative critical reaction which costume dramas, flourishing on the TV screens were given once the medium of television had matured in the 1980s could be associated with the negative spin the *Cahiers du cinéma* critics gave to the *tradition de qualité* film-making in the 1950s. In other words, objectively speaking costume drama made for television might have had more positive characteristics but those were unappreciated because of the cultural climate dominated by the *Cahiers* rhetoric which to some degree continues even until nowadays.

The criticism developed in the *Cahiers* from the early 1950s contributed to the development of the notion of an auteur, who was to be in full control of the creative process – writing, directing and sometimes even producing a film. This notion of auteur was contrasted with the division of labour, which dominated French studios at the times of the criticised *tradition de qualité*:

> The Nouvelle Vague and critics-film-makers have shaken the system, destroyed certain artistic norms, renewed the film-making, aired the system but they have also imposed an idea of an auteur, this notion of a total artist, who is capable of directing, script-writing and sometimes even producing. Apart from a few rare exceptions (Truffaut, Rohmer . . .) the majority of French film-makers are not capable of doing all of this. (Jousse and Toubiana 1992: 99)

The initiative of INA was welcomed because it embraced the notion of film auteur while trying to transplant it on the televisual ground hoping that the contribution of cinematic auteurs could also lead to the birth of new art of television with its own tele-auteurs. There is no reason to believe that such a development is not possible in television; and in many ways INA and ARTE prove that it is quite likely. However, this is hardly the point in the debates about television and about popular and commercial film-making. INA with its limited broadcast time could focus on and promote experimental works. But something quite different is at stake when there is an increase in the number of broadcasting hours of which many have to be filled with fiction. It is not possible that all of these hours will contain *films d'auteurs*, in part because they are not to everybody's taste and in part because there is simply not enough of them. Arguably, the need to produce a greater volume of films could be the first step towards compromising the notion of a single auteur. In other words television, with the exception of the INA, re-introduced into French cinema the discarded and criticised notion of the division of labour whereby 'some film-makers just write while others only film' (Jousse and Toubiana 1992: 100). The many costume dramas are in a way a bridge between the two worlds. In the future this division of labour was also to amplify the role of the producer which was welcomed by Canal+ whose CEOs argued that 'we have to make sure that the notion of the auteur does not diminish the importance of the producer' (Jousse and Toubiana 1992: 100). The rehabilitation of the producer was to be exemplified in the role Alain Sardre came to play in the destiny of Canal+.

During the INA period the film-makers saw some examples of television fiction production as a reflection of forms being developed in cinema. There were some particular forms of film-making that they valued over the others (experimental, avant-garde/Brechtian, *cinéma d'auteur*, reflective, combining the importance of the *mise en scène* with that of the dialogue). It is the recognition of television's potential to realise these filmic preoccupations in the medium of television which raised an issue of making films which could be broadcast on television and shown in movie theatres as well. However, even though this type of cinema can exist and survive thanks to television (especially, such channels as ARTE), it is a quite different kind of film-making, one criticised by all the auteur film-makers and one going against the grain of the *Nouvelle Vague* ethos, the cinema of spectacle, high values, costumes and classics adaptations that television ended up pursuing most vigorously especially when Canal+ appeared. However, there is one aspect of cinema that Canal+ learned from the points made by the INA auteurs — the fact that television should act as a distribution platform which can complement theatrical distribution. There was a recognition that television could act as a form of a secondary movie theatre with some wide-reaching benefits to itself. But this was only possible if the films shown on television were clearly labelled as cinematic films. Hence, the idea of accompanying TV distribution with the theatrical release was born and placed at the heart of Canal+.

Canal+

This role of television as a place for experimentation was terminated in the early 1980s. INA lost its production arm and became just an archive, the place where the wealth of the audio-visual material broadcast on TV was stored. This transformation of INA from production to archiving is quite telling since it coincided with the time when the first private TV channels appeared in France. This alone stepped up greatly the demand for cinema and films. The quantity of films available became as important as the quality since there was a greater quantity of broadcast time available via different channels, which had to be filled with various audio-visual materials, among which films were in particular demand. This outburst of television channels and the disappearance of INA only enhanced the prevailing negative image of television in France. The real story seems to be that, just like INA in the 1970s, Canal+ in the 1980s was the way to address the needs of cinema in the transforming audio-visual landscape.

Canal+ was established in 1984 as a state-owned channel focused on broadcasting films which was only available to those who paid the subscription. Even though cinema was the type of programming privileged by Canal+, the channel also broadcast various sports, football in particular, and also some soft porn. The profile of Canal+ not only changed the relationship of cinema and television but also the relationships within the world of television for 'this channel was envisioned as a challenge to other channels, to public television, which simply was the television at the time' (Buob and Mérigaud 2001: 64). Canal+ was also obliged to partake in the production of French films and then to broadcast them. In other words, Canal+ was to become a new way of producing and distributing films in France. Between the two distribution was more important than production. In 1984 when Canal+ was founded French cinema was doing very well; it took 53.4 per cent of the market while Hollywood had only 30.1 per cent. (Buob and Mérigaud 2001: 16). Thanks to the generous system of state subsidies French cinema did not really need the money Canal+ could contribute but 'it was not able to resist the attraction [of additional funding]' (Buob and Mérigaud 2001: 16). This view that French cinema did not have need for the financial support of television was reiterated ten years later by René Bonnell[6] (one of the Canal+ CEOs) who said that 'cinema is not about money; there is enough funding in France to double the film production' (Jousse and Toubiana 1992: 97). Thanks to the presence of Canal+ additional funding became available to French producers and film-makers. This did not result in better films but in films whose budgets were inflated and many incompetent or one-off producers were trying to make films.[7] This was definitely a negative result of Canal+ presence; however one can hardly blame the channel for this state of affairs. It seems that the French film industry was not quite prepared to deal with the influx of cash. Awash with money the system was not behaving enough like an industry, which should have been rationalised to deal with greater funds and greater budgets. In time this situation changed and the increase in the number of costume dramas produced for television could be seen as reflection of the rationalisation of the system and an attempt to deal with the increase of cash. This had an effect on the aesthetic quality of the films resulting in the high value productions which the producers, funded by Canal+, simply were able to afford. Obviously, this situation introduced even greater division between *cinéma d'auteur* and popular or genre cinema. Canal+, effectively the French cinema banker, ended up supporting both auteur and commercial cinema. Canal+ 'created Sautet, Tavernier, and Corneau, but also promoted Mathieu Kassovitz [*La Haine* (*Hate*, 1995), *Les Rivières pourpres* (*Crimson Rivers*, 2000)], Jan Kounen [*Doberman*, 1997] and Christophe Gans [*Le Pacte des loups* (*Brotherhood of the Wolf* , 2001)]' (Buob and Mérigaud 2001: 99).

Although there is no denying that Canal+ transformed the audio-visual landscape in France through offering an additional source of funding, its most significant impact was in the areas of distribution and exhibition where Canal+ emerged as a new platform. The channel's influence was so profound because Canal+ had to be attuned to the needs of its audience (being a channel 95 per cent funded by subscriptions). Some said that Canal+ dependence on its paying spectators led to the situation where 'cinema allowed television to dictate its choice' which was not a welcomed development (Buob and Mérigaud 2001: 64). However, the story is more complicated than that and perhaps more beneficial to cinema than it is widely acknowledged. After all Canal+ also contributed to the transformation of a profile of a cinema spectator through its programming. Perhaps when the distribution of films takes place not just through the theatrical release but also via TV, we could talk about a development of a new type of a spectator (after all it does not make much sense in such a case to speak about television and cinema spectators separately, because more often than not they are the same person.) Laurent Créton suggests that 'by broadcasting cinematic films, television attempts to appropriate for itself the symbolic value of the cinematographic work as well as the special relationship cinema has with the spectators' (Créton 1994: 71). He suggests that the impact of television breeds a new type of a viewer who is no longer a spectator but a spectator-consumer (*consommateur-spectateur*) (Créton 1997: 9). For Créton Canal+ can be found at the beginning of a long process of the development of the various media distribution platforms (multichannel television, cable, satellite, digital television and broadband internet) which have strengthened the identity of this spectator-consumer who 'experiences a profound change in the traditional media economy where rarity of the product used to be its defining feature while nowadays it is a profusion of the product' (Créton 2003: 32). We can say that Canal+ broke the cinema–spectator relationship which resulted in a triangle consisting of cinema–spectator (consumer) and television. It is that severing of this relationship which has created the greatest anxiety for the people associated with the world of cinema and those concerned about the results of dissolving the division between high and low art. The important point to keep in mind is the fact that many of the arguments about cinema as an art were developed in the intellectual climate which had a tendency to ignore the economic dimension of cinema. One of the biggest shocks experienced by the *Cahiers* critics-turned-film-makers was a realisation that cinema was a commodity as well, not just an artistic endeavor. Godard created a poignant testimony to this shock in his *Le Mépris* (*Contempt*, 1963).

At this stage it might be important to return to Susan Hayward's arguments about the Biblical and bloody story of the two mediums in France. In her evaluation of the role of cinema–TV relationship in France she did not take into account the role played by Canal+ and the way this channel, and earlier on INA, actually changed television in France by making it more cinematic (while also emphasising the business-side of cinema which many found very uncomfortable, distressing or plain boring). The influence of Canal+ had to do less with the impact of cinematic stylistic on television (although I would argue this happened as well through the growth of the development of costume drama into a cine-televisual genre) but more by television, Canal+ in particular, becoming a studio, which produced films for particular audiences which were shared between cinema and television screens. In this sense Canal+ gave rise to a new stage in the cinema–television interactions. The full expression of this new role of television was the establishment of the production branch of Canal+ (Studio Canal+) in 1990 which was essentially run by a film producer (who also made films with numerous auteurs) Alain Sardre, through his company Films Alain Sarde. At the beginning it was Films Alain Sardre, serving as a production branch of Canal+, which indicates what a clear line existed between distribution (via TV and cinema) and production (controlled by cinema people). Canal+ was required by law to contribute to cinema funding in France but it was not able to become a production company itself. It could have done two things: to create an alliance with an established producer who could give it a name and a face. The Studio would still finance the majority of its productions either completely or in part (this is close to the Hollywood principle where an independent producer makes films for a major). The other option was to engage in foreign productions, often Hollywood ones.

The Studio created close links with a producer, Alain Sarde, and participated in the productions of André Téchiné [*Ma saison* préférée (My *Favourite Season*, 1993)], Bertrand Tavernier [*L 627*, 1992] and Roman Polanski [*Bitter Moon*, 1992] (Buob and Mérigaud 2001: 97). Once Canal+ linked with Films Alain Sarde it could enter directly into co-production agreements with other companies or with independent producers. As a result in 2001 Studio Canal+ was participating in the production of 90 per cent of French films usually through pre-sales (Lecasble 2001: 153–4).

The objective of Canal+ from the very beginning of its existence was to get involved in all the stages of film production and distribution (Buob and Mérigaud 2001: 9). The presence of the Canal+ in the French cinema production context was appreciated because the channel was ready to inject large sums of money into film production. Its contribution resulted in some very well received films, such as Polanski's *The Pianist* (2002) and David Lynch's *Mulholland Drive* (2001) to mention just a few most recent ones. However, the ubiquity of Canal+ also created an anxiety because it is Canal+ which gets to make final decisions regarding actors, directors and scripts because it is involved in the production not just in broadcasting or distribution (Lecasble 2001: 154).

This fear was to at least some degree justified for there is no denying that TV channels in France, especially Canal+, became the main source of funding for French films. In 2000 Canal+ was financing almost half of the French film production. Canal+ has been also involved in the pre-sales of films and thus the channel's contribution constitutes about 18 per cent of an average film budget. This signals a significant increase (over 10 per cent) during the 1990s. While Canal+ is obliged by law to invest 9 per cent of its budget, other French TV stations, TF1, France 3 and France 2 have to invest only 3 per cent. Elisabeth Lequeret points out that 'while TF1 produces prime time films (very expensive, often comedies) and Arte opts for *cinéma d'auteur*, M6 broadcasts the leftovers of TF1, France 3 and certainly France 2 stagger its course between the spectators' ratings (Audimat) and its duties as a public broadcaster' (Lequeret 2000: 46–8). But then Canal + is a specialised cinema channel which broadcast about 450 films a year of which the majority is also French (Lequeret 2000: 46–7). Cinema's dependence on television in terms of funding leads Hayward to conclude that cinematic production is more and more geared towards the needs of television and thus loses its cinematic specificity. Laurent Créton points out that 'the channels want to produce quality TV films (téléfilms de prestige) but they are not able to get over the aura given to cinema by the festivals' (Lequeret 2000: 48). It is this aura of the festival, of dealing with a truly 'cinematic films', that resulted in the commitment of the channel to produce films which have a cinema release before they are broadcast on TV. Canal+ was thus a realisation of the film-makers' dream, dating back to the INA period, to have TV as an additional channel of distribution for their works. In this sense, it would be more precise to say that TV channels such as Canal+ did not contribute to the disappearance of the cinematic culture but to its profound transformation and in a sense proliferation which continues nowadays with the expanding DVD market. The cinematic culture of cinema-going underpins the very existence of the channel itself which in itself is a strange and particularly French phenomenon given the fact that in 1985 an average French person watched three films a year in cinema and sixty-two films on TV. In 1990 this figure dropped to two for cinema and raised to about a hundred for television (Farchy 1992: 64). At the same time, it should be remembered that the wider and more diverse TV public also demands a particular product, and the *cinéma d'auteur* is not always to their taste. Hence, this catering to popular tastes must necessarily contribute to privileging films from the middle ground if all of the Canal+ production is taken into account. In more general terms it is to be noted the ways in which cinematic representation reflects cultural and economic changes in the society. For instance, before World War II, in the 1930s, the characters played by a star performer of French cinema, Jean Gabin, were close to the popular audiences attending cinemas then. After the war, he tended to play professionals (doctors, lawyers, policemen, landowners) (Farchy 1992: 62). Canal+ is as diverse as cinema in France ranging from popular to *cinéma d'auteur*. It is a true version of home cinema; the one where somebody else is still making a choice of a film for you. This culture is rapidly becoming history. The real question nowadays is whether films paid for by television, shown in cinemas, and being streamlined online could still be considered 'cinema' at all. I think this will be the case if we believe that what we value most about cinema and what enthrals us in it goes beyond the dominant technological, distribution and production modes. As *Screen International* has editorialised, 'the future (of cinema) has nothing to do with technology – this is just a means of transport' (*Screen International*, 19 May 2006: 2). The art of cinema has proven again and again its extraordinary resilience while facing all various changes and revolutions. We should remain hopeful: for cinema has clearly proven itself to be an invention not without but with the future.

NOTES

1. See for example Jill Forbes 1992 and 1984.
2. Interview with Frédéric Bourboulon. Graham Roberts, Stephen Hay, Dorota Ostrowska, March 2005 (unpublished).

3. Interview with Frédéric Bourboulon.
4. The cultural anxiety surrounding not simply television but para-televisual phenomenon such as CCTV is still present nowadays and has been recently explored by Michael Haneke in his 2005 *Caché* (Hidden).
5. I am referring here to the heated debates regarding the cultural status of cinema conducted on the pages of *Cahiers du cinéma* and *Positif* in the 1950s and 1960s.
6. When Canal+ was established René Bonnell was made responsible for the feature section of Canal+ while Catherine Lamour was in charge of the documentary section (Buob and Mérigaud 2001: 16).
7. Interview with Frédéric Bourboulon.

4. ITALY: CINEMA AND TELEVISION: COLLABORATORS AND THREAT

Luisa Cigognetti and Pierre Sorlin

For a long time television was blamed for weakening the Italian cinema and reducing it to a very limited part in public entertainment. According to an Order in Council of 1947 radio and later television broadcasting was a State service entrusted to a public company submitted to parliamentary control (Monteleone 1992). When the RAI (Radiotelevisione Italiana) began its television broadcasting, on 3 January 1954, the Italian cinema was in its heyday. Many assumed, at the time, that once they would be offered pictures at home, people would have no reason to go out, so that cinema attendance would soon decline. However, with the passing of time, we see that the evolution of both media was not so straightforward; they were in competition but, at the same time, they complemented and influenced each other. Opinions about the impact of television on cinema changed during the second half of the twentieth century (Ortoleva 1999: 993–1012) Today, when new means of communication, more flexible and interactive, are appealing to a wide public, they can and must be defended from the point of view that a close collaboration is their only chance to survive.

Was the birth of television a hard knock for the cinema? Let us look first at statistics. In Table 4.1 the first line shows the number of film spectators, the second the number of television sets, both given in millions.

Two things emerge from these figures. On the one hand, the Italian public was not immediately conquered by the new medium. During the first years television sets cost about as much as the annual income of a country doctor and were too expensive for the great majority of potential clients. It took the television production companies five years to manufacture reasonably priced sets. As we shall see there were many more spectators than television owners, but theirs was a random use, which did not prevent them from paying a visit to a

Table 4.1 Numbers of Film Spectators and TV sets.

	1949	1955	1957	1959	1963	1966
Spectators (millions)	600	819	758	750	697	669
TV sets (millions)		0.18	0.67	1.5	4.5	5.5

movie theatre. On the other hand the decline of cinema attendance was not catastrophic. It is true that compared to the peak reached in 1955 and 1956, with more than 800 million tickets sold, the drop that occurred in the following years looked impressive but the takings of the mid-1950s had been exceptionally good and if we work out the average of the figures over two decades we come to the conclusion that television did not kill the cinema.

A NEW MEDIUM, NOT A CHALLENGER

Since the end of World War II the cinema had been the most popular form of entertainment. In 1938 Mussolini had put a ban on American movies. After the liberation in April 1945 spectators who had been starved of Hollywood pictures for six years flocked to the movie theatres. The Italian film-makers were quick to react. Lobbying for state intervention they obtained some restrictions on the importation of foreign films and various subsidies, which enabled them to boost production. On an average, 130 films were shot every year during the 1950s[1] and, in the second half of the decade, about one third of the screenings were of films of Italian national origin. Italian films found favour with the national audience all the more as neo-realist pictures and comedies of Italian manners were much appreciated abroad and won awards at international festivals. The number of picture houses steadily grew. There was a theatre for every 7,000 people and many institutions, especially the Catholic Church and the communist party, organised projections at a reduced price. Not only was it easy to watch films, but the movie theatres were also meeting places, where families used to go on Sunday afternoons, and where people liked to socialise.

Socialisation was precisely what made cinema exhibitors fear the new medium of television. Fascism, unlike Nazism, had not attempted to put a radio set in every home. For ideological reasons (and also because it was unable to develop an efficient wireless manufacturing) it had favoured collective hearing, Mussolini's speeches or important news were heard on public squares. On the other hand, the ownership of a radio set reinforced local hierarchies as rich people did some less fortunate friends or their employees the favour of inviting them for a much-appreciated programme. The same process occurred with television. It has been estimated that, in the 1950s, one out of five sets was the property of a cultural circle, a parish organisation or, more frequently, of a bar. Every time something gripping was on, spectators gathered in a bar and as far as 1959 only one third of spectators watched television at home. Loud applause, heated debates, small conflicts and above all a great atmosphere made collective hearing highly enjoyable; the performance was as much in the room as on the screen (Alberoni 1968; Anania 1997). The ownership of a television set was also a status symbol. In *La Sfida* (*The Challenge*), a Francesco Rosi film released in 1958, a mean trafficker, who lives in a poor district of Naples, becomes rich by swearing allegiance to a boss of the *camorra*; he immediately buys a big television set and people from the neighbourhood gather in his place, filled with admiration and respect.

Television was thus in competition with cinema but its impact was not as dramatic as had been feared. Spectators who liked to comment loudly on what they saw on television wanted to watch their favourite films in silence and did not abandon the movie theatres. Right from the beginning films were screened on television, usually twice a week, on Monday in prime time, in the middle of the week at a later time. Cinema attendance was so scarce on Monday that, in the provinces, many theatres closed that day thus the broadcasting of a film did not hamper the cinema proprietors. In the 1950s the Italian studios boasted of being the most advanced in Europe. Adopting colour film and Cinemascope they produced quality works more attractive than the old-fashioned, black and white movies that RAI rented for broadcast because they were cheap. It should be remembered that the much liked American pictures could not be seen except in movie theatres. The biggest times for cinema were Saturday evening and Sunday afternoon. On Sunday RAI put on the air *La domenica sportiva* (The Sporting Sunday), a sports magazine so badly shot and so clumsily presented that it did not appeal to the public, cinema audience, which was mostly familial on Sunday afternoons, did not decrease. There were more problems with the Saturday evening. RAI had scheduled a quiz, *Lascia o raddoppia?* (Double your money) which was immensely popular. Many did not go to the pictures because they wanted to follow the quiz, but the association of exhibitors came to an agreement with the RAI, the quiz was postponed to the Thursday and the previous order was restored.

The RAI managers gave in willingly about *Lascia o raddoppia?* since their aim was not to lead spectators away from the cinema. The majority of those involved in television broadcasting came from the radio. Theirs was a practical experience of sound, music, jokes, quick answers, but they lacked a 'culture of image'. Understanding that the small screen (and in the 1950s or 1960s the screens were really small) was not fit for wide landscapes or camera motions, they chose to give greater place to close-ups and talking heads. At the same time these people set themselves the task of educating the lower middle class. After the liberation, the Christian democrats had seized the information networks to prevent them from falling under the control of the communists, but also to provide the Italians with a common cultural background. The RAI managers were keen on extending a schooling that for many had been rather short. In their view what was at stake was not art but education. Unlike most of its European counterparts, Italian television had no research department, sophistication was banned and simplicity was the rule. For its inauguration the RAI broadcast a 'classic', a play by Goldoni, which set up the standard for the Friday programme *Theatre in TV*. There was no attempt at creating an original production; the shooting took place in a studio, with only three cameras, one of which filmed the whole stage while the others focused on the face of the actors. The didactic project led to giving much space to conferences delivered by lecturers who were content with talking, without trying to illustrate their lessons. The listeners were invited to ask for information about any kind of issue; an expert answered them in the way he would have done on radio (Bettetini and Grasso 1985).

Television pleased its public because it was not demanding and could be watched with detachment. It was fashionable, among intellectuals, to say that it was unable to contrive genuine, imaginative genres but a film-maker, Anton Giulio Majano, and a stage director and actor, Sandro Bolchi, accepted the challenge. Both men noted that the cinema which, in its first decades, used to adapt great literary works, had long given up, so that the general public, which did not read much, had no contact with the masterpieces of the past. Therefore they insisted that television, a popular medium, should make famous plays or novels suitable for broadcasting. From 1956 onwards they shot a series of television films taken from plays or novels. In their view, television was much more flexible than the cinema which was hampered by many constraints such as a conventional timing of the movies, the recourse to famous actors, the necessity of screening impressive scenes.

Majano, in tune with the management, wanted to create 'an illustrated library' (Romanò 1985: 101), or what he called a 'second school', which would put millions of spectators in touch with 'the great names of world literature'. He did not hesitate to tackle well-known, difficult novels, *Jane Eyre* (1957), *L'Isola del tesoro* (*Treasure Island*, 1959), *Una tragedia almericana* (*An American Tragedy*, 1962), *Citadel* (1964), *David Copperfield* (1964) and *La fiera delle vanita* (*Vanity Fair*, 1966). His was an original method, chosen because it differed strikingly from cinematic traditions. There was, before the beginning of the programme, a short presentation of the author and of their work – something that was impossible in a film. Then a voice-over, sometimes a dialogue, gave the main lines of the story, some passages of which were performed by actors. Majano was bitterly attacked by critics who reproached him for indulging in sentimentalism and betraying the texts he adapted. He, in turn, blamed the film-makers who gave too much importance to the scenery and costumes, and assumed that a television film, watched by the whole family, was like a book read by one of the parents, in front of the children. He added that while the cinema engrossed its public, a television programme provided its spectators with the rhythm and the simplicity of a written text and allowed them to understand and appreciate it.

Bolchi introduced to the small screen Dostoevsky and Victor Hugo, but was above all intent on popularising the Italian writers of the nineteenth and twentieth centuries. He considered television to be a vehicle that was more modern and more present-day than the cinema. Given the size of the screen it was not possible to offer imposing scenes but, far from being a shortcoming, such restriction obliged the director to emphasise small details or revealing gestures likely to express the psychology and innermost motivations of the characters. When he shot a serialised adaptation of a much liked novel, Manzoni's *I promessi sposi* (*The engaged couple*, 1966), *Il Corriere della sera* (11/12/1966), significantly, titled its review: 'Manzoni's masterpiece brought in mass culture' – an attack to which L'Espresso (22/1/1967) replied that, given the tremendous success of the programme, whose episodes had been seen, as a mean, by more than eighteen million people, Bolchi has created what the magazine called a 'new Manzioniani' among those who, otherwise, would never have heard of the book.

There were much confusion and doubts in the founding era of Italian television; some 6,000 people were working for the RAI2 and it was not easy to coordinate their projects. However something was certain: nobody wanted either to imitate the cinema or to compete with it; all agreed on the fact that television should be more a means of information than a form of entertainment and should contribute to draw the Italians toward each other (Cesareo 1979). Yet, there were many practical links between cinema and the new medium. All the operators came from cinema studios. Obliged to adapt to other manners of lighting and shooting, they brought nevertheless some cinematic formulas to television e.g. the use of key lighting, of establishing shots at the beginning of most programmes, of shot/reverse shot instead of medium shots in interviews and debates. The prospect of getting in touch with a vast public, popularising their image and making money appealed to many actors, especially to the youngest, Ugo Tognazzi and Vittorio Gasman, who were not yet the great stars they would become in the 1970s, and were all too happy to lead variety shows which made their names known to the whole country.

Stylistically the cinema could not learn anything from a television whose pictures and techniques were rather rudimentary. But the RAI introduced its public to new forms of recreation, which met with a warm response and could not be ignored. In the 1930s the cinema had adopted the newborn radio, using it either as a status symbol (the presence of a set told how well-off a family was) or as a device useful to communicate briefly important information. The television set was not granted the same function in films, as if film-makers were reluctant to admit its social relevance. It is striking to see how few TV sets appeared in the more than 1,000 films made between 1954 and the mid-1950s. Television, unlike radio, was presented in a sarcastic way. *L'oppio dei popoli* (*People's Opium*) is the title of a sketch in *I mostri* (*The Monsters*, 1963); a husband, glued to the screen, does not realise that his wife is deceiving him in the next room. Two films, *Totò lascia o raddoppia?* (1956), and *La domenica è sempre la domenica* (*Sunday is Always Sunday*, 1958) attacked from the front *Lascia o raddoppia?*, the famous quiz which pleased millions of spectators. In the former Totò, a well-known comedian who never had any significant part in television, is trapped in an absurd situation: wining or losing in the quiz will equally be fatal for him. While he was starring in the latter movie Alberto Sordi was leading a show on radio but was not yet introduced to television; in the film he played the part of an industrialist, crazy about television, who, being invited to a quiz, does not realise that the announcer manipulates him and accepts to make a fool of himself. Many, in the film business, despised television, criticised it but few, if any, refused when they were offered to appear on the small screen.

ON EQUAL TERMS

I promessi sposi (The Engaged Couple, 1967) ended the first stage of the RAI's history. Up to that date, television had used an expensive, complicated material and privileged the studio which met two necessities: high speed in pitching and adjusting the lights and full liberty of moving, with no electric cables or spotlights across the floor, in order to let actors and cameras move as planned without meeting any hitches. However the same period witnessed a slow penetration, generally overlooked at the time, of cinematic techniques in television. Adopting the light equipment and shooting on location, which was then fashionable, the Italian film-makers were able to shoot stirring, alive pictures, which met with an enthusiastic response from the public. Enough we confront the television adaptation of Manzoni's novel with *The Leopard* directed, in 1963, by Luchino Visconti, to see the difference. There is, in the latter, a sense of space, an agreement between the characters, their surroundings and their social condition totally lacking in the former, which, despite its qualities, looks very tight.

The RAI managers understood that it was not possible to persevere in that direction. The adoption of techniques inspired by the cinema was made easier by the opening of a second channel, in 1959. Raiuno went on broadcasting quiz, reports, serials and talks while Raidue was more oriented towards experimentation. Film directors and operators were invited to work for television (Caldiron 1976), light video cameras allowed shooting on location and made documentaries or news more alive, and a few films were financed in partnership with production companies. The finishing touch came with the long delayed adoption of colour.

During its first decade, RAI had used films as 'consumer goods', aimed at filling empty segments in the schedule. At the end of the 1960s it adopted a radically different scheme: since the cinema was an art, television, owing to its educational mission, must do what it was already doing for literature, that is to say introduce its audience to such heritage. There were extensive cycles dealing either with a genre or with a period; old pictures of the silent era or of the interwars period were pulled out of archives, restored and presented to a public which often had never seen them. The cinematic heritage of the peninsula was emphasised – a retrospect was baptised 'Italiacia, amore mio' (Small Italy, my love) and anthologies were dedicated to typically Italian themes or actors, the most popular being *Storia di un Italiano* (History of an Italian), a panorama of sixty years of Italian life edited with sequences borrowed from films in which Alberto Sordi had the leading part. Rediscovering and saving many forgotten pictures, RAI provided its spectators with knowledge of cinema unimaginable in the previous generations. At the end of the 1960s the television set had become a banal domestic appliance; the film-makers no longer distrusted television. Valeria Camporesi rightly notes that in *Dillinger è morto* (*Dillinger is Dead*), a film released in 1969, 'television is represented as a medium which stands in peaceful harmony within a society which is no better than its myth makers' (Roberts and Taylor 2001: 162).

A decisive factor in the relationship between television and cinema was the intervention of a famous film-maker, Roberto Rossellini. His movies, *Open City* and *Paisà*, had marked the birth of a new manner of filming, soon labelled 'neo-realism', and he had won international fame. Like most film-makers he first took a scathing look at television, but when he visited India RAI offered him a chance to film his trip. His *L'India vista da Rossellini* (India Seen by Rossellini), broadcast in 1957, was much appreciated and he found that work was much easier than in cinema: once a script had been accepted, money was supplied, technical facilities were granted, there was neither postponement nor ideological control. Changing his mind,[3] he criticised the cinema, which, in his view, did not provide people with clues likely to guide them in a rapidly evolving world. By contrast television, present in most homes, might become a wonderful cultural vehicle, it could explain where the present society was coming from and where it was going (his extremely polemical views have been gathered in Adriano Aprà 1997) as he wrote to an American historian, Peter H. Wood, in July 1972, 'I have abandoned commercial, traditional cinema, and have dedicated myself to developing new educational methods through the use of visual images.' He dreamt of a gigantic encyclopaedia, which, encompassing the whole history of mankind, would offer the key to contemporary problems but, although he furnished the RAI with more than eighty hours of broadcasting, he could only fill a small part of his vast programme.[4] His longest works were *L'età del ferro* (*The Iron Age*), a vast panorama of the importance of iron and steel in the history of human beings, and *La lotta dell'uomo per la sua sopravvivenza* (*Man's Struggle for Survival*), a twelve-episode programme broadcast in 1970–1. The general structure of the former, made of five episodes of about fifty minutes each, aired in February–March 1965, is typical of his method; he jumped from the Etruscans, who were meant to have improved the quality of forged iron, to the invention of gunpowder, drew a portrait of Alberti, inventor of crafty machines in fifteenth-century Italy, lingered on the manufacturing of armours, swords and other weapons, skimmed over the evolution of communication thanks to archival films, and ended with the biopic of an Italian metalworker who had been a resistant during the German occupation. Other films dealt with most limited periods (Acts of the Apostles, the age of the Medici) or with individuals (Socrates, Pascal, Descartes).[5]

It is difficult, today, to treat with due appreciation Rossellini's work for television; his films, according to our standards, look slightly awkward. The reconstitution of old machines or antique fabrication processes is excellent and there are wonderful landscapes, especially in the programme about the apostles. But, on the whole, the programmes are heavily didactic, the film-maker himself introduces and comments at length on some episodes, the actors who deliver long speeches look like schoolteachers explaining to their pupils the ideas of Socrates or Descartes, while the numerous non-professional actors, chosen to avoid affectation, perform in a clumsy way. There could be no sequel to these works and the RAI gave up the series after Rossellini's death. Yet, the great film-makers' intervention had a strong impact, it proved that television was able to introduce its public to arduous problems and it contributed to bridge the gap between the silver and the small screens. In the wake of Rossellini tens of film-makers paid a visit to television. Some were content with directing a script written for the small screen; a few seized the chance to make experiments that no film producer would have backed; Fellini, in *Prova d'orchestra* (*Orchestral Rehearsal*, 1978) took a light comedy from an orchestra rehearsal; Antonioni made the most of the palette and special effects allowed by the video camera in *Il mistero di Oberwald* (*The Oberwald Mystery*, 1980).

Two decades of close collaboration with cinema deeply influenced the Italian television. RAI broadcast regularly American series, which were followed by regular, enthusiastic spectators, but it produced few serials, which never exceeded four or five episodes. The reason was that people, in the RAI, preferred a film-like size, with closed, self-sufficient stories that would not go on after the word 'end'. Yet, initially, these short fictions had something in common with the serials; they were told in the present and, despite imperceptible ellipses, in 'real time', as if they were unfolding in front of their public. As has often been noted, serials, as a rule, do not pay much attention to temporal references and do no have recourse to flashback, while a return to the past, covering several years, or just a few moments is common in cinema. Italian television films progressively integrated narrative returns to the past; there were flashbacks, captions and voice-over to tell the audience that it was taken back to an anterior epoch. A device, current in films, was the recourse to black and white and even, at times, silent pictures, which pointed to events that had happened before the present moment, and television adopted the convention. Unlike serials which seemed to go by, in the same way as life itself, Italian television fiction broke with the linear story telling in favour of more subtle – more cinematic – narrations. For example in 'Non necessariamente' where, precisely, any kind of narrative necessity is bypassed.

During the sixty years preceding the beginning of public broadcasting the cinema had spread images, ideas, stereotypes and visual patterns. In Italy, especially after World War I, a recurring theme had been *la malavita*, in other words shady people, swindle, the misdeeds of the Sicilian mafia and of the Neapolitan camorra. Such orientation was linked to a revival of interest for regional life, for the provinces, their traditions, their landscapes and their dialects. Films had created, or reactivated, a cultural background, which passed to the RAI. Italian linguists have proved that television played a crucial part in diffusing a common form of language in a peninsula where, up to the middle of the twentieth century, many used prevalently, and at times only, local idioms (De Mauro 1970).

Contrary to the general rule, the recourse to dialects was not rare in television films, in concert with an interest in geography, natural scenery, countryside. Fictional characters travelled through Italy, stayed in villages, took a look at the surroundings, the mafia, the camorra, the problems of the south were tackled in television films as they were in movies (Lamberti 1988).

Studying here the relationship between cinema and television, we have stressed the impact of the former on the latter but many other factors contributed to the evolution of the RAI since the mid-1960s. The opening of a third channel, Raitre, in 1974, helped to diversify the programmes. Where cinema was concerned three innovations were of particular importance. Television news, which had long been a mere listing of random chosen, ill-connected events, gained more coherence and vivacity thanks to the introduction of reports with live commentary; the audience of television information grew so quickly that all newsreels companies had to close down (in 1965 for the most important ones but some lasted till 1972) and that exhibitors began to abandon the documentaries which completed their screenings. Variety shows, with dancing, singing and comedy acts, won a continued popularity and led to a series of hybrid outcomes. Faced with an increasing request on the part of the public, Raiuno scheduled one of its variety programmes on Saturday evening, of course to the detriment of cinemas. The change by far the most considerable concerned the sports coverage. In its original version *La domenica sportiva*, lacking material and pictures, left the audience cold. The 1960 Olympic Games, which took place in Rome, disrupted the routine; Raiuno established an authoritative afternoon programme in which soccer was predominant, although much space was left for cycling and car races. Presenters guided the audience through the rules and intricacies of the various sports and, besides sporting events, focused increasingly on individual personalities, on their past and private life. From less than one million spectators in 1960 the programme passed to two million in 1965, five million in 1970 – which, again, meant fewer visitors in the movie theatres.

Up to the end of the 1960s cinema attendance had decreased slowly. The decline speeded up in the 1970s so that, in the early 1980s, there remained only 200 million spectators – one fourth of the level reached in the peak years 1955-6. Television had a share in such recession, its offer of three different channels round the clock, its continuum of programming extending from sport to drama, from news to quizzes prompted people to stay at home; the number of television sets developed proportionally to the drop of cinema audience. However, if we take into account the social context, we see that even without television the cinema would have faced a serious crisis. There was, in the second half of the twentieth century a huge migration towards the biggest urban centres, Milan, Turin, Rome and Naples. The young left their villages or small towns and, since they were the best clients of pictures shows, one third of the cinemas were obliged to close down.[6] Settling in suburban areas deprived of bars, picture houses or dancing halls, often isolated among other immigrants, they were prone to buy a television set (Foot 1995). Suburbanisation coincided with the consumption boom of the so-called 'Italian miracle'; people who had purchased, on credit, cars and domestic appliances, in addition with their television, worried how much they spent. As exhibitors, to compensate for the loss of earnings, had doubled the admission charge, many gave over going to the pictures. Glued to *La domenica sportiva* on Sunday afternoons, they had a passion for competitive sport. Soon soccer substituted the cinema as the most popular form of entertainment.

Film producers and exhibitors were badly hit by the crisis and put the blame on television. Yet, if we consider the whole cinema business, we must admit that it was rescued by RAI, which not only provided technicians, scriptwriters, directors, actors with an alternate solution, but also helped them to carry on with a quality work consonant with the traditions of the Italian cinema.

FACING ADVERSITY

Throughout the 1970s politicians and industrialists attacked the state monopoly of broadcasting. Theoretically they were fighting for the freedom of expression hampered by the governmental control over the RAI. Their real purpose was less disinterested (Pilati 1987). Advertisement on radio and television was authorised in 1957 but remained severely limited. The big distribution networks, which provided only one third of retail trade in the peninsula, needed nation wide, insistent sales campaigns to increase their clientele. They carried the matter before the Supreme Court, which was obliged to acknowledge that no law hindered the creation of private stations. Immediately tens of local channels, sponsored by commercial enterprises, came legally into being. Many were weak. When they were in a state of collapse, they were bought up by a shrewd businessman, Silvio Berlusconi, himself owner of a cable station in Milan and of a supermarket, and who used his television to offer, on his screens, the goods he was selling. Combining image and sale Berlusconi was entering a new age of capitalism based not on the quality and reliability of manufactured objects, but on a permanent flow of commodities and a direct relationship with the consumer. In a few months he set up a television network, Mediaset, which was incorporated into his holding company, Fininvest.

There were thus, from now on, two national networks (Ortoleva 1995). If they were competing harshly, via terrestrial transmission, via cable or via satellites, to lure on the same audiences and seduce the same sponsors, their aims were rather different. Inside Fininvest, a commercial company, broadcasting was not intended to inform or educate the public, but to catch spectators' attention and prompt them to buy. In the holding's strategy television was a mere tool which produced only 10 per cent of Fininvest's total turnover, against 20 per cent for the advertising agency, 25 per cent for the distribution firms, 15 per cent for the press and publishing. Mediaset could, possibly, make some marginal profit but expenditure had to be cut down to a minimum. Three factors enabled it to implement such line of action. The first was the technological development that characterised the 1970s: light cameras did not require a specialised, well trained staff; while, previously, a journalist, a cameraman and a sound engineer were necessary to cover an event, a lonely operator was now able to go anywhere and follow anyone. Easy and economical coverage and simple rules helped to establish a new television fashion. A second element was the acquisition of cheap American series of the 1960s and of Brazilian *telenovelas*. Despising both the successful American melodramas, which gave emphasis to prominent male characters, and the romantic, happy ending Latin American tearjerkers, RAI had starved the Italian audience from these world-famous serials. Their broadcasting by Mediaset caused a sensation; millions of Italian spectators were hooked on them from morning till night. The third and by far most important change introduced by Mediaset was the disruption of the traditional schedule, with its precise timing and its well defined genres, in favour of hybrid programmes mixing up soaps, music, quiz shows, talks with media stars and debates (Forgacs 1993).

In a decade the project of expanding advertisement and making it the best tool of sales promotion was a success. From 1981 through 1990 the number of television adverts increased by 300 per cent, the sums spent on them raised by 900 per cent. The winner was Mediaset, which received two thirds of the money, against one third to the RAI. In the 1990s public service television had still the biggest audience but its advantage decreased year after year and, in 2003, it was Mediaset which went into a lead. The new system, which Umberto Eco has called 'neo-television', had a strong impact on the cinema. Beside the two national networks, with three channels each, there were a great many local or regional stations. These small channels, hoping that a good movie could bring them a few more thousand of spectators, had recourse to cinema. Inside Mediaset a channel, Rete 4, specialised in the transmission of films, which filled one third of its schedule. The other stations aired fewer pictures but, all in all, at the beginning of the twenty-first century, there were about 6,000 films broadcast every year so that, sometimes, people had to choose between twelve gripping pictures.[7]

It must be admitted that the transmission of so many films had a positive effect. Up to the 1980s, after a few weeks of exclusive showing in smart cinemas, films were screened for months in smaller theatres. Such long-lasting exploitation was suppressed in the last decade of the twentieth century, the films were screened during a few weeks, then definitely taken off: television was their only chance to survive. On the other hand, thanks to state subsidies or owing to the generosity of private sponsors, the Italian studios were able to shoot yearly about a hundred movies. For reasons which will soon be explained one fourth of them were never released, while another third were removed after a few days. Again television was their last resort. It is true that they were projected during the afternoon or at night but they were granted a series of presentations, two or three times on Rete 4, then on local stations.

Films took up a large slice of the schedule but such a high number did not harm the producers and directors; the real victims were the exhibitors. At the end of the twentieth century the video cassette recorders, whose image were often of poor quality, were replaced by digital equipment; people were enabled to watch, at home, pictures as sharp as on a silver screen. Cinema attendance shrank again, then stabilised with about a hundred million tickets sold every year. So, in approximately a decade, everything – not only the audience but also the theatres and the programmes – was modified. The independent cinema owners abandoned their picture-houses to large companies, which concentrated the viewing-facilities in the sixteen biggest urban areas. The small or medium-sized theatres were substituted with multiplexes consisting of one big auditorium and a series of smaller studios, all arranged around a unique projection room, so as to economise on staff. These multiscreen sites were located in shopping malls equipped with parking lots and providing a variety of stores, bars and recreation facilities.

Up to the 1990s going to the pictures was an autonomous activity taken by people in order to achieve a cultural or purely diverting aim. At the end of the twentieth century a film show became merely a recreation that might be chosen during a visit paid to a commercial centre. Multiplexes were managed like any other business; big international companies monopolised them in order to reduce the film rent and get better terms for screen advertising. They selected films using spectacular special effects, digitally originated graphics, computer generated devices and manipulated images, which would not have produced much impression on a small screen, but were likely to overwhelm spectators with emotion in a large hall fitted with a Dolby sound system. As the furniture and material of such theatres was costly, as hiring sophisticated films was expensive, the owners charged high prices. Attending a film show turned into a relatively luxurious form of entertainment and not within everyone's pocket.

It is generally accepted that it is impossible in advance to tell whether a film will be a big hit or a flop, but multiplex managers were able to improve the market condition by choosing a limited amount of pictures and releasing them the same day all over the country. Most blockbusters were American made; on an average two thirds of the screenings came from the USA, one fifth from Italian studios, one tenth from Europe or Asia. This accounts for the fact that two thirds of the Italian movies were either never released or taken off after a few days. However, cinema production kept on, partly because private or public investors continued to finance projects, but above all because televisions, especially the RAI, came to the rescue and, in two cases out of five, saved a film which was about to sink.

There was thus a close cooperation between the networks and the studios. The involvement of film-makers or screenwriters in television fictions was beneficial to both external contributors and television channels. *La piovra* (The Octopus) is a good example of how such synergy produced good results. This successful serial, the longest ever produced by RAI, sold to eighteen foreign television companies, was broadcast from 1985 through 1991. It is exceptional inasmuch as it allows us to observe the evolution of the shooting and editing techniques over seven years. The first episodes were quite traditional; there was, at the outset, an enigma, then an inquiry and a solution, filmed in slow medium shots, with prolix dialogues. A radical change occurred after 1987; the police investigation became a mere pretext, the characters met various people, entered places which were not necessary for the unfolding of the plot, the shooting was quick, nervous, motions, unexpected cuts, discontinuity, surprise encounters prevailed over talks. *La piovra*, in its last episodes, did not look like a classic television series and was more akin to an action film.

At the end of the twentieth century most film-makers worked alternately for television stations and for film companies. Some critics blamed the former for imposing their low standards upon the young, inexperienced directors and undermining the aesthetic quality of the cinema. Such influence cannot be denied; many were strongly marked by the ways of shooting and recording sounds they practised when working for television. Competition for audience led the main networks to privilege straightforward, easy viewing programmes like games, competitions between groups, quizzes, chats. Little creative effort was necessary to film these shows, the camera focused on the participants and followed lazily their motions and all of their words were broadcast, even when they were quite inaudible. Traces of this method of operating are perceptible in the films that newcomers shot at the time. Instead of framing what they wanted to emphasise, the operators seemed to be looking for absent characters, as they wandered clumsily in search of a face or an object. At the same time there were no coherent, pre-established dialogues; the actors, often non-professional, ad-libbed and spoke a cursory, idiosyncratic vocabulary. These pictures were not intended for distribution in movie theatres. Aimed at the rising generation, mimicking its habits, using its language and its music, they were edited in DVD and sold during a season. Then, they vanished forever. They did not belong to the system commonly labelled 'cinema', but they were films and a full class of age appreciated them.

'Dilettante films' were not the only fictions shot thanks to the help of a television channel. But, like clothes, records or sweets, they were manufactured in order to be 'consumed' and then thrown away; their fast obsolescence pointed to a change in the very conception of audio-visual products. In the second half of the twentieth century cinema and television had first ignored each other, then set up a hesitant but fruitful partnership; the former had helped the latter to diversify its programmes and made them more alive, and television had provided the studio workers with jobs and financed a good many films. In the first decade of the twenty-first century, when our story is nearing its end, both media are confronted with a new, uneasy situation. Thanks to the convergence between the computer, telecommunications and entertainment industries, audiences are given the possibility not only to interact with the screen but also to create their own programmes, independently from the movie-theatres or the television channels. This is not to say that these are about to close down; cinema attendance has stabilised, and Italian television sets are on, on an average, four hours a day. But unless they contrive new forms of addressing audiences, they might lose any appeal to youngsters and the advertisers would give their money to other, more profitable media. In such a juncture the cinema would become a pastime for the elderly, television a radio with pictures. Both media are under a serious threat; collaboration would help them face the danger.

NOTES

1. The mean of the annual statistics to be found in the yearly publication of the *Società italiana degli autori ed editori, Lo spettacolo in Italia.*
2. Mean of the statistics between 1962 and 1980.
3. His adversaries stressed the fact that after 1955 most of his films failed and that nobody would have ventured in helping him made new pictures. This may be true but Rossellini had the courage to embark on a new career when he was nearly sixty years old.
4. Here we do not take into account his most famous film, *The Taking of Power by Louis XIV* (1966), because it was shot for French television.
5. An useful overview of Rossellini's work for television is to be found in Sergio Trasatti (1978).
6. *Annuario statistico del cinema europeo*, Rome, Media salles ed., a yearly edition since 1989
7. For the most recent decades, up-to-date figures can be found at www.cinema. italiano.net or www.mediasalles.it.

5. SPAIN: BIPOLAR VISIONS, UNIFIED REALITIES: A GENERAL OVERVIEW

Valeria Camporesi

Almost everybody in Spain knows that one of the best known arty Spanish films, *El sol del membrillo* (The Sun of the Quince Tree, 1992), was originally conceived within a project that its director, Victor Erice, had been charged with by Televisión Española as had his previous, unfinished film, *El sur* (1983), whose filming was declared complete by its producer, Elias Querejeta, against Erice's will (Heredero 1997: 844–6). It ended up as an extremely cheap, totally independent production which gained international acclaim within a small élite of *cinéphiles* and intellectuals which seems so far apart from the very idea of a mass media as it can be in the contemporary world. Indeed, one could say that this film is in more than an instance a crucial document in the history of the relationship between cinema and television in Spain. On one level, its history shows how normal it is for an auteurish film director to work for television; on the other, it can perfectly serve the purpose of dramatically separating the two media as if they belonged to different worlds, with culture, art, and history on one side (the cinema side, of course), and superficiality, lack of commitment, and an eternal present on the other (the television side, of course). One is almost tempted to say that the place that *El sol del membrillo* has acquired within Spanish culture, its prestige, might indeed have something to do with the fact that it could be used and referred to, to show off a supposedly intellectual disdain towards the electronic media. If emphasis is put on how the history of its production ended, with Televisión Española going out of the picture as soon as serious content was getting in, it might be held to demonstrate that television cannot be seriously interested in such an innovative and intellectually daring enterprise. On the other end, if its meaning is given priority, no doubt can be expressed that, in general terms, television is depicted as the antithesis of what Erice thinks that culture, art, and cinema should do. Indeed, television occupies a rather crucial place in *El sol del membrillo*'s central plot, as Erice contrasts cinema's fixity with the televisive flux. That being so, it would not be anything peculiar: many film authors, as well as a good bunch of mainstream directors, from all over the world, have often portrayed television as the bad guy, ultimately responsible for our not being in contact with our own reality and emotions. What seems more peculiar, insofar as the Spanish cultural context is concerned, is that hardly anybody would point at this particular implication of Erice's vision of cinema, and discuss it.[1]

This story shows how difficult it is to draw an accurate, unbiased picture of the television–cinema relationship in Spain. Established visions which tend to represent the two media as inmersed in a hyperrealistic world which is interpreted as the scenery for the deployment of a paradoxical cultural schizophrenia are strongly widespread, and generally accepted as commonsensical.[2] To counteract its influence, this essay approaches the history of cinema–television relationship from an opposed point of view, and finds its main inspiration in the work of a group of scholars who are struggling to establish the history of Spanish television as a serious object of study.[3] The following pages are therefore aimed at establishing a more even-handed view of its subject. After a brief reconstruction of the industrial relationships which have drastically influenced the history of Spanish cinema at least since the late 1960s, attention shall be drawn to some major cases which illustrate to what extent the existing interchanges between the two media did work as a creative driving force. At the very heart of this intersection, one finds the film-makers, who would come back and forth from television to cinema, or reverse, asserting themselves as good professionals in the two media, and their programmes and films. To what extent at both levels it is possible to devise some kind of contamination between low–high (art and cinema) and low–low (television and, when times are ripe, videogames) culture, will be the central issue to be addressed, along with questions regarding the representation of television which is being depicted along the way.

THE LAWS OF POWER AND MONEY: THE INDUSTRY

Indeed, in the very early days of Televisión Española, what was mainly regarded as its most interesting social function had a lot to do with the longing of better living standards, conventionally defined as purchasing power. This is at least how cinema depicted it in the 1960s, when various films included the television set in their stories as a symbol and symptom of domestic welfare, while its programmes were mainly represented as a viable way to gain fabulous amounts of money, through the quiz and/or the amateurs' hour programmes. Hardly any credit was given to the possible cultural implications of its presence, and, when some attention was devoted to it, it usually was to portray more or less sinister, or simply idiotic, concerns, characters, and stories.[4]

At a primary level, these images might be interpreted as the inevitable outcome of the specific political, and socio-economic, circumstances of Spain.

Twenty years of dictatorship, and a prolonged economic agony, accompanied by a ferociously conservative social climate, might account for this bitter vision of television, which, it should not be forgotten, was regarded a child of the regime and a monumental instrument of propaganda. Nevertheless, what is startling about the way in which popular cinema dealt with television in its early days is the way in which those filmic images coherently fit into long term public attitudes towards the electronic medium, images which proved enduring, in different forms and versions, within changing political and economic contexts. The tendency to underrate television's cultural content, while at the same time develop a sharply clear perception of its political and economic power, maintains its grip over the public discourse on the medium well beyond the economic modernisation of the 1960s, Franco's death in 1975, and the transition to democracy.[5] Besides, all through these years, it ran parallel to an equally inconsistent, but no less durable, broadcasting policy.

According to the standard version of the history of industrial relationships between cinema and television in Spain, active cooperation involving the two media industries had been 'sporadic since 1967 . . . but never resulted in a continued policy . . . which was going to appear only in 1984'; and even then, continuity was only partial, and 'tensions continued to exist well into the end of the twentieth century' (Torreiro 1995: 375).[6] In most cases, up to the introduction of commercial television in the early 1990s, active cooperation meant that politicians in charge of the audio-visual policy would exert pressure so that TVE would support different projects to revitalise the film industry, traditionally depicted as in need of some kind of public financing. Thus:

> The concept of crisis is inherent to the discourse on Spanish cinema. The crisis was and is the inevitable premise in its representation and explanation of itself. It is a concept of crisis which never or very seldom might be taken to mean 'drastic change' but that is always a synonym of 'bad situation'. (Soto Vázquez 2003: 182)

In other words, the very origins of the industrial relationship between the two major audio-visual centres belong generally speaking to the realm of politics, and, more precisely, of policies to protect and support film production (*política de fomento de la industria cinematográfica*) which TVE managers would either willingly promote or reluctantly admit to and later neglect. This picture was not altered substantially up to the second half of the 1990s. The two major figures in this scenario would be José María García Escudero, in his second chance as Director General de Cinematografía, in 1962–7, and Pilar Miró, both as Directora General de Cinematografía of the first Socialist Government, in 1982–6,[7] and afterwards, up to 1989, as Directora General de RTVE; but what strikes most when analysing the whole period is its astonishing continuity, rather linearly marked by frustrating attempts which always failed to establish a clear, detectable legal framework to cooperation. What should also be mentioned is that, although its full consequences were only to be seen a decade later, in the 1980s an increasing number of programmes were produced by independent companies, a trend which is generally considered as a basic symptom of television contribution to the economic vitality of the audio-visual industry (Cuevas Puente 1994: 68).

The double trend which results from the coexistence of intermittent attempts at forcing television to invest in the film industry, and a slow, unstable, very thin, but growing, line of actual cooperation, is the basic feature of the history of the audio-visual industry in Spain and might be cause or symptom of the contradictory attitude to television which has been described above. The origins of this discourse belong to the end of one of the crucial periods in the industrial history of Spanish cinema, the late 1960s. By then, the decline in cinema attendance which had hit other national industries since the end of World War II had become evident. It might be instructive to see how it was dealt with.

As Spain was a relatively late comer to the world of broadcast television, it does not come as a surprise that the beginning of the crisis would be attributed to the competition of television, as indeed the story had been told elsewhere.[8] 'The social phenomenon of modernity which has had the major consequences on film showing', an influential account on the Spanish film industry situation stated in 1970, 'is with no doubt the appearance and fast growth of television. In every country, its influence has been, in principle, negative for cinema' (López García 1972: 81). 'As it has happened . . . in more developed countries . . .', another official report stated in 1975, right before Franco's death, 'the strongest competition (to the film industry) was going to emerge from the very heart of the audiovisual media: television'.[9]

If that was the diagnosis, the natural remedy in a monopolistic context strongly conditioned by authoritarian political priorities was that the medium which was taking advantage of the crisis would act responsibly, and reinvest at least part of its revenues to give back resources to the film industry, a recipe which the advent of democracy did not alter ostensibly. While TVE would start its unstable policies of cooperation with the film industry, private production companies would gradually slip into a practice where the intensive integration between the different media was increasingly viewed as normal, although uncertain and intermittent. Indeed, the same reports which had singled out television as a major cause in the impending crisis of cinema attendance had reckoned its benign influence on cinema, and mentioned its manifold impact.

> Television influence on production was less prominent and, in many cases, favoured it, either promoting production of films with a double outlet, cinema and television, or bringing back to circulation a remarkable number of titles which were deposited in storehouses of production companies; (besides) some cinema technicians and professionals would join television companies. (López García 1972: 81)

Industrial and labour relations have often been in the limelight, and they will be carefully revised here. However, it seems important also to stress how big a role television can play to spread affection for cinema. What happened in Spain under this regard might prove illuminating. As it can be expected, popular feature films which had enjoyed a remarkable success when shown in cinema theatres, repeated and magnified their acceptance when television decided to broadcast them.[10] Also, the hypothesis which links the closing up of peripheral and provincial theatres to this role being taken up by television seems quite reasonable under this regard. However, at a less visible level, perhaps, those films which were broadcast to more targeted audiences of would-be *cinéphiles* were also very influential, although quantitatively limited to certain specific urban middle-class, and lower middle-class publics.

> In November 1966 (as a by-product of the launching of the second public channel, TVE2) the key factor in the awakening of TVE cinematographic programmes was set in motion: the creation of 'Cine-Club'. . . . 'Cine-Club' marks a new era . . . Since its beginning it is structured as a succession of series devoted to, mainly, directors or cinematographic movements . . . (and) very quickly it wins over an enthusiastic and addicted public. (Baget Herms 1993: 180–1)

Indeed, it was just the beginning of a very long history of resurrections which, while subject to the sometimes frivolous personal preferences of some producers, nevertheless had a major impact in the promotion of a public affection to film history. Although no exhaustive study has been pursued on this phenomenon, it is repeatedly referred to in specialised magazines, either devoted to cinema or television. Within this fascinating story of a chameleonic cinema, the whole chapter devoted to the image that TVE projected of Spanish cinema and its history would constitute an intriguing sub-plot, sufficiently long and complex to deserve a much closer analysis than the one which can be pursued here. What is pretty clear is that the formats and meanings of the TVE programmes on Spanish films of the past and, more in general, on the history of Spanish cinema, depended utterly on the political climate. Contrary to what happens with the rest of the cinematographic output of Televisión Española, it is possible to detect here significant discontinuities and disagreements, clashes which are especially sharp in the first years of democracy. This is illustrated, for instance, the way in which Diego Galán, responsible for a three year long series on the history of Spanish cinema, between 1976 and 1978, describes his experiences in various articles published under the title 'Memorias del cine español' in *Fotogramas* in August and September 1978. In various moments, it was clearly perceived that dealing with Spanish film history implied being able to take some firm stance on Francoism, and its historical meaning. Although the actual impact of these programmes on the promotion of a public affection to Spanish cinema is not as clear as their political implications,[11] what should be stressed here is that film history as depicted by television does represent a significant phenomenon whose detailed analysis could contribute substantially to our knowledge not only of the various implications of the relationship between cinema and television, but also of the complex meaning, and the changing contents, of what, in different moments, is considered as the (official) Audio-visual History.

In any event, side by side with the precarious but determined political interventions in favour of television investments in film production, in coincidence with a more or less conscious, more or less sensible, policy of diffusion of feature films and their history, actual intercourses between television and the film industry were also growing, and conflicts became possibly less numerous than multiple areas of cooperation. As the then president of the Sindicato Nacional del Espectáculo (the show business union moulded on corporatist premises), Juan José Rosón, admitted in 1970, 'What is peculiar is that lately film directors and producers are working in TVE and reverse. What should be done now is to coordinate, more if possible, those works, and aim at doing films together' (*Teleradio*, 658, 3–9 August 1970). That being the situation, it might be interesting to explore its consequences and attempt to establish what kind of audio-visual products were conceived and realised as the outcome of that cooperation.

How did it all begin? Film-makers and television during Francoism

In spite of the strong political continuity represented by the dictatorship, it seems reasonable to establish a dividing line which separates two different moments in the history of the first decades of the cinema–television relationship in Spain. As for the first period, in general terms it can be asserted that between 1956, when the television service was established, and up to 1965, when the second public channel, TVE2, was launched, the cultural gap between the two audio-visual media in this country was very wide and mutually accepted:[12] during the first decade of its history, public television did not only identify itself with what was generally perceived as a degraded visual culture, but was also strongly intertwined with Francoist values, censorship practices, and traditionalism.[13] This is not to say that the film industry could consider itself at all free from the oppressive influence of the dictatorship. It simply was more complex, and, to a certain extent, more unpredictable, although within certain obvious limits.

Once again, it is cinema which accurately depicts the caricature of television which best describes these perceptions. *Un, dos, tres, al escondite inglés* (One, Two, Three, Let's Play, Zulueta, 1969) is a telling example of such a portrait. Its director was one of the 'TV brats' who had entered TVE a little earlier, and his story as an image maker will be told in the following pages. What seems especially interesting about this film is that, while explicitly inspired by Zulueta's television work,[14] it is built upon a drastic reprobation of the small screen, depicted as the repository of the most sinister traditionalist conceptions of popular culture. The movie, structured around ten songs, tells the story of a group of young musicians who disrupt a very conservative music festival as it is broadcast live on television. Strongly influenced by Richard Lester's Beatles films, as Zulueta himself admitted, its main argument implies a sarcastic attack on Francoist television, insofar as it identified itself with censorship and the diffusion of a retrograde aesthetics, and it self-ironically pledges for a fight against it in pursuit of a juvenile re-appropriation of public spaces.[15] Yet the history of the film's director and his experiences as a television director were at least as meaningful as the film's content. Indeed, the contradiction which can be detected between them might prove extremely revealing and do justice to the complexities of the changes which were under way.

TVE began to change in the first half of the 1960s, as the result of different factors. To begin with, the Spanish film industry was aware of the imminent impact in their country of the worldwide crisis in attendance in movie theatres. In a curious parallel, in those very years the extravagant economic situation of a public monopoly financed by private advertising had generated a generous financial bonanza for RTVE: 'In the second half of the decade (the 1960s), TVE lived its golden age. With no significant financial problems it worked as a money making machine' (Palacio 1996: 73). This was a situation which, accompanied by a growing professionalism, was suitable to generate modernising investments and a favourable attitude towards change. Besides, international trends in television were showing the overwhelming power of social penetration of the new medium, concentrating the attention towards the desirability of a multiplication of channels, and revealing the importance of the output contents in a similar way as it happened in other countries (Palacio 1996: 121). At a rather different level, quite far away from direct political power, it should also be recalled here that in 1963 Roberto Rossellini publicly declared that he was abandoning cinema to devote his energies to a pedagogical audio-visual project conceived for television. The weight of Rossellini's decision in the film-makers' world can hardly be overrated, as a symbol and symptom of the expectations that television was generating in various corners of the cinematographic world. Furthermore, it certainly helped to broaden its influence in Spain the fact that TVE would participate, along with ORTF, in the financing of two of Rossellini's programmes, *Gli atti degli Apostoli* (*The Acts of the Apostles*) in 1968, and *Socrate*, in 1970, which was also filmed in Spain.[16] *Gli atti degli Apostoli* was broadcast on TVE in Easter 1970.

When TVE2 came into existence, then, a series of circumstances were contributing to make television, as a creative workplace, as attractive as cinema at least in certain regards. As a consequence of these different factors, it is hardly surprising that a Francoist institution would participate in its own way in the context of the 1960s, and that Spanish public television might want to absorb and interpret these breezes of change. What seems important here is that TVE managers began to feel more at ease with the idea of the opening up of new types of productions, and were willing to give a chance to programmes which, although attracting only minority audiences, might nurture new ideas and tune television in with its own time. It was as part of this policy that in 1969 TVE began to take part in international television festivals. An effort was also being made to improve the intrinsic technical values of what was being broadcast.

Within this context, a direct relationship was established between TVE and the young graduates of the Escuela Oficial de Cinematografía, the publicly financed School of Film-making, which up until that very moment had lived in a different world from television. When the public broadcasting system opened up to seek help in its search for a renewal in its programmes, it found its obvious allies among those who not only had been trained as professional film-makers, but that also seemed to have developed interesting cultural personalities. On the part of the future television professionals, the fact that the small screen seemed to be heading towards a radiant future did also play a part. Pilar Miró was one of the young film-makers who joined TVE in that context. She was referred to in the previous pages as an influential figure in audio-visual policies; but her role in the story of the cinema–television relationship in Spain does not end there, as she began her professional career as a television, and, later, film director, and would later go back to it, after the collapse of her political career. As such, she was among a group of young film-makers who, in the mid-1960s, shared an optimistic view of the creative potentials of television. As Miró would recall, in the mid-1960s 'an interchange of ideas, experiences and a vocabulary' was established, and cinema and television began to nurture 'a certain renewed illusion, a search and an attitude which I should define as new, as improvisation was set aside and a series of theories, standpoints and realities were developed which were more tuned to the social and cultural context' (Miró, *Teleradio*, 1976). Within this vision, television was the driving force for the renewal, a conviction which was shared by a conspicuous number of young film-makers, whose main common feature was the desire to be good professionals, somehow tuned in with their society and times.

So it was that between the late 1960s and the early 1970s, right before the end of dictatorship, television was 'discovered' as an interesting medium which could accompany a delicate, and firmly controlled, transition to the filtering in of modern values and audio-visual innovations in Spanish visual (and social) culture. As another protagonist, Josefina Molina, would put it: 'all of a sudden we realized that television is a very important medium and also that under certain circumstances, RTVE might offer more opportunities for personal and creative expression than cinema' (*Teleradio*, n. 961 24/30 May 1976: 12–13). This is how a new climate was established which would give way to new ideas and programmes. Although important differences existed among the young men and women who were going to lead the new trend, they were instantly perceived as a generation, probably due to the strong relationship which existed between them and their context. Many of them were going to play an important role in the drawing up of future trends of visual culture in Spain, well after

Franco's death in 1975. Their experience in TVE can hardly be overestimated. Their names, at least some of them, form part of the history of Spanish visual culture. It might be worth it to observe what their television experiences implied and to what extent they can be considered as historically significant.

It all began with the discovery of the refreshing aspects of popular culture, the showiest being pop music. While Valerio Lazarov was attracting attention with his zooms and elaborate camera movements in musical programmes in the first channel, TVE2 began to look for styles and formats, especially designed to attract young audiences. It was in this context that that the director of *Un, dos, tres, al escondite inglés*, Iván Zulueta, could contribute one of the most interesting programmes of the history of television in Spain, both for its formal qualities and its unconventional content. *Último grito*, the weekly magazine he directed and produced in 1968 and 1969, was devoted to interviews, commentaries, news, and reports, of new trends in music, cinema, and fashion. Its style, main characters, ideas were a direct challenge to established culture and values. Filmed in 16mm, it was broadcast between May and December 1968 and between October 1969 and January 1970. According to Palacio, who reconstructed the programme's history, it was: 'one of the most interesting programmes of the history of television in Spain' (Palacio 1996: 38). Pedro Olea, Ramón Gómez Redondo (directors) and Jaime Chávarri (screenwriter) participated in its production.

While Zulueta was certainly untypical in his explicit lack of interest for social conventions, the energetic drive which he experienced in television was shared by quite a few of his colleagues from the Escuela Oficial de Cine. They all seem to have begun working in television with an unpretentious but at the same time wishful, and crystal-clear, purpose: 'I do not mean to be definitive, or to settle the world, but I do wish to record my time, my society; be a witness of what stands all around me, especially if this is something I do not like' (*Teleradio*, 630, 19–25 January 1970: 10). In some ways, television and cinema seemed to be equally useful for that purpose, as most of the directors who might identify themselves with this frame of mind went back and forth between the two media, many of them with creative purposes in mind. Quite a few of their names have been referred to above. José Luis Borau, former teacher at the Escuela Oficial de Cinematografía, founder of the production company 'El Imán', which produced advertisements as well as films and television programmes, was an important figure within the group,[17] no less than the already mentioned Pilar Miró, Josefina Molina, and Iván Zulueta. But many others shared their experiences, and were capable to introduce a new creativity in the audio-visual world. Among them, the following should be mentioned: Antonio Mercero, whose *La cabina* (*The Phone Box*, 1972)[18] won an Emmy Award in 1973 and stands as a piece of quality television, as well as of a critical stance against dictatorship; in spite of his premature death, Claudio Guerín was also a critical innovator, and played a crucial role in the creation of a cinematographic culture; then, Jaime de Armiñán[19]; Antonio Giménez Rico[20], Emilio Martínez

Lázaro[21]; Alfonso Ungría[22]; José María Forqué[23]; Antonio Drove[24]; José Luis Cuerda[25]; Jaime Chávarri[26], Francesc Bertriu[27]: they all considered it equally interesting, although diverse, to work in television and cinema.

Video was quite another thing. That same group of rather experimental, socially committed film-makers, who were able to see in television the opportunity to work within a context not so drastically determined by money, was at the same time quite resistant to renounce the quality of celluloid. Indeed, quite a few of them expressed their total rejection of the poor results of the then new technology of video recording. The most remarkable exception was Claudio Guerín, who, having been trained in traditional filming techniques in the Escuela Oficial de Cine, was nevertheless able to see the new possiiblities which electronic support might open up to audio-visual creations. Anticipated by the work of Josefina Molina and Pilar Miró, who also integrated video in their dramatic productions for TVE, Guerín is considered to have attained the best results in the application of video techniques to quality television (Palacio 1996: 129–31).

DIRECTING AND PRODUCING THROUGH THE POLITICAL TRANSITION TO DEMOCRACY TO THE LAUNCHING AND GROWTH OF COMMERCIAL TELEVISION

A striking feature of any interview with these young film-makers who changed the standard quality of television programmes in the late 1960s to early 1970s was a reference to 'well known limitations' which marked the otherwise free deployment of their creativity. No explicit reference could be made to censorship and the oppressive weight of dictatorship, but the allusion was clear. While different personal styles and predilections would lead to varied attitudes towards this situation, it is hardly debatable that those limits did condition the possible televisual culture which these young film-makers were trying to build up. These circumstances might explain that while their drive was capable of generating a new audio-visual style, it nevertheless fell short of any radicalism, either in its implications or formal solutions. The utopian, short living Rossellinian drive to use television as a medium to approach reality as it is was never viewed as an inspiration: if a collaboration and interchange of financial support, ideas and professionals was inaugurated, and brought about significant innovations and changes. No institutional structure seemed interested in coordinating the individual efforts so as to devise the map of a new mass culture which would be able to close the gap between elitist and popular culture. The few examples of good cultural programmes which Ortega and Albertos describe were conceived from outside the film-makers' world.

Franco died on 20 November 1975 and TVE could, gradually, participate in the transition to democracy. The end of the dictatorship represented under many respects the opening up of a new era, as the new political context had quite a deep impact on the way in which TVE was organised and the values it was called to propagate. Palacio draws up a sharp synthesis of the main changes which the advent of democracy implied for Televisión Española (Palacio 1996: 92–3) Yet, broadly speaking, the public image of television, and its relationship with cinema, did not experience a radical change. The new democracy, which had taken control of TVE, did not succeed in convincing the audience that the powerful electronic medium which they hosted in their living rooms was an energising agent of a new political era. On the contrary, between the late 1970s and the early 1980s, the new political climate seemed to be leading to a new juxtaposition between the two media, with television once more playing the part of the vulgar character. In June 1976, Emilio Martínez Lázaro stated that the uncertain months which followed Franco's death were witnessing a flight of young film-makers towards cinema, as television seemed increasingly indifferent to quality and contents.[28] Indeed, the first years of the democratic transition witnessed an explosion in critical cinema production. Besides, in spite of the dense panorama described above, television did still suffer from a profound lack of social legitimisation (Palacio 1996: 96–7), which might have favoured a peculiar perception of its future. Nevertheless, it was a short lived phenomenon. Soon, the film industry would go back to its poor revenues and pessimistic outlook, while RTVE recovered.

In the following decade, while creative forces were driven back to television, and to the preceding, continuous migrations between the two main audio-visual industries, the strongest trend in the integration of cinema and television implied a return to established canons of quality. Palacio describes it as the 'classic period' of dramatic production in TVE (Palacio 1996: 143). This trend accompanied what has been described above as the increasing financial presence of the television industry in film production. Conventional wisdom had it that the television of democracy had to work in pursuit of dignity and cultural refinement. In dramatic production, this goal implied the promotion of established good and reassuring series, often inspired by literary or artistic classics. These series were viewed as the ideal vehicle for the adaptation of what could be considered as the national heritage to the formats of mass culture. However, in spite of the supposedly consensual character of the ideal Spanish culture which was to be spread, the actual contents of these series would be more or less revisionist towards the official history spread during the dictatorship, depending on the government of the day. Palacio and Ibáñez have described how Juan Antonio Bardem translated his political and didactical audio-visual project on Spanish history into his television programmes of the late 1980s and early 1990s (Palacio and Ibáñez 2004: 141–51). While cinema, radio and comics were being the vehicle for new cultural values and styles, along with many other things, being able to rescue even a certain degree of underground culture, the television of democracy went back to established literary texts, biopics of great Spaniards, and audio-visual classicism.[29] The most interesting film-maker who came to be associated with this trend is Mario Camus.[30] He had made himself known as a good professional in the film industry, both as a director and a screenwriter, since the mid-1960s. 'It is hard to find in one of his contemporaries a similar will to be integrated in the industry and to live his activity as filmmaker strictly as a professional engagement' (Borau 1998: 182). It was is in the late 1970s that Camus began to be known as a sensitive, highly valued demiurge of good audio-visual adaptations of national literary master-pieces, being able to work on high technical standards both in cinema and tele-vision. Although it has to be reckoned that literary adaptations did imply very different processes in the two media,[31] it should not be underrated the very fact that Camus was one of the great translators of literary classics both in Spanish cinema and television at least since the late 1970s, thus creating an interesting instance of synchronic activity.

The 1980s did not seem to change in structure what had been going on since the mid-1960s. According to Palacio, the last chance to change radically the way TVE worked was gone when F. Castedo, Director General between January and October 1981, abandoned his job (Palacio 1996: 98–9). For many film-makers, television continued to represent a stable job as well as a less pushy and harsh workplace, as compared with the strict control which production exerted, according to them, in the cinema industry.[32] While experiments were still quite unusual, and direct financing of film production was experiencing a boom,[33] film-makers who had entered TVE during Francoism kept working along established lines. What was going to change the panorama, and deeply affect cinema–television relationships, was not the appointment of film-maker Pilar Miró as RTVE Director General, in 1986–9, but the 1980s different laws which broke up the RTVE monopoly in broadcast television, either in favour of local governments (since 1982), or of private enterprises (beginning in 1988). What was at stake, though, was not to be seen until the beginning of the new millennium, a decade afterwards.

The early 1990s did not mark a watershed, either, in terms of audio-visual creativity and innovation. While the number of hours produced increased dra-matically, most of its contents did not generate any abrupt change in the cinema–television relationship. The rapid growth of broadcasting hours estab-lished as firmly as ever the existence of two supposedly separated worlds, with television standing firmly on the side of low (mass) culture. Some film directors kept working to upgrade it, as they had done since the late 1970s. *El Quijote de Miguel de Cervantes* which Manuel Gutiérrez Aragón directed in 1991, for instance, was a renewed example of an inspired adaptation very much in the line of what had been done in previous years. Yet generally speaking, still at the end of the twentieth century, cinema insisted in portraying the dark side of tele-vision, and identified it with the moral decadence of 'reality shows', thus con-tributing to spread the idea of television as cultural garbage (*televisión-basura*). It is significant, for instance, that a rather popular and socially visible film like *Muertos de risa* (*Dying of Laughter*, de la Iglesia, 1999) would show at the end of the decade a TV audience which finds it very amusing when the two main characters, TV comedians, kill each other during a live show. Also Alejandro Amenábar's first two feature films, *Tesis* (*Thesis*, 1996) and *Abre los ojos* (*Open*

Your Eyes, 1997), while clearly different from *Muertos de risa* in their style and intentions, are nevertheless firmly installed in a rather negative perception of the domestic media. Years had passed by without altering radically the established model, and the increasing reciprocal influences did not seem to produce any significant innovation, either formal or cultural.

As an example of the paradoxical relationship which film-makers entertained with television, through the 1990s, some voices began to be heard which were capable of portraying a powerful critique of the mystifying power of media, while giving new media an ever renewed potential to challenge cultural conventions. The mock documentary which Basilio Martín Patino filmed on video in 1992, *La seducción del caos* (*The Allure of Chaos*), at the same time took advantage of the flexibility of its electronic support, and of the money of TVE, while launching a strong '*J'accuse*' against the manipulation of the representation of reality in television. Born in 1930, since the 1950s Patino was one of the most representative exponents of cinematographic dissent, during the dictatorship. His first feature film, *Nueve cartas a Berta*, dates back to 1965. He is the author of an important documental trilogy on Franco and the Civil War, *Canciones para después de una guerra* (produced in 1971; prevented from public exhibition for political reasons until 1976); *Queridísimos verdugos* (1973; released in 1977), and *Caudillo* (1976). Extremely open to new conceptions of the audio-visual, Patino is considered as the Spanish film-maker who has proved to be more sensitive towards 'the promiscuity which media and audiovisual forms of representation share in the contemporary world' (Borau 1998: 553).

TOWARDS THE TWENTY-FIRST CENTURY: CELEBRATING THE HYBRIDISATION

'The 1990s made television the major financing source for Spanish films . . . If in 1997 30% of the revenues of a Spanish production came from broadcasting royalties, in 1999 this percentage raised to 45%' (Abad 2002: 87). Eventually, the late 1960s utopian drive towards a substantial financial involvement of television to support the film industry has come true. That it would happen within the framework of a much less buoyant economic situation for television itself does not seem a major problem. What demands attention is that it seems to be generating a drastic change in attitudes.

Since the late 1990s, in coincidence with a growing decisive dependence of the film industry upon television financing and promotion tricks, it is also gaining momentum in what could be described as a brand new 'cultural' dependence, the first symptoms of a transformation in the discourse on cinema and television. The gradual proliferation of commercial and local television stations at the end of the period here analysed seems to have brought forward a change in the general trend of a more productive interchange of ideas between cinema and television. Increasingly, at the turn of the millennium, television is viewed not only as the solution to the film industry never ending 'crises' but as the provider of a new injection of talents and, not less important, social dimension. If one was to judge it by the 2005 annual ceremony of the Goya, the 'Oscars' of the Spanish Film Academy, the first decade of the twenty-first century did mark quite a watershed. Popular television stars were the main attraction to the point that *El país* hosted a debate on the questionable opportunity of this choice (Galán, *El país*, 3 February 2005). Hopefully, this might help to generate a more balanced view of the existing, and eventual, creative relationships between the two media. As an influential media commentator stated: 'today, television is certainly a big Taylorist factory, where work conditions are determined by the dictatorship of "share" and competence, but this did not give away with innovation and creativity' (Bustamante 2001: 41). While cinema is subject to strong financial restrictions, and cinema theatrical attendance is only one of many sources of returns, the blurring of borders between the two media might might be an interesting development for the good of challenging audio-visual products.

NOTES

1. See, for instance, Marías (1992: 118–31) and Arocena (1996).
2. In his analysis of *Cuadernos para el diálogo*, Josetxo Cerdán describes an influential case of unbalanced assessment of television within Spanish intellectual circles. See Cerdán 2005: 219–34.
3. An overall, balanced and informed report on quality programmes in TVE throughout its history can be found in Palacio 1992 and an analysis of the enduring negative social image of TVE in Palacio 2001: 75–90; see also Ortega and Albertos 1998: 61–74; and Smith 2003: 9–33.
4. My extensive description of a few examples can be found in Soderbergh Widding and Fullerton 2000: 149–58 (for a more detailed Spanish version, see V. Camporesi 1999: 148–62).
5. As an example of how this discourse is applied to the cinema–television relationships after the establishment of democracy, see Pérez Pinar 1985: 51–7.
6. A detailed description of the cinema–television agreements, and their confused preliminary and conseuences between the late 1960s and the mid-1990s can be found in Cuevas Puente 1994: 61 and 91–107.
7. As part of the 'Ley Miró' approved in December 1983, which was meant to deploy a strong policy in support of the national film industry, an agreement was signed between RTVE and the Association of Film Producers which, apart from making easier any kind of cooperation which would benefit the film industry, guaranteed that 25 per cent of the feature films which were broadcast by TVE had to be Spanish (Torreiro 1995: 402–3).
8. On the impact of foreign experiences on attitudes to television in Spain, see V. Camporesi, 'Stereotyping a Competitor' (2000).
9. *La exhibición cinematográfica en España (situación y condicionantes)*, Madrid, 1975, p. 34 (this document was brought to my attention by Alberto Elena as part of the research done within the framework of the collective project on 'El consumo de cine en España').
10. See reports on audience acceptance in *RTVE Anuario* since 1976.
11. No systematic study has ever been devoted to the 'invention' of a public discourse on Spanish film history. I am presently engaged in a first exploration of it as a part of my collaboration with the project 'El archivo del Dos de Mayo: mito,

conmemoración y recreación artística de una memoria compartida' (Hum2005-01612/ARTE; Head of project: Jesusa Vega).

12. See the testimony of Pilar Miró in 'Los de la Escuela Oficial de Cinematografía', in '20 años de TVE, 1956–1976', *Teleradio*, special issue, 1976.

13. As I argued in Camporesi, 'Stereotyping a competitor' (2000), the way in which Pedro Almodóvar depicts television broadcast news in a rather well known scene of *Mujeres al borde de un ataque de nervios* (Women on the Verge of a Nervous Breakdown, 1988) shows how clearl defined and strong is the image that TVE gained during Francoism, not only as a propaganda tool, but also for its old fashioned visual appearance. For a more intellectual description, see Palacio (1996), special issue on television in Spain; and Pérez Ornia, 'Peculiaridades de una televisión gubernamental' I and II (1989: 304–25).

14. According to Zulueta, the film represented 'the opportunity to do on a big screen what I was doing in my television programme' (Gabardos, Interview to I. Zulueta, 1969).

15. For a very balanced assesssment of this film, see Heredero, n.d.: 25–6. *Arrebato* (1979) is unanimously considered Zulueta's best film.

16. *Gli atti degli Apostoli* (The Acts of the Apostles, 1968) was broadcast on TVE in Easter 1970. See *Teleradio*, 639, March 1970, pp. 10–11. *Teleradio* published a report on the filming of Sócrates in Peatones (on n. 663, 7–13 September 1970). See also the reconstruction in Quintana (1995).

17. A very prestigious film director, Borau was a professor in the Escuela Oficial de Cine in the mid-1960s. Among his students were many of the film-makers whom are mentioned here. Borau also directed television programmes between the late 1960s and the mid-1970s.

18. For a sketchy history of *La cabina* and the resistances it awoke, see Baget Herms 1993: 264–6.

19. 'Theatre is very complicated. I feel more at ease in television, I can better express what I want to say', *Teleradio*, 630, 19–25 January 1970.

20. Although Giménez Rico began to work in television due to the flop of his 1969 feature film, *¿Es Usted mi padre?* (Are You My Father?), his conception of television was far from utilitarian only. See 'RTVE- Directores. La nueva generación (III): Antonio Giménez Rico', *Teleradio*, 983, 7–13 June 1976.

21. Martínez Lázaro would direct his first feature film in 1977, but went on to gain major popularity as a film director only in the late 1980s.

22. Judged as a politically controversial director, eiher for his too outspoken critique to Francoist values during the dictatorship, or to certain radicality in the democratic context, Ungría maintained a conflicting relationship with the film industry, and was forced to work in television.

23. A multifaceted film director, Forqué managed to maintain a rather consistent personal style, and a certain independent tone, all through his professional life, which began in 1951. He worked in important series in TVE between 1981 and 1988.

24. For his interesting television programmes, see Borau 1998: 296–307.

25. Although he is now mostly remembered as the discoverer of Alejandro Amenábar, Cuerda has an impressive curriculum as both television (since 1969) and film (since 1982) director. See Borau 1998: 264–5. As for the coherence in his audio-visual productions, see, for instance, 'Entrevista co José Luis Cuerda', *Teleradio*, 1356, 26 December 1983 – 1 January 1984.

26. The director of one of the most influential documentaries of democratic Spain, *El desencanto* (The Disenchantment, 1976), a challenging work more for its style than for its contents, questioning the life of one of the most influential official poets of Francoism, Chávarri considered his television experience as crucial in his identity as a film-maker. See 'Entrevista a Jaime Chávarri', *Teleradio*, 1320, 15–21 April 1983.

27. Very interested in formal innovations, Bertriu's most interesting contribution to the history of the interaction between different media is his literary adaptation of *La*

plaza del Diamante (1982), which had a cinema and a television versions.

28. 'RTVE- Directores. La nueva generación (IV). Emilio Martínez Lázaro', *Teleradio*, 965, 21–27 June 1976. Ramón Gómez Redondo confirms: 'A few years ago, Josefina Molina said that the true Spanish cinema was being made in television, and she was right. Two years ago it was true. Not any more: programming in RTVE is chaotic' ('RTVE- Directores. La nueva generación (V). Ramón Gómez Redondo', *Teleradio*, 966 (28 June – 4 July 1976). Indeed, Molina directed in 1981 *Función de noche*.

29. For a very comprehensive and acute description and analysis of literary adaptations in Spanish television, see Palacio 2002: 519–38.

30. As an example of the prestige which Camus had acquired see Cobos 1983.

31. As Palacio convincingly argues in 'Enseñar deleitando' (2002: 519–21). For a contemporary vision on the common traits of cinematographic and televisive adaptations, see '*Los santos inocentes*. Gañanes y señoritos', *Fotogramas*, May 1984, p. 32.

32. See 'Directores de cine en TVE', *Teleradio*, 1332, 5–14 July 1983, and 'Los que hacen la televisión', *Teleradio*, 1336 (5–11 August 1983).

33. See Danieri 1983.

6. GERMANY: SCREEN WARS: GERMAN NATIONAL CINEMA IN THE AGE OF TELEVISION

Margit Grieb and Will Lehman

In 1935, the city of Berlin and the National Socialist government of Germany officially inaugurated a new era in visual technology with the broadcast of its first television programme with the purpose of 'plant[ing] the image of the Fuhrer indelibly in all German hearts' (Reich director of broadcasting Eugen Hadamovsky, quoted in Uricchio 1996). Television, the technology and the institution, were already in development in the 1920s, before the National Socialists came to power. However, in 1933 the Reich's Ministry for Enlightenment of the People and Propaganda (Reichsministerium für Volksaufklärung und Propaganda) was officially put in charge of its development and significant advances in the technology made the 1935 broadcast possible. Nazi government officials remained sceptical as to the usefulness of television in the quest for ideological manipulation. Radio and cinema seemed much more effective in the dissemination of information, such as public addresses, and the staging of public political spectacles (Hickethier 1998: 36). Nonetheless, one year later Hitler's resourceful and media-savvy propaganda machine put the new medium television to effective use for transmitting the 1936 Berlin Olympic Games. Interestingly, the next event to reach a significant viewership in Germany was sports-related as well, the broadcast of the 1954 World Cup of Soccer (also the first televised World Cup). Germany's win in Switzerland against the more fancied Hungarian team became known as the 'Miracle of Bern'. This televised game had particular significance for Germany as a nation in the immediate post-war years. In the words of Franz Beckenbauer: 'Germany became someone again. We gave ourselves the feeling of self-respect again' (*German Hero*, 2003). This win, seen by millions of people on television, announced to the world West Germany's budding national confidence and the onset of the nation's Economic Miracle (Fassbinder uses the World Cup broadcast as a concluding moment in his *Marriage of Maria Braun*, but as an auditory event broadcast on radio).

To enable sufficient public access to the broadcasts, the city of Berlin built special viewing locales, called *Fernsehstuben*. There was a decisive push by the Propaganda Ministry to turn television into a medium tailored to attract group audiences (not unlike film) rather than promote viewing as a private, home-bound experience (analogous to radio). However, after 1939, television technology was implemented predominantly in military operations which hindered its commercial development.

While it exceeds the scope of this chapter to trace the early history of German television in more detail, suffice it to say that this connection to fascist political enterprises served as a precarious foundation for German television's development as a mass medium in the decades after World War II. Although this medium was embraced by the general population and quickly spread into almost every household in Germany (at least in the West) in the 1950s and especially in the 1960s, many film-makers believe that TV's potential for ideological manipulation, unsavoury connection to mass entertainment, and ties to commercial interests ultimately diminishes its prospects as a serious medium for artistic expression; many continue to view TV as a medium with much less creative potential than its cousin, film. Although film could be characterised in a similar fashion, the way in which television became institutionally organised rendered it ultimately more suspect. Even several decades after television's ominous public debut, directors such as Wim Wenders denounce it as 'purely fascist'.

Television in West Germany: Film subsidies, the demise of small theatres, and aesthetic hegemony

German independent film-making [. . .] is unthinkable without television. (Elsaesser 1999: 202)

Television in Germany represents an especially interesting case within Europe due to the country's division after 1949 into two sovereign nations, with radically different trajectories concerning the role of the arts.[1,2] After World War II, developments in television commenced in the Federal Republic of Germany (FRG) and resulted in the establishment of the first public broadcasting station, the NWDR, in 1952 and two years later, the ARD. In the 1950s and early 1960s initial attempts to establish a productive relationship between cinema and television were underway and feature films began to be broadcast on TV. However, these cross-media experiments were not well received by critics or the public and were given the derogatory label 'Pantoffelkino' (slipper cinema) (Hickethier 1998: 142). Furthermore, many within the film industry blamed the dramatic decrease in cinema spectatorship on the emergence of television, tainting the reputation of the latter. The then popular slogan 'not a meter of film for television' (Seidl 1987: 40) aptly describes the antagonistic attitude prevalent at the time.[3] It was not until the 1970s that television began to play an important role in the development of a German national cinema.

While popular cinema in the FRG during the 1950s and early 1960s produced mainly entertainment films, such as *Heimatfilme*, pornographic features (comedic and educational), and schoolboy comedies, West Germany's film scene changed drastically after the emergence of a distinctive movement, termed New German Cinema, and the establishment of the *Filmförderungsgesetz* (FFG, Film Subsidy Bill) in 1967. Naturally, not all cinema productions fitted into these established genres. In the 1950s alone, German cinema produced over 1,000 films, covering a gamut of genres and themes. Although light entertainment films were most successful at the box office, a number of more serious films also screened in cinemas (such as Rolf Thiele's *The Girl Rosemarie* from 1958) (Seidl 1987).

Although the FFG initially sponsored projects mainly based on a film-maker's previous commercial success, that is film-makers had to have a *Referenzfilm* (reference film) that had grossed at least 300,000 DM to qualify for government subsidies, subsequent revisions of the bill (especially the revision of 1974) and its administrative body, the *Filmförderungsanstalt* (FFA, Film Subsidy Board), focused on the sponsorship of high-quality, artistic films and the advancement of an alternative film culture.[4] As a result of this subsidy system, a particularly productive relationship developed between television and the emerging creative explosion of the New German Cinema movement; this association had a significant influence on the latter's achievements. The productive relationship between television and film was by no means one-sided. As Thomas Elsaesser notes, TV used films to 'advertise [its] own appeal to a mass audience. Television everywhere has co-opted the cinema and its history in order to create a more special viewing experience for its own captive audience' (Elsaesser 1999: 33).

The Television Framework Agreement of 1974, an accord between state-run television (various channels were administered by state and regional governments) and the FFA, allowed for a specific percentage of the television budget to be used in sponsoring feature films, an arrangement which, over time, turned television into the principal financing body and primary exhibitor of New German Cinema films. The subsidy system, regulated by the FFA, enabled West Germany's television to exert a greater influence on cinematic productions than was the case in other European nations. Unlike contemporary Britain, for example, television stations in Germany procured a significant number of broadcast programmes from external sources. That is it acquired material not originally intended for television (Elsaesser 1999: 32). This business approach allowed for many New German Cinema films, originally conceived as cinema productions, to reach a substantial domestic audience on television, despite their often poor box office performance. Elsaesser points out that many of the

NGC films never made the top 50 at the German box office (Elsaesser 1999: 36). He traces the enormous impact of television on German films to two main factors:

1. television executives who were previously active in the areas of film-making and film criticism had influential positions and votes on the Film Subsidy Board, and
2. commissioning editors at television stations decided what films to co-produce – 'television administrators [turned] into executive film producers' (Elsaesser 1999: 112).

The intimate relationship between television and film had a particularly decisive impact on projects of women film-makers. Through special television events, such as the ZDF's (second German television channel) *Das kleine Fernsehspiel* (the little teleplay), which showcased a large number of women's pictures, many female film-makers acquired considerable access to public venues and received more funding for their films than ever before (Elsaesser 1999: 34, 115). Women film-makers, for example Jutta Brückner, also turned to the ZDF and *Das kleine Fernsehspiel* to get financing for their first-time projects, which many other funding sources would not support due to the risk of sponsoring an unknown film-maker.[5] Additionally, the directors Rainer Werner Fassbinder, Alexander Kluge, Rosa von Praunheim, Helke Sander, and many others, showcased their films in this television venue. While New German Cinema became popular and acclaimed with an art house cinema audience abroad, television represented the main conduit for New German Cinema films to reach a domestic viewership. Peter Jansen comments on this phenomenon, describing Germany as a film-rich yet cinema-poor country (Elsaesser 1999: 32).

When television first emerged as a mass medium it was seen by many as the likely hangman of the cinema, triggering the development of technologies such as Cinemascope, which sought to lure viewers back to the cinema. The advent of cable and pay TV and the dissolution of governmental control over television in Italy only exacerbated this perceived threat in Germany. In the early 1980s, the Arbeitsgemeinschaft Kino e.V., a group of small movie theatre owners who provided a venue for films by New German Cinema directors, declared: 'Cable television's establishment, the emergence of private television organizations and ever-increasing broadcasting of fiction films in state and publicly controlled stations are causing conditions under which the majority of German cinemas will eventually cease to be able to exist' (Arbeitsgemeinschaft 1987: 55). Indeed, as Udo Klein points out, in 1956, 818 million tickets were sold in 7,085 cinemas while almost thirty years later, after television (private and state-sponsored) had established itself firmly as a mass medium in Germany, tickets only reached the 125 million mark in a mere 3,660 cinemas. Concomitantly, in 1985, over 350 feature films were aired on German TV (Klein 2000: 39–41). These figures certainly lend credence to the anxiety felt by theatre owners toward television. However, the statistics also show that television was becoming a bigger threat to the institution of cinema than to the medium of film. In the 1980s, during the years of emerging private television in the FRG, much criticism focused on the negative economic impact of television on theatres rather than on its effects on film aesthetics. Nonetheless, filmmakers and critics increasingly perceived television's gradual aesthetic influence as shaping, defining and, for many, corrupting the look and feel of West German national film productions.

To be sure, many films by Wim Wenders and Werner Herzog in the last few decades exhibit an unmistakable hostility toward the television aesthetic. One aspect that sets traditional television images apart from film is the tendency to favour medium close-up over distance and panorama shots mainly due to the reduced image resolution and size of the television set. In Wenders' films there exists an abundance of long shots, a pre-occupation with scenery (especially in his road movies) and usage of film formats that exceed the size of traditional 35mm film stock. Wenders has commented in the past that, 'television has eliminated the long-shot, which so beautifully conforms to the human eye, and replaced it with the tedium of close-ups' (Wenders 2001: 356). In the last few years, in order to increase the dramatic effect of his widescreen images, Wenders has employed Cinemascope format in several of his films, such as *The End of Violence* (1997) and *The Million Dollar Hotel* (2000), and 70mm in *Until the End of the World* (1991), a format which he claims has not been used for any other European film in twenty years (Wenders 2001: 286) and which many cinemas are no longer equipped to project. Cinemascope is much wider than standard film formats, and in order to be displayed on a typical television set much of the filmed material has to be omitted, manipulated by the 'pan and scan' technique, or shrunk to a narrow band. By using formats such as Cinemascope and 70mm, Wim Wenders strives to offer 'filmic' images – images that are, at least to some degree, hostile to television technology.[6] Thus, Wenders' intentions can be seen as analogous to those of the inventors of Cinemascope forty years earlier: to lure viewers away from the TV set.

In Werner Herzog's case, a similar preoccupation with visually dramatic landscapes mark his films as distinctly cinematic. Films such as *Aguirre, Wrath of God* (1972) and *Fitzcarraldo* (1982), but also more recent films, such as *Grizzly Man* (2005), use exotic locations to showcase the visual beauty of the natural environment in which the stories are set. As in Wenders' films, Herzog's images do not translate well onto the television screen with its limited resolution and size.

FRIEND OR FOE? EXPERIMENTS WITH TELEVISION AND VIDEO:
WIM WENDERS AND ALEXANDER KLUGE

Television began to incorporate video into its formal and institutional organisation in the mid-1950s. Before video became a technological viability, film constituted the only medium with which television broadcasts could be recorded. Video technology had a profound effect on almost every aspect of television's output capabilities, acutely affecting programme content and broadcasting times. Presumably, television could never have aspired to reach its by now axiomatic cultural significance without video recording technologies. Gregory Ulmer notes in *Teletheory* that television and video are intimately coupled because the former can be thought of as 'the institution that has arisen to manage and distribute the medium of video' (Ulmer 1989: x). In other words, Television has become virtually synonymous with video, as it is the latter that constitutes TV's primary vehicle for recording and broadcasting material on the air. It is not surprising then that many film-makers approach video not as an artistic medium in its own right, but as an extension or even surrogate of television.

Wenders: A rebel with a cause

While West Germany's popular film productions (mostly low-brow entertainment films) enjoyed a more or less seamless cooperative relationship with television in the decades after World War II, film-makers within the New German Cinema movement were much more reluctant to embrace television as an artistic ally. Wim Wenders' case probably illustrates best the ambiguous relationship that existed between directors and film productions in one corner and video and television in the other. Although throughout Wenders' more than thirty years of film-making, his *œuvre* creates the impression of being exceedingly receptive toward new media, especially television technologies (such as HDTV), but his experiments also exhibit a certain ambivalence, a concomitant distrust and enthusiasm. From Wenders' earliest attempts to use a video camera in *Nick's Film: Lightning Over Water* (1980) to further examinations of this technology in the essay film *Notebook on Cities and Clothes* (1989), to high definition experiments in *Until the End of the World* (1991) and digital video use in *Buena Vista Social Club* (1998), his artistic application of new imaging technology often exhibits a cryptic constitution. In the 1980 film *Nick's Film: Lightning over Water*, for example, Wenders records the last days of the dying American film-maker (and Wenders idol) Nicholas Ray, who has directed such Hollywood classics as *In a Lonely Place* (1950) and *Rebel Without a Cause* (1955). Wenders and Tom Farrell, a student of Ray's, film the sick man who is suffering from cancer not only with conventional film equipment but also on video. Wenders intends to draw an analogy from the video technology to the invasive cancer within Ray's body. Besides using video to record images, Wenders also incorporates this technology into his films as both subject matter and thematised object. *The End of Violence* (1997), for example, features a video surveillance system, and the presence of television in one form or another is a ubiquitous element found throughout Wenders' films, from *Kings of the Road* (1976) to *Million Dollar Hotel* (2000). Alter points out that, 'TV has forcefully intruded into Wenders' films, insinuating its supposedly malevolent, totalitarian, fascist presence into every nook and cranny of filmed everyday life' (Alter 2002: 125).

In 1982 Wenders recorded a short 'documentary' film at the Cannes film festival entitled *Chambre 666* in which he takes issue with the medium television. Wenders set up a camera and filmed the reaction of several directors (Spielberg, Antonioni, Herzog, Fassbinder, Godard, and others) to the following question:

> Increasingly, films are looking as though they had been made for television, as regards their lighting, framing and rhythm. It looks as though a television aesthetic has supplanted film aesthetic. Many new films no longer refer to any reality outside the cinema – only to experiences contained in other films – as though 'life' itself no longer furnished material for stories. Fewer films get made. The trend is towards increasingly expensive super-productions at the expense of the 'little' film. And a lot of films are immediately available on video cassettes. That market is expanding rapidly. Many people prefer to watch films at home. So my question is: Is cinema becoming a dead language, an art which is already in the process of decline? (Wenders 2001: 182–3)

The formulation of the question makes abundantly clear how Wenders views television and video and that his apprehensive stance is based chiefly on his fears that they will not only corrupt, but actually *replace his* artistic medium, namely films made for cinema. The reactions to Wenders' question varied, from Fassbinder's self-assured argument that films deliver what film-makers infuse into them, and that television's money can help realise the film-maker's individual vision, to Spielberg's criticism of economic pressures produced by Hollywood's insistence on propagating blockbusters (in retrospect a rather ironic reaction from a director who has arguably supplied the blockbuster phenomenon with more steam than any other). Michelangelo Antonioni declares that 'what we should really do is adapt ourselves to the future world and its modes of representation [. . .] We must turn our minds not to the immediate but to the distant future', and he somewhat prophetically predicts that 'high-quality video cassettes will soon bring films into people's homes' (Wenders 2001: 189–90). Antonioni defends video as a medium worthy of experimentation, especially if it harbours the ability to conquer film, as Wenders predicts in his original statement

Although certain aspects of video, especially its association with television, estranged Wenders from this medium through the 1980s, the subsequent decade witnessed a complete reversal in Wenders' attitude – not toward conventional video technology, but to emerging digital video and television technology. After his experimentation with early HDTV in *Until the End of the World*, Wenders recorded his music-documentary *Buena Vista Social Club* entirely on digital tape with the Sony Digi-Beta camera. Since then, he has become an avid user of digital video equipment, especially for his non-fiction work and his music videos.

Wenders' use and self-professed, albeit reserved, admiration for video in the film *Notebooks of Cities and Clothes*, the 1989 essay film on Tokyo fashion designer Yohji Yamamoto, was to be his final experimentation with conventional video technology. However, it was not the last time he directed a film which thematises emerging visual technologies and their relation to the established medium of film. With *Until the End of the World* he revisits his interest and pre-occupation with any technology which has the potential to displace or negatively affect the cinematic image. In *Until the End of the World* Wenders does not simply depict video as a technology pitted against film as he did in *Lightning over Water*.[7] Instead, the film uses a digital video technology, namely HDTV, which is much different from the standard video Wenders had used in the past, and he integrates it in a much more problematic and, at the same time, interesting manner into the film's fiction and form. In *UtEotW*, Wenders explores the future of video and television (represented in the film by HDTV) in a society that is saturated with images. In the fictional adaptation and in the technical realisation, video's prospective status as a cultural determinant is dramatised in anything but a positive way.

During a talk at the IECF in Tokyo in 1990 Wenders comments specifically on his use of HDTV (called 'High Vision' by the Japanese) in *Until the End of the World* and his vision for this medium's future. He stated:

> High Vision could balance the loss of reality by the gain in image resolution. [. . .] High Vision, and this is my dream, could help to sharpen our sense of reality; my nightmare is if High Definition in the long run only continues to undermine any remaining faith we may have in the truth of images. (Wenders 2001: 358–9)

In *Until the End* he appears to have turned his own nightmare into a cinematic reality. The film's high definition images neither reflect reality (they depict dreams and subjective memories) nor do they evoke faith in any type of true images because they are so highly manipulated. In the rare sequences where the high definition images depict 'life-like' subject matter, their content is challenged in other ways. In one of the initial sequences Claire, the main protagonist, passes by a large rectangular wall monitor as she is leaving a party. On this monitor a music video offers some of the first high definition video images of the film. High definition video is the source material for HDTV, and it is very fitting that the music video depicts a group conspicuously evoking the TV as a medium with its name, the Talking Heads, a derogatory reference to television's habitual use of the close-up.

UtEotW, true to the genre of the road movie, does exactly the opposite: it presents the viewer with many sweeping long-shots of landscape and scenery, including shots of the entire globe as viewed from space. It is only within the segments filmed in video that close-ups abound in the film. In other words, the film visually celebrates its otherness, that which sets it apart from television. As early as 1960, the media theoretician Marshall McLuhan noted that one of the main reasons for TV's abundance of close-ups is its screen size and resolution (McLuhan 1994: 314). HDTV, however, with its improved resolution and larger aspect ratio is no longer tied to close-ups. It is bound to change the aesthetics of TV significantly. Wenders, however, appears sceptical in his film.

In the filmic techniques employed in *UtEotW*, Wenders does not treat video as an ally either, but rather showcases it as a rival to what he calls his '"sacred" celluloid images' in *Notebook on Cities and Clothes*. Although high definition video's principal advantage over conventional video is its image clarity and realism, *UtEotW* primarily uses it for the dream sequences, memory play-backs of recordings showing the main character's acquaintances and family, and the highly stylised music video-clip. The images that are presented to the viewer in these sequences have undergone drastic manipulation. They are fuzzy, distorted, and not at all representative of their source material. Instead of capturing HDTV's primary improvements over conventional video, Wenders obscures them through another divergence, digital mutability. As if to lay bare HDTV's inability to project 'truth in images', Wenders foregrounds the digital nature of the recorded dreams and memories, thereby highlighting their constructedness, through various techniques, such as intentional pixilation.

Kluges *Fernsehen* (Intelligent TV)

Wenders' experiments with television are not singular in the context of West German *Autorenfilm*. Another German *Autor*, Alexander Kluge has been using cable television as a creative medium to further his 'public sphere' project since 1988 with 'Kulturmagazine' shows such as *10 vor 11* and *Primetime/Spätausgabe* on RTL, with *News & Stories* on SAT.1, and with *Mitternachtsmagazin* on VOX. His experiments, sometimes referred to as 'kluges Fernsehen' (smart TV), commenced in 1985, when he founded the 'Arbeitsgemeinschaft Kabel und Satellit' (AKS), which later became the TV production company Development Company for Television Programs (DCTP).

In television, Kluge has found a medium to further pursue his notion of a productive 'public sphere', based on Habermas's theories. Such a sphere calls for democratic societies to provide spaces in which information can circulate, guarantee an unfettered exchange of opinion and ideas, and actively encourage public debates. This space should exist independently of the state and remain isolated from private and corporate interests. Despite the fact that Kluge's public sphere appears antagonistic to the norms and practices of private television stations, the director has managed to carve himself a niche in this commercial realm which has enabled him to realise his ideological goals. Although viewer ratings for his programmes are dismal, he is allowed to continue his *Kulturmagazine* experiments through special provisions which German law attaches to television channels.

In addition to pursuing his public sphere project, Kluge also insists that no matter which medium he employs in his productions, he will always and foremost be an *Autor*. With much enthusiasm and ideological fervour he poses the question 'Why shouldn't there be a "TV for the *Autor*"?' (Kluge 2004). In a 2003 speech Kluge amended this view by labelling his work in television that of a translator rather than an *Autor*. For Kluge, collaboration between TV and film is far more productive than simple enmity, and he sets out to establish a relationship where television and cinema can each be used as venues for the other's wares, especially in cases when a format does not fit into the parameters or conventions of the specific medium (Uecker 2000: 34).

Kluge derives his motto from a Günther Hörmann film title: 'Those who fight may lose, those who choose not to fight have already lost' (Wetzel 1987: 252). Although, like Wenders, Alexander Kluge is not ready to give up his status as elite cultural producer, he represents a point at the opposite end of the creative spectrum from Wenders. He shows television as a platform from which any ideological and aesthetic project, no matter how politically progressive or anti-capitalistic its message, can be launched.[8]

While Kluge's productive utilisation of private TV's distinctiveness as a medium and institution illustrates that New German Cinema directors' collaboration with television is not confined to the financial realm, it cannot be ignored that his creative involvement with cinema has all but ceased in recent years, turning Kluge effectively from film director into full-time TV moderator. The director's commitment to his television work, to the exclusion of filmmaking, may be rooted in his belief that TV has supplanted cinema as the most influential agent in today's media landscape. In his 2003 acceptance speech of the prestigious Büchner literary prize, he characterises television as a Leitmedium (a medium that dictates direction):

> When a catastrophe occurs, such as September 11, people don't look out of the window or consult manuals, but watch television. The US president turns on CNN when there is a crisis, and only afterwards does he read the Secret Service briefings. The audience invests much trust in a *Leitmedium*, an investment paid by concrete individuals. (Kluge 2003)

Kluge sees it as his responsibility as an artist to respond to this audience investment of trust by providing a counter-sphere to, but also within, mainstream television. Apart from Kluge's affirmative stance toward television as a medium there are also other voices calling for less antagonistic views toward a productive television/film relationship.

MERGING FILM AND TELEVISION: GÜNTER ROHRBACH'S 'AMPHIBIOUS FILM'

In the late 1970s, Günter Rohrbach, then head of film production at the TV station WDR, made the case for an 'amphibious film', one that bridged the gap between television and the cinema, both aesthetically and technically, and would do equally well in both exhibition venues.[9] He announced:

> Cinema and television will be able to live with one another, because they must live with one another. We who work in television and love the cinema will do our best to contribute to this. Long live the amphibious film! (Sandford 1980: 150)

Rohrbach verbalised what for many film-makers had already become (or was at least threatening to become) a reality: the transfiguration of the film aesthetic to conform to television specifications. Critics likewise had characterised many New German Cinema films as bearing the invisible stamp 'made for television' and prompting an international perception of German film as excessively cerebral:

> The tendency to make '*films à these*', films that demonstrate a topic or a theme, where images *support* dialogue and debate rather than being the primary source of inspiration, the tendency, in short, to create 'illustrated radio plays', is a characteristic of television that has left its distinctive mark on the New German Cinema. (Sandford 1980: 150)

Sandford adds that the high number of literary adaptations in New German Cinema can also be ascribed to television's financial sponsorship. According to Sandford, television corporations were highly interested in such adaptations because they fit in with their mission to be an 'educational' medium in addition to providing entertainment. Also, such material was seen as *Kulturgut* (cultural treasure) and therefore political themes or subtexts could be attributed to the source material rather than seen as an ideological endorsement by the station (Sandford 1980: 151).

The underlying technological determinism in these types of characterisations ignores the historical complexity that is endemic to image production in Germany. It could be argued that a preoccupation with dialogue over image, privileging the rational over the visceral, stems from film-makers' attempt to engage critically with the historical baggage of Germany's past, especially the ideologically driven media and image manipulation employed by the Ministry of Propaganda of the National Socialist regime.

Regardless, in the 1980s, Rohrbach's vision of a film/television convergence became more and more a reality. Against the backdrop of New German Cinema's gradual demise and the onset of a changing attitude toward German historical awareness, several successful film productions moved comfortably from one medium to the other. Wolfgang Petersen's blockbuster *Das Boot*, produced by Rohrbach, appeared not only as a theatrical version in 1981, but also screened on German television in 1985 as a miniseries. When Petersen shot the film originally, he had plans to release it simultaneously in both, the theatre and on television, but distribution limitations initially allowed only for the theatrical debut. Rather than maximising the film's economic potential through dual distribution at the original release date, Petersen was given creative freedom to realise the miniseries only after the film's enormous box-office success. Petersen commented: 'I always thought that even though the film version I delivered worked well it would be wonderful to one day go back and cut my own ideal version – to ask what is the best way for me tell the story of *Das Boot* based purely on creative rather than commercial considerations.' Petersen's comments regarding creative versus commercial factors notwithstanding, the economic advantages of an amphibious film, as voiced by Rohrbach, still eventually panned out for the director.

It is to some degree indicative of the changing landscape of Germany's film industry and television of the 1980s, that Doris Dörrie's *Men* (1985), a film originally made for the television channel ZDF, became an astonishing box-office success with German audiences and launched a new era in German film history; a shift from the high-brow New German Cinema to a lighter, more entertaining and commercially successful national cinema. *Men* conformed perfectly to the amphibious film concept, both in terms of economics and aesthetics. Since Dörrie conceived *Men* originally as a production to air on the small screen, its aesthetics fit this medium as well. *Men* is one of the first in a series of *Beziehungskomödien* (romantic comedies), a genre that came to dominate German popular cinema in the 1990s. *Beziehungskomödien* often employ domestic settings rather than panoramic scenery; they are character and story, not image driven. This genre also appeals to a broad audience which serves it well in both venues, television and cinema. *Men* inaugurated an era of less ambiguous cooperation between film directors and television as an institution and medium.

Eric Rentschler has dubbed Germany's cinema of the 1990s a 'cinema of consensus', made possible by employing popular genres (especially comedy), recognisable stars, and commercial marketing techniques. According to Rentschler, German directors of the 1990s, such as Dörrie and Wortmann, looked toward Hollywood for inspiration, rather than modelling their productions on the 'old' New German Cinema. This Cinema of Consensus, he argues, has emerged as a consequence of four major developments: a change in policy regarding subsidies (from a cultural to an economic focus), increasing presence of TV officials on film boards, centralisation and consolidation of financing sources (TV stations and film boards join forces), and an industrious collaboration between film schools, TV stations and commercial production companies (Rentschler 2000: 267). In other words, film-makers, subsidy officials, and audiences have ceased to see film as antagonistic (aesthetically, technically, and politically) to television. On the contrary, as Ian Garwood suggests, contemporary German cinema is 'indebted to the "low" cultural form of television (through its persistent use of a shared genre, the domestic comedy), rather than the high arts' (Garwood 2002: 203), as was the case for New German Cinema. One could argue that melodrama, a genre favoured, for example, by Fassbinder, is also closely associated with television; in New German Cinema films it was employed as an ideological tool, rather than an emotional one, as was the case for TV productions. Regardless of the specific causes, Rohrbach's hope for Germany's film industry to conform to his amphibious model has been fully realised in the last two decades. This transformation involved not only individual agents, such as directors and producers, but is also a product of the changing global media landscape. Rohrbach faithfully continues his campaign for German national cinema to pursue the amphibious film model in the new millennium. In a public lecture in Munich, he resurrected this idea in the context of financing troubles in the German film scene, arguing: 'The first alternative [to bring about change in the German film scene] is a steadfast answer addressing the contemporary situation. If the contemporary German feature film is nothing other than nicely made-up television, then we should stand by it and abolish the superficial distinction between cinema production and television production' (Rohrbach 2001). It should be noted that in the last couple of years Günter Rohrbach has made frequent public comments regarding the state of German cinema as an institution to which several critics have responded in prominent German newspapers, such as *Süddeutsche Zeitung*, *Die Zeit* and *die tageszeitung*. Much of the criticism concerns the German Film Award which, beginning in 2005, is being awarded by the German Film Academy headed by Rohrbach himself. Critics charge that allowing the selection of prize winners to be made by industry insiders will lead to preferential treatment of box-office successes over 'small' films. This charge likely receives some of its fervour from Rohrbach's repeated comments regarding the necessity of German film to be a commercially viable product.

From New German cinema to a 'New' German cinema: The next generation confronts television

In addition to the commercial advantages that amphibious productions promised, several media events caused audiences and visual artists alike to take note of television and its capacity as a powerful conduit for important socio-political events, in this regard a much more effective agent then the cinema. The US television series *Holocaust* (Chomsky, 1978), broadcast in Germany in 1979, and Ronald Reagan's 1985 televised visit to a Bitburg military cemetery sparked heated discussions and debates that affected West German society on many levels. As Anton Kaes remarks in the case of *Holocaust*: 'It was as if for the first time an entire nation dared to remember and to look at its past' (Kaes 1992: 313). Edgar Reitz's television miniseries *Heimat* was less of a watershed than *Holocaust*. Nonetheless it added another dimension to television's powerful new status as a vehicle for thought-provoking, home-grown historical drama. Television's command of the decade culminated with its compelling coverage of the fall of the Berlin Wall and the round-the-clock barrage of images depicting the first Gulf War. It took a decade for film to confront these events with any broad effect on audiences, whereas television offered an immediate response. These media spectacles established television as a medium with serious potential, with both audiences and artists alike, because it could represent and control the perception of significant national and historical events while they were still in the making. The 1980s also witnessed the birth of privately-funded television stations, satellite and cable TV, which further propelled television as a mass medium of formidable size and a magnet for a large audience. However, these developments failed to alarm Germany's new generation of film-makers, and instead laid the foundation for an era of significantly less tension and ambivalence between film-makers and television.

Although much changed in Germany's media environment after New German Cinema, much also remained the same. *Das kleine Fernsehspiel*, which had its premier on television air waves in 1963 and developed into an important launching pad for new directors in the next two decades, continued to play an important role in the 1990s, exhibiting and financing the debut films of the biggest names in Germany's film industry today, such as Tom Tykwer, Fatih Akin, Oskar Roehler, and Sandra Nettelbeck, to name but a few. Television sustained its role as a financing source for many film projects, and the added revenue from commercial stations in many cases increased this synergistic effect. In 1991 Arte, the German–French cultural channel (in partnership with several other European TV stations), was founded, which began broadcasting in Germany one year later. Arte has developed into a major venue for German feature film exhibition and a premier financier of many film projects. Arte also confirms the increasingly transnational character of television, and by extension cinema, specifically with respect to Europe. Whereas New German Cinema represented a movement that, for many, epitomised film endowed with a specific national identity, post-Wall German cinema reaches out to a transnational audience with a pronounced emphasis on 'compromise between artistic and commercial interests' (Hake 2002: 180) in order to appeal to a large number of domestic and international, small and large-screen spectators alike.[10]

Film and television's harmonious cooperation in Germany's post-Wall era has seemingly converted even its staunchest critics. In 1990 Wim Wenders remarked:

> The close ties between television and advertising have also done much to shape – and deform – the language of television. In short: video culture has undermined and largely destroyed [the language of film]. Films nowadays look almost indistinguishable from television productions [. . .], the audience is so accustomed to TV pictures that it now expects them even in films. [. . .] television has replaced cinema by [*sic*] something inferior. (Wenders 2001: 357)

Yet, a decade later Wenders found a whole new way to relate to television and its commercial outlets. In a *Der Spiegel* interview, Wenders pointed out that in prior days: 'Ingmar Bergman and Federico Fellini still had to make advertisements in secret, and even Woody Allen was still embarrassed about his first spots. Today, commercials are in many ways the avant garde of visual art'(Wenders 2001: 194). Notably, Wim Wenders has been filming television commercials himself since 1994.

Throughout the last century and into the new millennium, television and cinema in Germany experienced a gamut of emotional, artistic and financial connections resulting in an astonishing mêlée of cooperation and antagonism. Although it is difficult to trace this interplay as either productive or hostile to either medium's development, it can certainly be characterised as a formative relationship. A projection of future developments would likely include an analysis of the technological advances in television technology, such as HDTV, which are converging more and more with film and predict a final realisation of Rohrbach's 'amphibious' film. Whether current and future directors in Germany will work with or against these developments remains to be seen.

NOTES

1. We will confine our discussion to West German fiction film production (at least up to reunification). Although non-fiction films and documentaries, and especially the film industry of East Germany, were also affected by television's ubiquity, it would exceed the scope of this chapter to include them in our arguments.
2. We will not trace the full development of television and cinema in East Germany here. However, some noteworthy parallels need to be addressed. As television became ubiquitous in the GRD and the psychological warfare of the Cold War heated up, many film-makers abandoned cinematic production altogether in favour of the fast-response medium of television. Those who continued making films at the DEFA studio monopoly often became embroiled with government censors for failing to abide by the strict aesthetic requirements of socialist realism, which resulted in the official and unofficial banning of several films, particularly after the Eleventh Plenum of the SED in 1965.
3. In the original: 'Keinen Meter Film für das Fernsehen'. For a concise discussion of the interrelationship between film and television in the 1950s see Knut Hickethier (1989).
4. For a more detailed account of the history and effects of Germany's government subsidy system see Elsaesser 1999: 18–31.
5. *Das kleine Fernsehspiel* celebrated its Forty-year anniversary in 2003. To this day, it remains a venue for unknown film-makers and first-time features. Its motto, as displayed on its website and in advertisements, boasts *Deutschlands erste Adresse für den Filmnachwuchs* (Germany's number one place for a up-and-coming film generation) and *Wo Filmkarrieren beginnen* (where film careers are made). Rainer Werner Fassbinder, Alexander Kluge, Jim Jarmusch, Tom Tykwer, Oskar Röhler, and Christian Petzold all used the *Fernsehspiel* as a spring board to successful careers.
6. The international popular press has picked up on this aspect of Wenders' style as well. In a *Time International* spread, under the title 'The Visions of Wenders,' the director is depicted with his (now ex-) wife as a bride against the backdrop of a panoramic picturesque Idaho landscape.
7. I will henceforth use the acronym *UtEotW* to refer to *Until the End of the World*.
8. For a detailed and concise analysis of Alexander Kluge's television projects see Uecker (2000) and Schulte and Siebers (2002).

9. In addition to his involvement with the WDR, over the years, Rohrbach has been active in most areas of television and film production and organisations.
10. For a more detailed account of trends in German national cinema after 1989, see Sabine Hake's *German National Cinema* (2002: especially pp. 179–92) and Eric Rentschler's 'From New German Cinema to the Post-Wall Cinema of Consensus' in *Cinema & Nation* (2000).

7. DENMARK: THE ELEMENT OF CHILDHOOD FROM CHILDREN'S TELEVISION TO DOGME 95

Dorota Ostrowska and Gunhild Agger

The former military barracks in the suburbs of Copenhagen, Avedøre, are home to not only Lars von Trier's film company Zentropa, but also to the Film School for Children and Youth: 'Station Next'. The old fencing hall for soldiers is a greenhouse for young film-makers housing professional editing suites, studios and decoration sets. It is a place for children to learn about visual media, to become aware of the complexity of the film-making process and production and a way to gain some professional training. They are learning the craft of film-making at daily courses and summer camps run by film and television professionals, by students of the Danish Film School, with an occasional visit from their famous neighbour Lars von Trier. They can shoot using props from the sets of *Breaking the Waves* and *Dancer in the Dark*: the church benches where Betsy prayed to her God and the courtroom where Selma was tried.

In the corner of a projection room, which looks like a church, right next to the screen, which takes place of an altar, there are life-size cut-outs of the Dogme 95 'trinity': Lars von Trier in a kilt, smiling Thomas Vinterberg and Peter Aalbæk Jensen, the godfathers of this cinematic playground for Danish children and youth. This idea of children and teenagers playing film-makers, editors, directors and producers has uncanny resemblance to Dogme 95, which put film-making in the strait-jacket of ten rules with the expectation that discipline and transgression will lead to the rediscovery of joy, purity and innocence of film-making.

The shared ethos of Dogme 95 and 'Station Next' is reflected in *Idioterne* (*The Idiots*, 1998), probably the most emblematic and enigmatic of the Dogme films, where a group of people chooses to return to the state of child-like innocence and live together in a commune in a leafy and affluent Copenhagen suburb, not dissimilar to that where Station Next and Zentropa studios are located. Acting as mentally impaired the 'idiots' demand respect and recognition for their condition from the outside world. What the film does is to question the moral boundaries of the contemporary Danish society, which has become complacent in its social model. Members of this strange community just pretend to be 'idiots' in order to question the limits of individual reason and of collective rules, which structure interactions in the Danish society. As we learn from Stoffer, the leader of the group, it is necessary to find the 'inner child' in order to articulate the alternative to the existing status quo. Dogme-style film-making alternated with interview sessions supports and gives visual expression to these performative acts which make *The Idiots* contemplation on the power of art and performance to change the world. The film starts with the conviction that it is the underrepresented, the minorities, those without any claim to political power, like the mentally-impaired or children, who possess moral authority to question society. At first this premise seems banal, but it gains in power through the idiots' confrontation with acute pain of the two lovers who must part, and with the pathos of Karen's suffering, who mourns the loss of her child. The idiots seem less self-assured and the group's convictions fade. But the questions posed to society about double standards remain taking shape of Karen's and the young lovers' troubled bodies, which the camera is desperately trying to invade through close-ups that seem like the unwelcome breath of a stranger who gets too close to us, and in so doing violates our private space. *The Idiots* is a film about role playing, cheating yourself and others, hitting a sore spot and getting burnt every once in a while. Along with other Dogme 95 films, *The Idiots* signals a cinema of moral peek-a-boo and is a good starting point to open a debate about this new generation of Danish film-makers, children's culture in Denmark and how they both relate to the media.

Accounts of Dogme 95 often identify the French New Wave as its predecessor. In its lack of inhibition in the treatment of the visual medium, Dogme 95 had another home-grown, far more obvious, but never mentioned model for its 'games', that is, the Children and Youth Department of the DR (Børn og Unge, B&U), which in its own time created as much riot, scandal and media-coverage as von Trier and co. have recently. As a department, B&U was formed in 1968, replacing the BUS-department (Børn, Unge, Skole: Children, Youth, School), which combined educational aims with television entertainment for children and youth. Mogens Vemmer, leader of the department from 1968 until 2000, cut the traditional association between children and learning and started an exceptional development in the history of Danish children's media. Within a very short period of time, B&U turned into a forum for public debate for children and youth, where questioning of traditions and social mores was conducted in an oppositional and anti-authoritarian fashion giving rise to a new and challenging televisual aesthetics. Especially during the roaring 1970s, satirical programmes flourished in which the world was represented from the children's point of view. During the 1980s an urge to tell less socially conscious and less realistic stories succeeded in appealing to children's imagination. Poul Nesgaard, a children's TV personality, cultivated some of the best of the tradition of 1970s children's television.[1]

The older Dogme brother, Søren Kragh-Jacobsen (born 1947), worked in B&U for many years before he shifted into children's film-making and then adult film-making. The path from children's television to children's film-making and finally adult film-making is also followed by some young film-makers nowadays. Natasha Arthy made a feature debut *Mirakel* (*Miracle*, 2000) and then went on to direct *Se til venstre, der er en svensker* (*Old, New, Borrowed and Blue*, 2003) after working in B&U and is now 'turning her attention to genre films and other types of films in the big wide world, and away from the "classic" tradition of Danish children films' (Michelsen 2003: 6). Anette K. Olesen has taken a similar path, starting with the youth programme *Transit* in B&U. In 1997 she made the adventure film *Tifanfaya*, and in 2002 she directed the dogme film *Små Ulykker* (*Minor Mishaps*). Throughout their childhood and youth in the 1960s, 1970s and 1980s respectively, the Dogme generation of directors from the younger Thomas Vinterberg (born 1969) to the older von Trier (born 1956) belonged to the child audiences which congregated in front of TV sets to watch B&U programmes broadcast by DR, the only channel in Denmark. Denmark launched a public television channel in October 1951, by and large modelled on the BBC. The Danish TV2 started in 1988. It was 'a rather unique construction, based both on commercial funding and licence and with built in local affiliations' (Bondebjerg and Bono 1996: 2). In 2004 TV2 was sentenced by the EU court to pay back a part of its licence because the station had not fulfilled its public-service obligations in a satisfactory manner. Since 2004 the licence fee for TV2 has been suspended.

In many ways B&U presented television as a place of experiments and freedom. Von Trier also had an early experience with children's TV when at the age of twelve in 1968 he acted in a youth-oriented four-part TV series, *Hemmelig sommer* (*Secret Summer*), directed by Thomas Winding (Stevenson 2002: 11). Television as a site of experimentation preserved its attraction for von Trier even in the times when there was little connection between television and cinema worlds in Denmark. In 1988 he directed a single TV play *Medea* using his own distinctive visual strategy to adapt Carl Dreyer's screenplay from 1965–6. *Medea* represented an early experiment with the aesthetics of television. Technically, it was shot on ¾ inch videotape, transposed to 35mm film, and again copied to 1 inch videotape. The last part of the process was due to the graphic elements produced by the 'Paint Box' software (Pryds 1991: 141–56). The result of these transformations conveyed a very rough impression, experimenting with the very structure of the raw material, pointing to the medium of television. Visually, this was a forerunner for the technique in *Riget* (*The Kingdom*). The effect enhanced the eternal question in visual aesthetics:

What do we see and from which angle? What is true and what is illusionary? The focus on the four elements – water, earth, air and fire – further sustained the mixture of ancient and modern perspectives. However, von Trier seemed to be less occupied by the characters and their destiny than by the atmosphere and the surprising visual effects.

According to Vibeke Windeløv, the producer of von Trier's films, he decided to make *Kingdom* (parts 1–4, 1994; parts 5–8, 1997) for television in order to prove himself as a film-maker who could work with actors, make a genre production and entertain popular audiences and thus alter his film-making profile:

> [von Trier was regarded as] a very technical, cool director and nobody believed that he could do a drama. If he wanted to make another *Europa*, another cool, intellectual, academic-type-movie, it would have been easier. But the problem was that he wanted to change genres and nobody believed that he could direct actors in that way.[2]

When Dogme 95 was launched, Jytte Hilden, the Danish minister of culture at that time, was delighted and offered financial support for the first four films. However, the Danish Film Institute (DFI) was not willing to dispense from its usual procedures, and Hilden could not act without the Institute's approval. This financial dilemma was finally solved in 1997 when Bjørn Erichsen, then director of DR TV, offered a financial support of 15 million kroner (£1.4 million) (Schepelern 1997: 227). Later on it was the attention that the two Dogme films, *Festen* (*Celebration*) and *The Idiots*, received in Cannes that allowed Henning Camre, the Head of the Danish Film Institute, to re-negotiate the Film and Media Agreement with Danish television stations, which legally obliged them to be involved in the production of Danish films. The Media Agreement stipulates how much TV stations must spend to support film production in Denmark. The majority of films are thus financed by the Film Institute, by television and by other investors. Purely commercial films cannot partake in these arrangements. DFI publishes every year *Fact and Figures*, a survey of key figures concerning production, development, distribution etc. in Danish cinema (available at www.dfi.dk/English). This survey shows the budgets of the supported films. According to the public-service contract, DR and TV2 have to invest 60 million kr. each in film production on a yearly basis during the period 2003–6.

Lars von Trier's films and Dogme 95 performed an important part in changing the relationship between the worlds of cinema and television in Denmark when it came to production, funding and the circulation of talent between the two media. These connections could only be successfully maintained if there was also a creative and conceptual connection between the two media. The kernels of the cross-fertilisation of this type can be found in the ideas about creativity shared by children's television and Dogme 95.

Dogme 95 and the cinema associated with this movement try to recapture a certain youthfulness of cinema and review some of the film-making conventions developed in the hundred years of cinematic history.[3] It is paradoxical but possible to suggest that Dogme 95 attempted to infuse film-making with excitement about the novelty of the visual medium only known from the film-makers' exposure to the early days of television, especially children's television. The new relationship with cinema was inspired less by the examples from the cinematic history, especially the French New Wave, than by children's and youth television. The suggestion is that this open, anti-authoritarian kind of TV has the same relationship to the world of visual media, including cinema, as children's culture has in relation to the culture at large whereby children's culture is based on 'a conception, which places the innocence of the child and the primary state of language and/or culture in a close and mutually dependent relation' (Rose 1984: 9). In other words, children's television could possess some elements in common with Dogme 95 phenomenon.

This chapter sets out to examine the importance of television, both children and adult, for the emergence of Dogme 95. It explores how first children and then adult television has been constantly present in the private and professional biographies of the Dogme 95 brothers shaping their careers, tastes and to some extend their concept of film-making. It is the transformation of television in general and its gradual opening to the idea of collaborating with the cinema world, first instituted by B&U, which created foundations for the success of Dogme 95. Our line of inquiry is inspired by David Buckingham's observations made in relation to British media context that 'in studying children's television, we are inevitably raising question [. . .] about the social and cultural functions of television as a medium' (Buckingham et al. 1999: 2). In our case the examination of children's television will yield some insights into the social and cultural role the medium of television played in the emergence of Dogme 95. Some of the Dogme 95 film-makers grew up watching children's television, others actively participated in the production of programmes and films for children, which made children's television a source of their personal and professional upbringing. Gradually, television underwent a profound transformation and became a source of funding and a way of exhibiting films. This change coincided with the launching of Dogme 95.

The new generations of film-makers, which emerged following in the wake of the Dogme 95 success, grew up spending about an hour a day each day and Saturday mornings watching programmes prepared by the Children and Youth Department of DR TV:

> If you talk to people of your age, they all grew up watching B&U TV. In a way they had the same language. You could always talk about something you had seen on telly and it was something, which was new, interesting and provocative.[4]

The uniqueness of the programmes, as there was only one TV channel, and the common reference it offered for the Danish public was something that von Trier, Vinterberg, Kragh-Jakobsen and Levring were trying to recapture in their experimental programme on the Millennium New Year's Eve when different elements of the same TV drama were broadcast on all seven Danish TV channels. It was not possible to be in Denmark, watch TV and miss it (Roberts 2003: 550). This suggests that even though at first sight any connection between children's television and Dogme 95 may seem tenuous, the closer examination of the character of the department, its unique ethos, the type and form of its programming make the Dogme's historical link with children's media less preposterous and more acceptable. In fact, many of the experiments which were done in B&U seemed to echo in the creative ideas embraced by Dogme 95 such as challenging of authority, focus on collaborative and experimental aspect of film-making, playing with the form and searching for new ways of expression. And according to Zarita Christensen, this ethos is not far from Zentropa's actual aims:

> I would like to develop a kind of B&U department in Zentropa where younger directors feel that they can belong. [. . .] In my opinion, all too often you only gamble on the safe horses. It is important to create oases where newcomers can get some help to develop their ideas and their relations. (Christensen 2006: 4) [Translation: GA]

The impact of children's culture in general, not just of children's television, could be also detected on the level of representation in Lars von Trier's and Kragh-Jacobsen's films. The fact that their films are populated with child-like figures with the heart of gold who struggle against the cruel world until death brings to mind fairy-tales and children's stories. The figure of Bess in *Breaking the Waves* was apparently inspired by a children's book *Guld Hjerte* (*Golden Hearted*) (Schepelern 1997: 215–18). Von Trier's predilection for creating fantasy worlds of the mentally impaired in *The Idiots* and true Americans in *Dogville* as spaces of moral example also has some overtones inspired by the world of children. The same can be said for Søren Kragh-Jacobsen's *Mifunes sidste sang* (*Mifune*) where child-like innocence of the mentally impaired Rud is magnified by his moral sense, which makes him the conscience of the film.

Programmes broadcast by B&U were a mixture of drama, animation, short films and documentaries aimed at different age groups. While the youngest group targeted was up to three years of age, the upper limit was less clearly defined. Presenters and programme-makers themselves, as well as their boss, Mogens Vemmer, were very close in age or only a few years older than their teenage audiences. Poul Nesgaard, one of the most interesting members of staff at B&U, was only sixteen when he started working in the department. The closeness in age between the makers of the programmes and the audiences created an unusual situation for children's programming. Children's television, as well as any other type of children's culture, such as fiction, is often criticised for being a creation of adults for adults; it is a projection of adult desires (Rose

1984: 137). But in the case of the older audiences of B&U the situation was different. The fact that teenagers and young adults had some voice on public television was unprecedented and extremely important as it happened in the late 1960s and early 1970s when Danish society was undergoing a cultural revolution sweeping across Europe and the West. For the generations of von Trier and Vinterberg, B&U was not just children's television but a space for youth to participate in public debate, formal experimentation and the questioning of the moral boundaries in Danish society. This ethos of children's television coincided with the ways in which Lars von Trier was brought up. His mother 'was committedly laissez-faire when it came to disciplining or setting rules for young Lars. It was left to the boy to decide if he needed to go to the dentist, whether he should do his homework and when he ought to go to bed' (Stevenson 2002: 8). The content and form of the youth programmes on B&U were creating controversy in Denmark, often becoming an object of public debate in the national press, with the head of the department even being summoned to explain himself to his superiors. This strong reaction to the programming on B&U shows that not only children and youth but also cultural workers, teachers and sometimes even politicians were watching B&U programmes. This was the arena for the contestation of the values and beliefs of Danish society on television. This debate also revealed the true nature of children's culture, which irrespective of cultural differences brought in by the national context, is always 'a site of conflicting values, goals and expectations' (Jenkins 1998: 1–37).

What was so controversial or new about these programmes? It was both the content and the form. Girls and boys drinking beer in B&U programming proved to be questioning as well as talking about sex and hinting at smoking illegal substances in the studio. 'We were all communists there' seems to capture for some the essence of the challenge to the mores this B&U programming was representing.[5] It also expresses a social-cultural climate of the period and the attitudes of the Danish intellectuals who identified children and youth as disfranchised group in the society.[6] Some programmes, which were considered too risky for the evening broadcast, were shown in the afternoon.[7] The controversy caused by B&U programming was so great because the roots of B&U could be found in the quite conservative conception of children's culture, which emerged in the post-war period when 'the social welfare system established throughout the Nordic countries had placed the family at the centre-stage in all political decision-making and legislation' (Marcussen 1995: 15). On the other hand, Danish families were quickly changing as the women joined the labour market in the 1960s and 1970s. As a consequence small children to a large extent were taken care of in kindergartens. This helped to develop a unique children's culture and a specific debate about the needs and rights of children, interesting both to the professional staff in the kindergartens and to parents. This children's culture was based on the idea of treating children with respect and giving them rights to freedom of expression in society even before they become grown-up citizens and recognising their status as a unique minority group. It was connected to a long-standing pedagogical tradition in Denmark, which has its roots in Rousseau's ideas about education and also in the Nordic ideology of the welfare state.[8] In a Danish educational context this tradition had its origin in the ideas of N. F. S. Grundtvig, the founder of the Danish folk high school. He resented the 'black school' and during the 1850s and 1860s he fought for the enlightenment of common peasants by way of the 'living word'. This tradition was partly contrasted and partly supplemented by a more radical strategy, inspired by Georg Brandes, the international literary critic and cultural personality. Georg Brandes fought for individual freedom and the right to criticism under all circumstances. In the 1930s Poul Henningsen and others of his spiritual heirs formed a movement whose ambition was to put the need of the child before anything else in upbringing and education (Borish 1991). As a consequence of these ideas, special funding was offered to museums, theatres, cinemas and libraries to prepare programmes aimed specifically at children which in turn gave an unprecedented and unique presence to children's culture in the wider context of Danish culture. According to Marcussen, 'there emerged a new awareness of the necessity of offering children meaningful cultural experiences – at first, in terms of literature. This was later put in broader terms, embodied in the concept of "children's culture", which became an expression of the highest virtue in the 70s' (Marcussen 1995: 15).

In the case of B&U, the initial focus of the department on the educational value of the programmes and through the staffing of the department with teachers reflected the conservative underpinnings of the children's media project. It was part of the public-service culture, which 'was seen as an expression of bourgeois ideology' (Marcussen 1995: 7). However, B&U underwent a very rapid transformation, which shifted its main focus from education into what can be described as learning through entertainment. In institutional terms it was expressed by the decision to separate the educational arm of children's television from the rest of B&U, which paved way into a new kind of more experimental television, mixing education with entertainment: 'It was fun to entertain children. It was fun to teach them something. To combine the two would be a hell of a lot of fun.'[9]

It was part of the process of a wider redefinition of public-service culture, which as a result of the 1960s liberalisation 'lost some of the paternalistic ideology and style' and resulted in the criticism of 'the notion of a homogenous national culture' (Zeruneith 1995b: 7). In the late 1960s B&U became the space where children and teenagers could exercise their right to freedom of expression in the context of social changes which did not preserve but challenged systematically traditional family values and granted greater freedom to individuals. Poul Nesgaard pointed out that 'an important element of B&U was that it was a satire directed at authorities, at people in power and it was thus the way of controlling those in power'.[10] Per Schultz believes that B&U was about finding out 'how to make TV and how to get a political message through as well'.[11] In this way, B&U was not just about the respectful treatment of children but about the whole society which refused to be treated in paternalistic ways and attempted to break down the existing hierarchies and forge new alliances which superseded traditional family bonds.

Such a critique of society and a suggestion of alternative communities is expressed in Kragh-Jacobsen's first (now classic) children's film, *Gummi Tarzan* (*Rubber Tarzan*, 1981). The main character of the film, seven-year-old Ivan, is bullied at school by older boys, who are more athletic and stronger than he is, and at home by his father, who upholds a traditional model of masculinity as defined by the character of Tarzan, whom he wants to become Ivan's hero and role model as well. Ivan's only friend is a crane worker, who helps the boy to muster some self-confidence and shows some understanding of his problems. Their friendship flourishes, which serves as a clear sign that the oppressed, the minorities and working classes should come together in their struggle against outdated and oppressive social structures. The same spirit of revolt against the established status quo is also part of Dogme 95, especially in the treatment of authority figures in their films, such as fathers and social workers. The search for alternative communities is especially pronounced in von Trier's *The Idiots* and *Dogville* and Kragh-Jacobsen's *Mifune*, while Vinterberg's *The Celebration* represents the crisis in the traditional communities based on familial bonds and kinship.

Formal experiments practised in B&U made contribution on the level of representation. Working outside the studio with handheld cameras, natural lighting and direct sound, and using phones to report live to the studio from the remote corners of the country introduced an element of 'live television' to the B&U programming. B&U also contributed to the democratisation of the visual medium, which in some way prefigured the impact of Dogme 95 in the digital age. B&U sent 8mm cameras in the 1960s and video cameras later on to different distant parts of the country asking children to report from there. This had an additional effect of undermining the power of the unions of TV technicians who could not control the use of the film-making process once it was taken outside studios. Initially, the union regulations did not allow B&U staff to handle cameras, edit or mix sound.[12] B&U was unique in having its own studio and production facilities in DR TV. Because it was able to use all the technological innovations in a very creative way, it was given privileged access to new technologies.[13] There was a wide scope for experimentation during the making of programmes, which attracted many people interested in television work to B&U:

> We had editors, sound engineers and technicians and most importantly everybody was working together. That was really something. When you were in the cutting room, you could always ask your colleague to come and have a look at something you were working on and hear their comments. The spirit was very creative and it was very special.[14]

Experimentation was so common in B&U because traditional forms, for instance documentary, had to be reinvented in order to attract the interest of children. Mogens Vemmer believes that B&U staff was responsible for the invention of the docudrama, because the elements of drama had to be introduced into a documentary in order to keep children's attention.[15] B&U also recognised the important differences between the social practices of cinema and television. When films were shown as part of television programming, it became essential that they were introduced in a way which recaptured for children the more familiar experience of watching films in the company of adults at the cinema. In a way television took on the role of a parent or a child caretaker. It was such efforts, which in the long run, blurred differences between the medium of television and cinema.

The children who were exposed to this type of television programming constitute the bulk of adult audiences today. Their taste for 'info-tainment', docudrama and fiction was to at least some degree formed by this early exposure to B&U programmes, where 'there was no separate sections responsible for a particular part of programming and this was what allowed them to cross borders, experiment, mix fiction and documentary and eventually arrive at new genres'.[16] Bodil Cold-Ravnkilde also points out that 'Mogens Vemmer required everyone working in the department to be able to do fiction writing, documentaries and radio programmes.'[17] Staff competence in all different genres and formats may be the reason why B&U trained very versatile professionals capable of working in both television and cinema and of moving smoothly between the two media. While talking about the most famous television series that he developed, a Christmas calendar (*Jul og grønne skove*, *Christmas and Green Woods*, 1980), Poul Nesgaard points out its affiliations with Dogme 95 aesthetics. The whole programme was based on formal limitations and was developed as a very simple idea, similar to the method Dogme 95 was following.[18]

Since most of the programmes were for children, the technical standards were not as strict as in adult film-making. The basic argument was that children would not notice if you made a mistake, which made children's television just like any other form of children's culture, for instance literature, 'where nothing is really taken seriously – and therefore where almost anything can be said, the privilege of both child and courtly fool' (Morris 2000: 6). This allowed for B&U to become a training (or learning) ground for many technicians and future television practitioners. Mogens Vemmer allowed everybody to make a mistake every day 'but not the same one'.[19] There was also lots of scope to try new ideas with other artists, painters and writers, who passed through the B&U studio, and to develop interesting collaborative projects. Elith Nykjær, for example, combined several talents. He was a musician and a property man in DR when in 1977 he became the partner of Poul Nesgaard at B&U. This informal partnership lasted for eleven years. A famous experiment balancing between innocence and scandal was *Baggårdsredaktionen* (*The Back Alley Editors*, 1980–2), a programme that dealt with public matters and well-known personalities, by presenting them in unusual context. *I Sandhedens tjeneste (In Honour of Truth*, 1987) and *Arvefjender (Hereditary Enemies*, 1993) were co-produced with Christoffer Barnekow, a Swedish producer who funded the game of Nesgaard and Nykjær exploring conventional truths in an apparently naive manner.

Mogens Vemmer believed that anybody working in B&U should learn all the parts of the television craft. For this reason, all members of staff worked in turns in different stages of production, which created practitioners with a thorough and extensive knowledge of television making without anybody having only narrowly defined expertise. It has always been extremely difficult to study at the Danish Film School due to the limits imposed on student numbers. For this reason, B&U functioned not only as a creative section in the Danish media culture, but also as a space where young people wishing to embark on a career in TV could learn the basis of the television-making craft. For some, the work at B&U was a way of entering film-making. Another reason why television became a training ground for some budding film-makers had to do with the fact that most ambitious young professionals trained to work in cinema were not interested in working in television. Hence, television had to train its own staff, which in the long term ended up moving into film-making. One such person was the Dogme brother Søren Kragh-Jacobsen.

Kragh-Jacobsen revealed that 'crossing from television to film-making was natural to him and crossing from children's television to children's film-making simply made sense'.[20] This shows B&U did not only have impact on Danish cinema in terms of audiences but also in terms of training opportunities the department offered. According to some critics, Thomas Vinterberg's debut *Drengen der gik baglæns (The Boy Who Walked Backwards*, 1994) is 'one of the most finely felt achievements in Danish children's films' (Skotte 2003: 16). Vinterberg got the DFI children's funding for this film, the 25 per cent subsidy for children's film-making which was set up by the Danish government in part thanks to the intervention and lobbying of Mogens Vemmer. The government support for children's film-making started in 1973 with the decision of the Danish Film Institute to grant one million kroner to the making of children's and youth films. In 1976 the Film Institute employed a consultant responsible for the production of children's films. Finally, in 1982, a decision was made to use 25 per cent of all state subsidies for film-making to support the production of children's and youth films. In the 1980s, which was really the peak period of children's film-making, Kragh-Jacobsen moved into film-making using this subsidy as a vehicle. He made two of the most famous Danish children's films *Vil du se min smukke navle (Want to See My Beautiful Navel*, 1978) and *Rubber Tarzan*. For the next twenty years Danish cinema was known abroad for its children's and youth movies rather than adult film-making. In 1982 in Berlin Kragh-Jacobsen received UNICEF's first-time children's film award for his *Rubber Tarzan* (Zeruneith 1995a: 36). Since its establishment this subsidy was a way for many first-time film-makers to enter the industry in the way that working in television was before. Apart from Kragh-Jacobsen other members of B&U staff who entered film-making via television were Michael Wikke and Steen Rasmussen. Wikke and Rasmussen were famous for their satirical programmes on DR, for example *Tonny Toupé Show* (1985–6) and *Sonny Soufflé Show* (1987), devising characters of parodic dimensions with the same disrespectful appeal as Nesgaard and Nykjær. In their films and TV dramas they went on mixing childish elements and grown-up naivité, most successfully in the TV serial *Johansens sidste ugudelige dage* (*The Last Ungodly Days of Johansen*, 1989), *Russian Pizza Blues* (1992) and the children's films *Hannibal and Jerry* (1997) and *Flyvende farmor* (*The Flying Granny*, 2001). The worlds of television and cinema, even when it came to children's film-making, were kept very separate with different budgets and distinct management and they were subject to quite different rules and regulations. Twenty-five per cent of the total film subsidy was given to children's and youth film-making, but only about 11–13 per cent of the total DR TV budget was given to B&U, even though Mogens Vemmer was fighting to increase this sum to the level of 25 per cent.[21] Cinema was then associated with heavy studio-based equipment and barriers regarding the entry of young people. Television, especially the B&U component, was still open to television enthusiasts, which created a very different atmosphere around television.

The common view was that cinema, whether for children or adults, was 'art' and television, whether for children or adults, was 'business' and there was little interaction between the two. In spite of its roots in television, children's film-making supported by government subsidy, just like the rest of the Danish cinema, 'was shaped by ideological agendas in the 70s and by the focus on "art" and quality in the 80s' (Zeruneith 1995a: 47). It led to a certain murkiness in the accounts of children's cinema in Denmark, which like Zeruneith's chooses to ignore completely the television roots of children's film-making when she says that 'in the spirit of our Nordic work with children's film, right from the start, arose from love and concern for children, but it was supported by an affection for film art' (Zeruneith 1995a: 27).[22] At the same time, she does not comment on the tradition of television series being made into cinema films. It is enough to mention Bille August's 1984 TV serial *Busters verden* (*The World of Buster*) or Søren Kragh-Jacobsen's 1986 TV serial *Guldregn* (*Shower of Gold*), which were turned into feature films.

Another example is Jannik Hastrup's beloved animation series *Cirkeline* for small children. Nineteen episodes beginning in 1967 were screened by B&U. Three animation films about Cirkeline followed in 1998, 1999 and 2004. In 2000 Martin Miehe-Renard wrote and directed the feature film *Pyrus på pletten* (*Pixie Panic*) on the basis of a series of Christmas calendars on TV2 (1994, 1995, 1997). The latest example is *Jesus & Josefine*, a Christmas Calendar screened by TV2 in 2003. In 2005 the director Carsten Myllerup transformed it into a feature film, *Oskar & Josefine*.

The joint production of adult TV serials and cinema formed the background to the TV–cinema collaborations regarding the production of children's fiction.

In the 1970s the Department of Entertainment at DR TV collaborated with the old film production company Nordisk Film on a number of long-running sitcoms and dramas, including the famous sitcom *Huset på Christianshavn* (The House on Christianshavn, 1970–7) and the ever-popular historical family saga *Matador* (1978–81). The popular formats were huge audience successes and kept Nordisk Film busy in a time of acute competition between the media. Erik Balling, the director of *The House on Christianshavn*, refers to television as a medium of rescue for film producers in the 1970s (Trautmann and Bang 1980: 20). In 1978 a co-production agreement between the Film Institute and DR was made. In the 1980s various kinds of collaboration were strengthened when TV2 was founded modelled after the British Channel 4.

From the late 1980s television became one of the main sources of funding for cinema, which complemented the subsidy coming from the Film Institute and from private producers. The introduction of TV2 in 1988 changed the established model of public support for national television and cinema. TV2 was a channel without any production facilities except for production of the news, which forced it to purchase all of its programming from the outside producers. TV2 was not simply allowed to buy all of its programming, but was obliged to fund it, which in the long run made TV responsible for supporting indigenous media production in Denmark. As it is much cheaper to buy the end product rather than investing in the production, the funding obligation imposed on television was seen as a subsidy for cinema. The transformation of the media landscape in Denmark and the introduction of new forms of financing cinema brought the worlds of television and cinema together. This cooperation was clearly seen in the establishing of Dansk Novellefilm, a new funding project launched in 1994. The target was to promote short fiction films (ten to fifty minutes) that could be screened at film festivals and on television. DR and TV2 financed the initiative together with the Ministry of Culture, the Danish Film Institute and Statens Filmcentral (a government-financed centre for distribution of films, established in 1938). This type of cinema–TV cooperation could help to preserve the single format for television drama, which was threatened by the series formats that began to dominate Danish TV drama from 1990. The short films had a short life in the cinemas. They gained a larger audience when screened and repeated on television. Besides, they served as a place of experiments and development for promising young directors and script writers. In 2003 Dansk Novellefilm was replaced by a new organisation directly aiming at developing the new talents *Talentudvikling* (Talent Pool).

Dogme 95, whose films were paid for by television before even the Film Institute decided to invest in them, was the result of the new ways of funding Danish film-making (Hjort and Bondebjerg 2003: 8–22). On the whole, Danish films during the period 1995–2005 impressed its national audience, which responded by buying more tickets than in the preceding years and by taking interest in public discussions about the films. Some of the most interesting films managed to attract an international audience as well. However, because of the limited national Danish audience and insecure prospects of distribution beyond international film festivals, many films have not been profitable even though television invests in them with the intention of recouping its costs:

> When you're putting a film project together, you spend a third of your time rising money for the project, a third of your time making the film, and the third of the time explaining what went wrong with the project and trying to start a new one.[23]

Due to these uncertain returns, TV investment in cinema feels more like a fee paid for the rights to broadcast.[24] It is also important to remember that producing feature films is more expensive than making television drama series, but takes less of the broadcast time and thus can attract lower levels of advertisement (although this is not relevant for DR, which doesn't carry advertisements).[25] These tensions between cinema and television came fully to the fore in 2002 when TV departments became responsible for allocating 35 millions of Danish kr. (£3.5 million) into feature film-making – a funding which amounts to about ten to twelve feature films a year.[26] This new financial relationship influenced in an unprecedented way the type of films which are being produced. Since feature film production is costly, films must be shown at prime times and attract the widest possible audience consisting of different generations for television to recoup its costs. Instead of films for adults and for children, the focus now is on producing 'family films'.[27] The new law does not specify how much of the 35 million must be spent on children's film-making, but because 25 per cent of the Film Institute subsidy must be invested in children's films, it is natural that television stations, both TV2 and DR TV, make a contribution to a quite large number of children's films.[28] Media critics and professionals point out that the making of family rather than children's films is not only linked to the impact of television, but also to the limited audience constituted by children and youth. According to Henning Camre, if the target audience is the eight to eleven age group, the film cannot get more than 60,000 entries.[29] This number increases if the film has a larger appeal. This economic factor relating to a minority audience in a small country such as Denmark could have been ignored if the principle of market-regulations did not have to be taken so clearly into account, which was the case until the late 1980s. Kirsten Drotner points out that it was the small size of the market and of the audiences rather than the impact of Hollywood and globalisation that was responsible for the low number of youth films produced in the 1990s. The competition for the audiences between DR TV and TV2 only exacerbated the problem but TV stations are not ultimately responsible for the current levels of children's and youth film-making in Denmark. Hence, the ideals regarding the support for children's and youth films much be checked against production reality, which imposes some constraints on the realisation of these ideals. The problem is connected with the debate about the role of public-service television and the impact of globalisation on the media.[30]

Perhaps one of the reasons why the connection between children's film-making and B&U was originally underplayed, or tacit rather than explicit, has to do with the belief that children's film-making should be a way of educating future cinema audiences. Quite rightly this belief is still upheld by film-makers working today, who argue that 'the higher attendance frequency by the youngest segments is laying the groundwork for a greater interest in film when they [children] grow up [. . .]' (Havn 2003: 21). The point was to make sure that cinema does not lose out to its competitors, including television. The view of television as a serious competitor of cinema was behind the decision to introduce a series of laws (in 1972, 1989 and 1997) aimed at protecting cinema production in Denmark.[31] This fear shared by cinemas across Europe might have been particularly dire in Denmark, a cultural space with a very limited audience for Danish-language films, where cinema's designation as an art could save cinema from the competition from television but also gain it support from the government which was needed for Danish cinema to survive the competition from foreign films. TV programming was generally not seen as art at the time. It was vital for cinema to preserve this label for itself. Mogens Vemmer's and other members of B&U staff's contribution to the world of cinema clearly shows that imposing any barriers between the world of cinema and television is artificial. In the case of children's film-making, it was children's television more than anything else which gave rise to children's cinema. In the same way opportunities presented by television offered a kick-start to Lars von Trier's career and was one of the factors contributing to the Dogme phenomenon. Hence, historically, in its different forms, television supports cinema rather than competes with it.

The view of public television as a supporter of rather than a rival to Danish cinema could be also explained through the shared goal of all public or government-sponsored media, which was to support Danish national culture. Talking about children's film-making, Ulrich Breuning said that 'the idea of Danish children films was motivated by the desire for self-preservation of a small cultural area which is Denmark. They wanted films in Danish, about Danish children and set up in Danish surroundings. There was something quite nationalistic about it'.[32] As part of the only Danish TV channel, B&U, just like the rest of television, 'for much of the earlier period was a national phenomenon, strongly regulated by the nation state and given a cultural task as a public service medium' (Bondebjerg and Bono 1996: 1). Another important fact is that neither cinema nor television at that time was subject to commercial or market constraints. It is only in such a non-commercially-minded world that the idea of children's film-making could have been born. It was a wild idea that Mogens Vemmer had, which seemed to show his great confidence in children's audiences. The truth is that he did not have to worry about the audiences at all or the box-office success for that matter. By the time von Trier entered film-making, television became an opportunity to break into cinema, but the rules of the game were very different.

It is clear that this split between cinema and television was reinforced for a long time by the government funding for cinema and television, which made it unnecessary for cinema to turn to television for funding. The lack of financial concerns on the part of the Danish media, be it television or cinema, is pointed out by Søndergaard, who sees it as a result of the domination of the Danish politics by the Social Democrats, which meant 'that radio and television have primarily been considered as matters of cultural politics, while their economic and industrial aspects, given significant weight in other countries, have only had a limited influence on their Danish development' (Søndergaard 1996: 13). It was only in the late 1980s, with the advent of liberal economic policies, that the division between the two media started to be breached and made cinema more responsive to commercial concerns. However, to say that it is television that commercialised cinema is a mistake because cinema and television met the market challenge at the same time. Television enjoyed the same subsidies as cinema and no competition (until TV2 was introduced). What it lacked was the cultural prestige coming from the recognition of its aesthetic and artistic potential, which has been recognised to a much greater extent in the case of cinema. The silences and blind spots in the accounts of the interaction between children's television and children's cinema could be thus seen as a microcosm of the relationship which television and cinema in Denmark entertained in general even without some of the film-makers, such as Kragh-Jacobsen, treating children's cinema as a vehicle to enter film-making for adults. There are some parallels between children's television and Dogme films, which are often overlooked because cinema and television production, especially children's TV broadcasting, is never examined together.

One of the central ideas evoked to characterise children's film-making is what Danish critics describe as 'magic realism'. This concept didn't necessarily contradict the critical, social orientation prevalent in Danish children's films. The cooperation between Flemming Quist Møller, the cartoonist, illustrator and jazz musician, and Jannik Hastrup, animator and jazz musician, can illustrate this. One of their first productions was *Hvordan man opdrager sine forældre* (How to Educate Your Parents, 1966). It represented a critical reversal of the traditional generation roles. This way of reversing authority was an inspiring element in the animation film *Bennys badekar* (Benny's Bathtub, 1971). Benny's life in the suburbs of Copenhagen is rather boring. However, in his tub he discovers a life of magical dimensions with all kinds of talking fish, octopuses and mermaids in breathtaking dramas. It only takes a tub and a child's imagination to develop this 'magic realism', which was further developed by both Møller, Hastrup and later animation directors such as Stefan Fjeldmark. This tradition formed the background of the adaptations of books by Ole Lund Kirkegaard, for example *Lille Vergil og Orla Frøsnapper* (Little Virgil and Frogeater Orla, Gert Fredholm, 1980), *Rubber Tarzan* (1981) and *Otto er et næsehorn* (Otto is a Rhino, Rumle Hammerich, 1983). This is a typical characteristic of children's drama which 'is less bound by the constraints of realism than adults';

magic, fantasy, fairy-tale and slapstick humour are staple ingredients, which producers, writers and performers find liberating' (Messenger Davies 2001: 97). If you keep believing, the power of your dream will change the reality. This is the case in *Rubber Tarzan* (and *Mifune*) and it is also an element of Lars von Trier's film-making – naive faith of Bess in *Breaking the Waves*, which results in a miracle, the fantasy world created by Selma in *Dancer of the Dark*, which turns a factory floor into a music-hall stage, and Thomas's reveries of a better *Dogville* where Grace becomes an unwilling victim. In *Breaking the Waves* the harrowing realism of Bess's and Jan's suffering subdues the fantasy until the final scene when the moment of Bess's ascendance into heaven and Jan's miraculous recovery is conveyed through a vision of church bells ringing in the skies. The fantasy is codified into a musical genre in *Dancer in the Dark*. It is most complex in *Dogville*, where the bare stage and the absence of props confine Thomas's vision to the imagination of the spectators until the final graphic sequence of Grace's relentless revenge. One inspiration behind *Dogville* was the *Verfremdung* (alienation) technique of Brecht's epic theatre, and the final revenge of Grace clearly echoes Jenny in *Die Dreigroschenoper* (1928). But also in this case, TV has a part to play. As pointed out by Schepelern, David Edgar's adaptation of Charles Dickens' *The Life and Adventures of Nicholas Nickleby*, performed by the Royal Shakespeare Company in Britain (1982), was another source of inspiration. The TV adaptation was performed on an empty stage floor, and the single video camera displayed its mobility. It was screened in Denmark in 1986 when von Trier watched it (Schepelern 2003: 26).

Von Trier's and other Dogme 95 film-makers' preoccupation with ethical problems is another characteristic they share with the genre of children's film-making and television. According to Bodil Cold-Ravnkilde children's films are marked by humanism, which can be also identified as a feature of recent Danish film-making. There exists an explicit commitment in children's film-making to maintain the integrity in the representation of reality, which can be also identified among the objectives of Dogme film-making. Yet another, perhaps, more trivial connection which exists between Dogme 95 and film-making for children is that just like nobody remains a children's film-maker forever, the Dogme brothers did not plan to continue making Dogme films. Children's film-making happens in a particular moment in film-makers' lives, usually at the beginning of their career, or at the time when they have their own children and become more interested in their problems and lives. This was the case with Søren Kragh-Jacobsen, who made children's films when his own children were young and then stopped.

Certainly, it would be a gross error to suggest that the Dogme 95 project to recapture the innocence of film-making through introducing a set of rules had the same result as the experiments with television as initiated by Mogens Vemmer, who allowed television to become a training ground for future television and cinema professionals. However, children's television was the space of creative experimentation the way digital cinema was for the Dogme brothers.

In order to (re)discover the medium you had to experiment with it. In order to recapture the true nature of the cinematic medium, it was necessary to set up rules to be broken, but also limits and discipline – these were some of the markers of childhood expressed in the revolt that B&U pioneered.

Nowadays, the connection between television and cinema is vital for the well-being of Danish film-making. On the whole, the former resentment has been replaced by a spirit of mutual acknowledgement. Previously, young directors and scriptwriters often suffered hardships trying to further their careers in film-making. Now the necessary alliances are generally made at the Film School, and following the tradition of DR's long running serial *TAXA* (1997–9), many of the new directors start by making programmes for television or by making films and productions for TV alternately (Niels Arden, Ole Christian Madsen, Lone Scherfig, Anette K. Olesen, Carsten Myllerup, Per Fly, Henrik Ruben Genz, etc.). In terms of biography, there are two symbolic expressions of the bridging of the two worlds. The first is represented by Camilla Hammerich, a film-maker who started directing children's films, becoming the head of the Drama Department of DR 1994–8. The second, indicating the historical importance of B&U for this process, was when Poul Nesgaard's became the Head of the Danish Film School in 1992. His appointment not only connected the worlds of television and cinema but also highlighted the role of B&U in this process. Working with a creative group of people and sharing their expertise at different stages of film-making is not just an inherent part of working in cinema but also something which Poul Nesgaard learned while working in the B&U. He tries to encourage students to work on many different projects during their school years, which is very helpful in the move between cinema and television when they begin their professional careers. His efforts 'are underpinned by the deep respect for children and art'.[33] Poul Nesgaard's efforts to infuse film-making with the collaborative spirit he experienced and enjoyed while working in B&U are echoed in the Dogme 95 project, which emphasises collaborative aspects of cinema by refusing to credit the director. Even though the public obviously identifies Dogme films with particular directors, what is significant here is the fact that the Dogme brothers felt it was important to de-emphasise the director as the only person responsible for the film. This may be seen as a sign of a broader transformation undergone by the Danish media and the culture of drama production and film-making resulting from the media liberalisation which created 'a shift from individual artist approach to a more group-oriented and collaborative one'.[34] The convergence of media diffuses the idea of cinema as art and director as an omni-talented individual and proposes a film-maker as a versatile professional capable of working in different media contexts.

The story of the relationship between film and television is full of surprises and paradoxes. One of the latter is that the rather anarchic upbringing and televisual education of the Dogme generations resulted in a set of rules. Taking that background into account, however, it is not astonishing that some of the rules were broken. The rule of not crediting the director was never taken seriously by the Dogme brothers, all of whom worshipped the idea of the auteur. Another rule banished genres even if genres are almost inevitable in film, as is demonstrated by for example *Mifune* and *The Celebration* (Bordwell 2004). Still another paradox is that this set of rules reflected the liberty of experiments in B&U that had been formative for the future film-makers – thus working as an appropriate vehicle for the renewal of the art of cinema. And after all, this renewal is what it was all about.

Notes

1. This development is documented in Christa Lykke Christensen, 'Børne- og ungdoms-tv's historie' in Stig Hjarvard (2006).
2. Interview with Vibeke Windeløv, Dorota Ostrowska, June 2004 (unpublished).
3. In the following the term Dogme 95 is used in a broad sense about the cinema of the generation of film-makers inspired by the manifesto. David Bordwell uses the concept in the same way in his survey 'A Strong Sense of Narrative Desire: A Decade of Danish Film', available at www.dfi.dk/English.
4. Interview with Bodil Cold-Ravnkilde, Dorota Ostrowska, June 2004 (unpublished).
5. Interview with Per Schultz, Dorota Ostrowska (June 2004) (unpublished).
6. Dorota Ostrowska is grateful to Kirsten Drotner for pointing this out.
7. Interview with Per Schultz.
8. Dorota Ostrowska is grateful to Kirsten Drotner for pointing out these elements of the Danish tradition in relation to children. See also the ideas developed by Ellen Kay, a Swedish thinker who wrote *Barndommens århundrede* published in 1902. This book became very influential not only in professional, pedagogical circles, but also in common debate, and it was translated into seventeen languages. The latest edition: Stockholm 1996. It was first published in English in 1909 under the title *Century of the Child*.
9. Interview with Mogens Vemmer, Dorota Ostrowska, June 2004 (unpublished).
10. Interview with Poul Nesgaard, Dorota Ostrowska, June 2004 (unpublished). Máire Messenger Davies' observations about children's television in general show that the subversive element is something Danish television shared with other children televisions. She writes that 'a creatively liberating aspect of children's material is its carnivalesque subversion of the respectabilities of adult authority' (Messenger Davies 2001: 96–7).
11. Interview with Per Schultz.
12. Interview with Mogens Vemmer.
13. Interview with Mogens Vemmer.
14. Interview with Bodil Cold-Ravnkilde.
15. Interview with Mogens Vemmer.
16. Interview with Poul Nesgaard.
17. Interview with Bodil Cold-Ravnkilde.
18. Interview with Poul Nesgaard.
19. Interview with Bodil Cold-Ravnkilde.
20. Interview with Søren Kragh-Jacobsen, Dorota Ostrowska, June 2004 (unpublished).
21. Interview with Per Schultz.
22. The view of children cinema as art continues nowadays and is expressed in the perspective embraced by the current Centre for Children and Youth Films, DFI. Its aim is among other things 'to encourage the debate of children and youth films as art and as a mass medium' (translation: GA), cf. the Centre's homepage at www.dfi.dk.
23. Interview with Per Schultz.

24. Interview with Per Schultz.
25. Interview with Camilla Hammerich, Dorota Ostrowska, June 2004 (unpublished).
26. Interview with Camilla Hammerich.
27. Interview with Camilla Hammerich.
28. Interview with Camilla Hammerich.
29. Interview with Henning Camre, Dorota Ostrowska, June 2004 (unpublished).
30. Telephone interview with Kirsten Drotner, Dorota Ostrowska, June 2004 (unpublished).
31. The motivations behind this first law are discussed in Niels Jørgen Dinnesen (1980) and *Honoré* (1994). See also Bondebjerg and Schepelern (1997). The subsequent two Danish laws of 1989 and 1997 could be seen as further reactions to the transformations in the Danish audio-visual landscape brought about by the introduction of the second TV channel, TV2, and finally the liberalisation of the media market in Denmark.
32. Interview with Ulrich Breuning, Dorota Ostrowska, June 2004 (unpublished).
33. Interview with Poul Nesgaard.
34. Interview with Per Schultz.

8. POLAND: COSTUME DRAMAS: CINE-TELEVISUAL ALLIANCES IN THE SOCIALIST AND POST-SOCIALIST POLAND

Dorota Ostrowska and Małgorzata Radkiewicz

In the 1960s across Europe and the United States the production of large-scale, spectacular and costly historical blockbusters was seen as an expression of the battle between silver and small screen in which cinema was trying to attract the spectators with the spectacle they would not be able to see on their television screens. Cinema was to overwhelm and to become a true assault at the senses. In the socialist bloc countries such as Poland the same period was marked by quite a different development; instead of competition there was a deep synergy between the two media regarding production and exhibition of lavish adaptations of the classics of national literature, which were compared to the Italian peplum, to westerns, to family melodramas and to historical romances. *Przygody Pana Michała* (*Sir Michael's Adventures*, 1969) was compared to a western film; *Noce i Dnie* (*Nights and Days*, film 1975, TV serial 1977) were compared to a family soap opera by Maria A. Hessel (Hessel 1969); *Hrabina Cosel* (*Countess Cosel*, film 1968, TV serial 1968) was praised for being a spectacular historical romance full of balls, duels and galloping horses (Toeplitz 1968: 1). Each of these major productions was accompanied by a television serial, which was an extended version of the cinematic film shot using the same casts, crew, directors, locations and decorations as films, but adjusted to the needs of television. TV serials were characterised by an extended narrative scope and the division in episodes. At the time when television could only broadcast in black and white, the TV version of *Przygody Pana Michała* (*Sir Michael's Adventures*, Paweł Komorowski, 1969) was shot in black and white, and its cinematic version, *Pan Wołodyjowski* (*Sir Wołodyjowski*, Jerzy Hoffman, 1969) in colour. However, since TV serials were essentially extensions of cinematic films there were no fundamental formal or aesthetic differences between the two.

In the period between 1968 and 1977 there were six such joint productions.[1] Polish cinema was not competing with television but rather supporting it by providing it with its most expensive and elaborate products. These joint productions of films and TV serials indicate that the nature of the cinema–television interaction in the Eastern bloc countries was quite different from the dynamics encountered between these two media in the West. In the socialist East unlike in the West the development of the television culture was not associated with the growth of a new production infrastructure, which in a relatively short period of time became capable of producing drama destined for television. In Poland the decision to produce extended TV versions of the most expensive cinema films was a reflection of the economy of shortages characterised by limited resources. Until the late 1970s TV lacked its own production infrastructure to produce fiction and relied on the cinema resources (studios, equipment and talent) to create content such as films and serials which were the most desired by the audiences. As in Western Europe, television in Poland was committed to broadcasting high-quality programming on its single channel. The extension of cinematic adaptations of literary classics into television serials was seen as a solution to the various problems faced by the new medium.

The nature of the TV–cinema collaboration changed in Poland in the second half of the 1970s when television finally developed its own infrastructure to produce films. In 1978 a new Faculty of Radio and Television was opened at the University of Silesia, Katowice, with the aim of providing training and education in all areas relating to television and film-making (Zajicek 1992: 212). The trained practitioners were expected to work in TV rather than cinema productions. TV's own production company (POLTEL) was established as independent from the existing studios producing fiction, documentary and animation films. TV was no longer interested in simply broadcasting cinematic films adjusted to the needs of television but wanted young film-makers to make films and serials which were specifically meant for television exhibition. This was the time when young film-makers such as Krzysztof Zanussi and Krzysztof Kieślowski began their film-making careers. Each of them made numerous films for television. In the period under discussion both Krzysztof Kieślowski and Krzysztof Zanussi were working for one of the most important of the production units, TOR. While working for TOR Zanussi made five TV films: *Zaliczenie* (1968), *Twarzą w twarz* (1968), *Góry o zmierzchu* (1970), *Za ścian* (1971) and *Hipoteza* (1972), which marked the beginning of his relationship with television which is continuing today. Also as an employee of TOR Kieślowski made three TV films: *Przejście podziemne* (1973), *Personel* (1975) and *Krótki dzień pracy* (1982). Both film-makers produced TV serials: Kieślowski's *Dekalog* (*Decalogue*, 1988, ten episodes) and Zanussi's *Opowieści weekendowe* (*The Hidden Treasure*, 1996–2000, seven episodes). From the late 1960s until the late 1990s the unit produced ninety-four films made for cinema exhibition and sixty-three films for television broadcast (among those there were five serials made by K. Kieślowski, K. Zanussi, Filip Bajon, Antoni Krauze and Henryk Kluba). Bajon's career, especially his engagement with television, is very similar to that of Kieślowski and Zanussi. Bajon made five films for television and one TV serial: *Powrót* (1977), *Rekord świata* (1977), *Zielona ziemia* (1978), *Wahadełko* (1981), *Engagement* (1984) and *Biała wizytówka* (1986, six episodes). He made three films for cinema (of which *Magnat* was a shortened version of a TV serial *Biała wizytówka*) (Hollender and Turowska 2000). Kieślowski's television serial, *Dekalog* had two episodes shown in cinemas in changed versions: *Krótki film o miłości* (*A Short Film About Love*, 1988) and *Krótki film o zabijaniu* (*A Short Film About Killing*, 1988).

In the 1970s a number of historical serials by prestigious directors were produced which were only shown on television. These serials included Andrzej Wajda's *Brzezina* (*The Birch Wood*, 1970), Janusz Morgenstern's *Stawka większa niż życie* (*More Than Life at Stake*, 1970), Jerzy Passendorf's *Janosik* (Stachówna 1994: 184). In some cases when a serial was particularly popular with the TV audiences, its shortened version was also given a cinematic release e.g. Jerzy Antczak's *Wystrzał* (*The Shot*, 1965), the first episode of Andrzej Czekalski and Konrad Nałęcki's *Czterej pancerni i pies* (1966), a shortened version of Jan Rybkowski's *Chłopi* (*The Peasants*, 1973), Kazimierz Tarans's *Szaleństwa Panny Ewy* (*Follies of Miss Eva*, 1985), Jan Rybkowski's *Rodzina Połanieckich* (1978) and Janusz Majewski's *Epitafium dla Barbary Radziwiłłówny* (*An Epitaph for Barbara Radziwill*, 1983) (Stachówna 1994: 184)

The role that television played in the mid-1970s in the lives of young filmmakers is perhaps best reflected in Andrzej Wajda's *Człowiek z Marmuru* (*The Man of Marble*, 1977), where a film school student Agnieszka makes her graduation film using television resources while the film itself is destined for the broadcasting on TV. In this sense *The Man of Marble* is an important film reflecting the role of television as a producer of films in Poland. The growing role of television was linked to the government's realisation that the medium of television could be a very important and effective propaganda tool (Pikulski 2002: 192).

After 1989 and the collapse of the socialist regime in Poland Polish television decided to return to the old formula of showcasing serialised versions of the prestigious adaptations of the literary classics made by established film-makers. By the year 2002 there were four more such joint TV–cinema productions: *Ogniem and mieczem* (*With Fire and Sword*, Jerzy Hoffman, film 1998, TV serial 1999); *Quo Vadis* (Jerzy Kawalerowicz, film 2001, TV serial 2002); *Wiedźmin* (Marek Brodzki, film 2001, TV serial 2002); *Przedwiośnie* (*Before Spring Comes*, Filip Bajon, film 2001, TV serial 2002). At the same time, television became the main source of funding for young film-makers. It is quite surprising that in 1990s television, by then an established institution, which in the new market-driven economy also discovered advertisement as a new source of revenue, embraced again the serial-making formula, which dated back to the medium humble beginnings. Hence, when it comes to the consideration of the joint TV serial and cinema production there is not just a question of a distinction between the West and the East media production drawn along ideological, economic and political lines marked by the Cold War divisions; there is also an issue of the continuity of this media production between the socialist and post-socialist period in the Polish context. The commercialisation of public TV and the transformation of the mission of the Polish TV from being a propaganda machine of the communist party to becoming a public broadcaster fundamentally did not affect the relationship between Polish TV and cinematography. Rather, the relationship between Polish TV and cinema established in the 1970s was preserved in the 1990s with some adjustments resulting from the transition to the market economy and liberal democracy. This means that the distinctive nature of the television and cinematic interface in socialist and capitalist systems is not enough to explain the existence of the joint TV–cinema productions in Poland as they continued after the end of socialism. Why did Polish TV decide to revive the formula of the TV serial productions, which belonged to a different time both in terms of the television history and of the history of the country as a whole?

The production of the TV serials, which were extended versions of cinematic films in the 1968–77 and the 1997–2002 period can only be understood in the context of unique historical, economic and political circumstances in which Polish cinema and television found themselves in the course of their history. The main question regards the production of the serials, which were spin offs of the cinematic films, which would have been made irrespectively of the serials. Thus, it is the recurring reliance of television production on cinema, rather than the other way around, which is central to the story. The contention is that through engagement with cinema, television managers were trying to enhance the symbolic value of the televisual production at the time when production capacities of television were very limited. The decision of the TV managers to commission the making of the TV serials based on cinematic films over the two periods was also motivated by competition for scarce financial resources allocated by the government according to the rules of the centralised planned economy. The debate regarding the political role of television in the 1966–77 period and the role of television as a public service provider in the 1997–2002 period was underpinning the history of the cinema/TV interaction in Poland which could be examined by tracing the history of joint cinema/TV productions. We can identify cultural, economic and political aspects in the interaction of cinema and television sectors in Poland exemplified by the production of TV serials whose shortened versions were granted theatrical release.

EPISODE ONE: 1968–77

A comparison between the capitalist West and socialist East regarding TV and cinema production in the first decades of the history of television reveals an important difference between these two parts of Europe. The Western production context seems to be revolving around some notion of difference between television and cinema production, which was established on the basis of the divergence in the production values and aesthetic dimension of cinema and television. Wide-screen star-studded high-production value epic spectacles were deemed suitable for cinema but not for television screens, which were smaller and for a long time lacked colour. When it comes to the Eastern European context economic and aesthetic categories are not enough to draw the distinction between television and cinematic product. In fact these categories do not mean much in the Eastern European case where the economic dimension was commonly overwhelmed by political concerns and where television serials were an extension of cinematic films rather than separate productions destined for television broadcast or cinema exhibition respectively. We can postulate that in the East the process of determining the specificity of the televisual product was a function of politics rather than economics or aesthetics. It was the politics with the small 'p' referring to the struggle for power and influence of TV managers competing with cinema managers for favours from the government, which determined the cultural status of television and its product. The distinction of the televisual production from the cinematic one occurred when the government started to appreciate the ideological potential of television in the 1970s. That's when TV became part of politics with the capital 'P'. The government's recognition was followed by the creation of the production infrastructure of television, which made it independent from cinema production units (*Poza ekranem*).

Since the end of World War II, cinema production in Poland was organised into film units. These were groups of professionals involved in the making of films financed by the central government. They consisted of directors, cinematographers, scriptwriters and artistic managers. The number of units differed at particular periods in the history of socialist Poland as the government was tightening and relaxing its control over the cinematic production depending on the current political climate and the government's objectives. Since the early 1960s units were made responsible for all the TV film production. The units agreed to do that but the reasons of cinema managers were not purely altruistic for they hoped to recoup their costs with the money the serials and the films would earn when sold abroad (*Poza ekranem*: 172–3). Cinema managers were also trying to preserve their monopoly on the audio-visual production in Poland and actively lobbied with the government for the development of TV's own production infrastructure. As there were plans to launch another TV channel, the estimates of growing needs of television regarding content were presented to the government to show that film units were not enough to address TV's increasing needs. This meant that the television production was going to resemble the cinematic one as long as the TV production remained dominated by the film units. Hence, television was born into the media landscape dominated by cinema and from early on the televisual product was determined by cinema. In fact, by and large televisual productions were cinematic productions. Paradoxically, the first production mounted jointly by television and film units was to be the exception to this rule.

It was at the end of the 1960s when the first joint TV serial and film production took place, the film *Sir Wołodyjowski* (1969) and the TV serial *Sir Michael's Adventures* (1969). One Polish television historian, Katarzyna Pokorna-Ignatowicz, defines the 1960s as the period when the cultural role of television was still more important that its role as the means of mass communication. For this reason, even though the potential use of television in the ideological struggle for advancement of socialism was recognised, television was not yet to be openly exploited for the propaganda purposes (Pokorna-Ignatowicz 2003: 16). For this reason the results of this first joint TV serial and film production can be seen first and foremost in aesthetic terms. However, a glance at the credits of the serial and the film makes them look like two quite different productions. They have different titles, the film is 141 minutes long and the serial consists of thirteen half-an-hour long episodes, the film is shot in colour while the serial is in black and white. Even more importantly, they have different directors (Jerzy Hoffman made the film and Jerzy Komorowski shot the TV serial). The productions were done independently from each other. The similarities are equally striking as well: the script for both is written by Jerzy Lutowski, the crew and the cast are virtually the same, as are many of the locations, decorations and extras. Both productions were financed from the cinema budget. Ultimately, it was the differences that gave the serial and the film a rather distinct look. It was the first time in the history of the co-existence of the two media that televisual images seemed to be emancipated from the cinematic one. However, the mobilisation of two different production infrastructures for film and serial was not to be repeated ever again for purely financial reasons. The high cost of producing a TV serial was used to criticise the film-makers' incompetence in managing the resources at their disposal. The film-makers were reproached for using costly decorations, rejecting narrative forms and shooting techniques unique to television such as 16mm film-making and later on video. The idea was that film-makers did not quite grasp what television was about and what were the new medium distinct needs.

To produce a serial and a film separately was considered too expensive by the TV managers and the decision was made that it would be cheaper, faster and more efficient to shoot the film and TV serial at the same time. Clearly, a serial shot by the same director simultaneously with the film would carry even more resemblances to the film, which, as we will see, is in fact the case with two of Jerzy Antczak's productions created this way: *Countess Cosel* and *Nights and Days*. The problem is that the economic argument made by the TV managers regarding the separate costs of filming a film and a serial is not really convincing in the context of the centralised planned economy of the socialist Poland. Even though it might have been more expensive to shoot a film and a television serial separately, the very idea of producing TV serials in conjunction with a cinema film was a very costly endeavour. Edward Zajicek, a historian of Polish film industry, gives some interesting insight into this story. He has argued that Polish television was full of individuals whose passion for cinema equalled only their ignorance concerning the film-making process. As a result, when examining the scripts of the films proposed for TV production, these TV executives often overlooked only apparently minor elements of film production, which ended up raising substantially the film costs. Incompetence of the TV managers was a real reason why films produced for television were often more expensive than the ones made for cinematic exhibition only. The TV managers' arguments in this period demonstrate their complete reliance on film units as far as TV production is concerned and their lack of any experience or knowledge regarding production for TV. In fact it took them about ten years, five high-values joint productions with film units, the advent of videotape and the development of TV's independent production infrastructure before they decided to discontinue doubling expensive historical films into TV serials. According to Zajicek, until mid-1970s TV managers were trying to hijack cinematic production in Poland and seize control over cinema by lobbying the government in various ways. For this reason they were criticising film-makers in a variety of ways and undermined their efforts, which resulted in an atmosphere of suspicion and distrust in the Polish film world. Script-preparation for the films, which were to become the basis for the extended versions of serials, became an important point of contention (*Poza ekranem*: 194–5).

Television managers were trying to use scriptwriting as a way to gain some control over the televisual product created by film-makers. TV was lobbying for a creation of a script committee which would set guidelines for the types of programmes film units would produce. Such a committee would select filmmakers who would make such films, it would approve scripts and evaluate a film or a serial once it was finished (Produkcja filmów dla programu telewizyjnego, 1963). All the scripts had to be presented to the Cinematographic Committee which was part of the Ministry of Culture where a special section made up of people derived from television decided the scripts' political suitability for further development and production. The people making the decisions were chosen because of their understanding of the censorial nuances governing the cultural politics of the socialist state. Then the decision of the committee had to seek a final approval from the Head of the Cinematographic Committee, who happened to be an individual who had gained experience running the National Television Committee (*Poza ekranem*: 228). The development of these decision-making structures was an attempt on the part of the government to extend its control over the cinematic production in order to curb its independence and make it more suitable for the achievement of the party's political goals. Ambitions of the TV managers to influence the cinema community coincided with the objectives of the censorship committee. They also signalled a privileged position TV was to have as the propaganda machine of the socialist state as it was expressed in a statement issued by the Party convention in July 1973: 'the Party and the State are very concerned about the development of Radio and Television as these are the most mass-oriented and effective means of implementing the public with the Marxist ideology and gaining the support of the Party policy'.[2] Clearly, television's potential as means of mass communication was finally recognised and shortly it was to become the central concern of television superseding any aesthetic or cultural ones.

Control on the level of scriptwriting was not the only way of keeping a close eye on cinema production. Another strategy was evident in the attempts to influence cinematic production by reducing the role of a film-maker as a creator of a work of art to that of a cultural worker who was accounted for the metres of film strip used during filming, the costs and the time of production. At the same time, only limited references were made to the aesthetic value of the films (and serials). For instance at the end of the report from the shoot of a sequence of *Ziemia Obiecana* (*The Promised Land*), there is a piece of information telling the readers that: 'according to the script, 250 people participated in the shooting of this 300 meters long sequence' (Wertenstein 1974: 16). In the same way, Czesław Petelski, the director of another of these joint TV–cinema heritage productions, *Kopernik* (*Copernicus*), said that 'the film is 3,700 meters long. After the recent viewing we cut out 300 meters. These are the scenes, which could be incorporated into the television serial' (Petelski 1972: 9). When the film-makers talk about the metres of the celluloid film by which their films need to be shortened or extended, they appear to be workers, a kind of 'film cutter', rather than artists. Such shift in the understanding of the film-maker's job was most welcome by both the government and TV managers.

In spite of the negative and demeaning rhetoric the possibility of extending the film into a TV serial with the use of all the outstanding material was something which was actually welcomed by some film-makers. They felt that such a process could help them preserve the integrity of their artistic vision in relation to a particular film. We can see this clearly with the view of the adaptation expressed by Antczak, who said:

> Like the novel, the film *Nights and Days*, has a very specific climate. Sequences and scenes combine into a network of microcosms, which form the narrative basis of the film. These are different from a thriller or a historical romance where narrative shortcuts are necessary to maintain the dynamics of the film's action and create suspense. The material of *Nights and Days* is very complex, difficult to touch, to describe in detail. (. . .) For this reason, in my opinion, *Nights and Days* is not a film where you can cut out whole sequences without destroying the architecture of the whole film. (Antczak 1975: 1)

Antczak's serial was very unique because the two versions were shot simultaneously resulting in two negatives, one for cinema and the other one for television. This allowed the director to establish a more organic connection between the two versions, which had some aesthetic implications.[3] This serial and film not only enhanced the cinematic production but at the same time television serial could establish something of its aesthetic specificity. In his reflection on the shooting of *Countess Cosel* (his earlier film/TV serial which was shot in the same way as *Nights and Days*) Antczak admitted to the challenge of 'creating separate episodes [in the serial], and a consistent whole [in the film]' (Antczak 1968: 13). This shows that not only the film but also the serial was treated by the director as an independent artistic endeavour.

High standards for serial productions established by film-makers such as Antczak led to the development of serial aesthetics and established a clear distinction between cinematic and televisual forms. Making a serial could be as challenging and rewarding as the making of the film on which it was based. TV versions were praised for the construction of episodes, which were whole in themselves while at the same time being a part of a longer totality (Pieśń o Małym Rycerzu 1969). There existed some formal standards regarding the construction of episodes of TV serials. It was emphasised that TV serials required their own narrative structures, which meant that TV serials should not be just the film cut into pieces but an independent piece of work. A reviewer of the script of a TV serial *Ogniem i Mieczem* (*With Fire and Sword*) argued that every episode should have a main motif or a narrative axis around which it is structured. A serial should present a richer portrait of film characters and include events and developments, which are often compromised in a shorter film version.[4] Reviewing a script of another serial *Pierścień i Róża* (*The Ring and the Rose*) a critic pointed out that often film-makers make a mistake of treating a film version like a knickers' elastic which could be simply extended into a TV serial.[5] As though in response to this critique some serials, such as *Nights and Days*, were believed to reach new heights in the history of adaptations for television. Recognised as significant artistic achievements they were giving the aura of quality and prestige to TV programming as well.

The serials and films' source in literary classics was also an element which enhanced the value of films and TV serials based on them. TV benefited from the high symbolic status of literature. Wajda signalled a particular suitability of the television serial for the adaptation of the novel such as *The Promised Land*:

> *The Promised Land* is a novel comprised of loose stories connected by the three main characters. Such novel construction enables the division of the narrative into parts – in this case four fifty-minutes episodes. (. . .) In this sense the television version is closer to the original idea of *The Promised Land*.[6]

Television allowed film-makers to create adaptations of literary classics which were more faithful to the original literary source than the cinematic version. The film-makers' recognition of the formal value of television could be seen as an expression of the politics of containment cinema practised towards television at the time when TV's popularity was growing, TV managers were lobbying constantly for the increase in the TV production capacity and the government was paying more attention to it. To agree to produce a film and its extended TV version could be also seen as a strategic decision on the part of film-makers to maintain their production levels and standards and at the same appease TV by addressing some of its needs.

The absence of independent production infrastructure is probably the main reason why it was so difficult for the televisual product to develop its own formal identity in spite of few exceptions, which were Antczak's adaptations. This finally happened in the mid-1970s when the popularity of TV was growing, the number of TV sets was increasing and the ideological potential of television was acknowledged. This was also the time when thanks to the long-standing film-makers' contribution to television production the medium of television began to demonstrate an increasing degree of formal evolution as well. With the political support of the Party and ambitious plans for future development, TV managed to work out an agreement, which coordinated the workings of TV and cinema by virtually subordinating cinema to television. It was argued that 'the production of films and artistic programmes for the television broadcast is the main element shaping the media market and the televisual-cinematic industry'.[7] As Zajicek points out, 'until mid-80s, cinematography was the main producer of TV films and serials, which consumed about half of its production potential'.[8] The distinction between television and cinema was constantly blurred as popular episodes of TV series were given theatrical releases. This lack of clear formal distinction between the two types of productions is one of the reasons why it was quite easy to return to the formula of joint productions of TV serials and cinematic films in the post-socialist period.

Television contributed to the development of the atmosphere of competition in which television and cinema practitioners were trying to win favours from the government because both communities were dependent on and deeply implicated in the system both financially and politically. Television ended up as a favourite of the government, which was a turn of fortune for cinema from the times when cinema had been the government's main media beneficiary. Even if throughout its history cinema was more daring in contesting the socialist regime than television, it was doing it in the context of the very regime, which controlled and financed every aspect of film production, distribution and exhibition. After World War II following Lenin's dictum that 'cinema is the most important of all arts', the state became committed to the construction, development and support of state cinematography, which was to become the main tool of the state's cultural policy. Interestingly enough, the political and social opinions of the post-war film-makers coincided with the goals of the newly-born socialist state. They shared their commitment to the education and enlightenment of the masses through art, which included cinema. The film-makers who began their careers after the war where part of the leftist part of the Polish intelligentsia all of which historically had been committed to the education of the nation. Supported by the state, cinema, and later on television, was to continue the historical mission of the Polish intelligentsia.

The alliance of the state and the artists was severed in the next forty years because of the repressive nature of the state, which was cracking down on opposition, freedom of speech and had a terrible record of human rights violation. The state curtailed the creative freedom of film-makers through censorship and failed to fulfil many of its investment promises regarding the development and improvement of the cinema infrastructure. We must remember that censorship worked in complex ways and sometimes with surprising results. It might be even possible to indirectly credit the existence of censorship for the existence of the unique visual style of Polish cinema recognisable in the world. Furthermore, the existence of censorship showed how important cinema was for the cultural policy of the state. There was an understanding between the film-makers and the state regarding their reciprocal dependency as the film-makers needed the state as much as the state needed them. This allowed generations of film-makers who regarded themselves as part of the intelligentsia to play a role of spiritual and moral leaders of the Polish nations. The Film School in Lódź, which helped to cultivate the ethos of Polish intelligentsia, was one of the most elitist and selective in Poland. As a graduate school it recruited among mature artistically talented people with a humanities background and encouraged them to think critically about the surrounding reality. Given the very high costs of educating these people and the fact that they often made films, which were censored and thus never distributed, it is obvious that running film industry in Poland was a costly and unpredictable experiment, which can hardly be called a business. But this did not surprise anybody because cinema making in Poland was never meant to be entertainment industry. Like everything else in the socialist Poland it belonged to the sphere of politics, which dominated any economic concerns.

EPISODE TWO: 1997–2002

Since 1989 the film-making community in Poland has been involved in a debate concerning the shape of the national cinematography. The debate has focused on the necessity to change the state legislation regulating the functioning of the Polish film industry. The unresolved issue of the film industry in Poland has been a source of great anxiety for the people employed in the field. The legislation introduced in 1987 has functioned with slight changes until 2005. At the same time, the post-communist transformation has managed to introduce some important changes and bring new players into the area of the Polish film industry. The liberalisation of the market led to the introduction of private Polish and foreign investment in the film industry which includes independent film producers and commercial television stations. Some parts of the national film industry were also changed in order to suit better the market economy. The main Cinematographic Committee was divided into three agencies dealing with pre-production and development, production and distribution in order to facilitate the functioning of the integrated national film industry in an increasingly more competitive environment. As a result for a long time the Polish film industry has been a mixed bag of private and state elements.

In spite of the fact that the state participation in the film production is so considerable, many experts in the field of Eastern and Central European cinema tend to see the Polish industry as already functioning fully according to the market principle. The films cited by the critics include historical and national heritage super-productions, popular cinema and socially-concerned cinema. In their opinion since 1989 'while the industry structure has continued to change, earlier thematic concerns persist that there is continuity in topics and style' (Iordanova 2003: 149). At the same time, the critics do not offer any explanation as to why the film production in Poland did not change artistically if the production structures have been altered so dramatically.

The artistic output is similar to the one known from the past because the pattern revealed by the Polish film industry is not that of rupture with the past but rather that of continuation and overlapping of the old and new structures. The past production structures have been transformed to only limited degree. They fused with new ones, which could emerge because of the transformation of Polish economy, its liberalisation and inclusion into the global economic matrix. The return to the joint cinema–television productions of serials and films is an expression of the continuities between the two systems. In the 1990s Polish television came back to the formula of producing TV serials on the basis of film, which was forgotten for over twenty years. The 1990s just like the turn of the 1970s was a difficult and uncertain time when both television and cinema in Poland were looking for new identity and new ways of co-existing in the reality where a new and brutal law appeared – market economy. Both television and cinema were forced to become subject to this new law. The decision to co-produce films and serials together was an attempt to survive in this new reality.

In spite of the liberalisation of the market in the early 1990s, which allowed for the creation of private TV stations, the Polish audio-visual landscape changed very little in the first decade after the collapse of the socialist regime. Polish public television, broadcasting on two channels, was the most attractive partner for local film-makers because of its funding capacity based on the highest penetration of its broadcast among the audiences, which made public TV channels a desirable partner for TV advertisers. It was the most established TV stations, TVP1 and TVP2, which had extensive contacts with the Polish film world dating back to the socialist times. The stations were very attractive to film-makers because they had a financial capacity to fund both lavish super-productions and smaller low-budget films. TV was also attractive to film-makers and independent producers, because through co-productions with TV they could gain access to cheaper TV production facilities. This was an important difference with the 1968–77 period when TV was relying on cinema for an audio-visual infrastructure.

The reviving of the old formula of extending cinematic films into serials offered public television a competitive edge, which helped it face its main competitors, private channels Polsat and TVN. Public TV was using serials based on the cinematic adaptations of literary classics as a way of attracting money from advertisers. Polsat or TVN were broadcasting mostly originals and Polish remakes of popular sitcoms and soap operas, which were hugely popular with the audiences thus making the stations very attractive to the advertisers. TV could guarantee that serials would bring in front of the small screen a large family audience consisting of parents and children who were all familiar with canonic stories of Polish literature from their school literature classes. The serials were also attractive because they carried high symbolic value, which helped the audiences reinforce their sense of national identity through engagement with familiar literary texts in the confusing times of transition from socialism into a new socio-political system.

The decision of TV managers to engage in the production of the films which were also extended into serials was also motivated by the TV's role as a public broadcaster financed in a large part by the TV licence money. In the statement about the mission of Polish TV we can read that 'Polish TV programmes aim at strengthening a sense of national identity and community, at protecting the Polish language, at expressing Polish tradition and national heritage in all genres, in particular in film'.[9] In the period leading to the production of these serials Polish TV was reproached for having too many American serials and not enough Polish ones. The 1995 and 1996 research revealed that in one month two channels of Polish TV showed thirty-eight episodes of different serials among which twenty-six were made in the US. By the end of 1996 out of forty-three episodes of serials broadcast on Polish television thirty-four were American.[10] Hence, the decision to engage in the production of films, which were adaptations of the classics of Polish literary canon, could be a way of fulfilling the mission of the television as a public broadcaster. Extending these films into serials would also help outbalance the presence of American serials on Polish TV. Public television also appeared very different from the fare shown on Polsat and TVN.

In spite of the change in the political environment Polish cinema is still defined in terms of the national message it carries which can be more or less politicised. Such understanding of Polish cinema was promoted by the socialist government. However it is important to note that the socialist government with its propaganda obsession was not the only one responsible for this situation. In fact, the understanding of the Polish cinema in political terms was very much the result of the fact that it was the political films, which made it abroad and shaped foreigners' understanding of Polish cinema in the context of the Cold War. Thus, the reshaping of the political context did not change the fact that in Poland Polish national cinema is defined in terms of literary adaptations to the exclusion of non-political films, popular genres and TV series. Film production, which is the building block of the popular culture historically, has been marginalised in Poland at the expense of more ambitious and challenging cinema although it has remained very prominent in the Polish consciousness. It has not so far been taken into account when the decisions about what constitutes national cinema have been made. It has not become part of the debate regarding the shape of the national cinematography.

The transformation from communism has altered the context in which the television–cinema game is played. Public television is no longer used to advance the political goals of the Polish state. Now it is expected to fulfil its mission as a public broadcaster in the context of market economy. The economic factor often prevails over the political or public concerns creating a ruthless and competitive environment for the film production. Public television not only invests into cinema production on the basis of its income derived from TV subscription and commercials but it also has a decisive role in the creative development and production of the projects which are going to be funded by the government. This powerful role played by public television in relation to national cinematography is a result of the structural relationship established by the communist government in the 1970s. At present the film-makers present their scripts to the state agency which recommends them for development and production. The actual process of development and production does not take place within the structures of Polish cinematography but within the television production structures. This means that television does not just fund Polish cinema but it essentially shapes it according to their needs which are dictated more by the market concerns than by the objectives set up in its mission statement as a public broadcaster.

The rationale behind co-producing serials such as *Quo Vadis* is that TV would not be able to produce a serial like this on its own.[11] This is the same financial argument which was used in the 1960s. The total cost of a film and serial such as *Quo Vadis* produced in 2002 was to come to about 40 million zlotys (£7 million). TV invested about 11 million zlotys (£2 million) which means that it got the serial for about a quarter of the total cost of the film and the serial.[12] The idea behind this arrangement was quite simple – it aimed at getting two for the price of one. As we will see TV was only getting one – the serial and no rights to the film. So, the financial argument seemed to have its flaws. From the perspective of television what seems to count most is being able to obtain this high quality product, the serial, which it would not able to produce on its own. Or so it claimed.

The co-production contracts signed between TV and independent producers all shared one distinctive feature. Although TV was always a co-producer of both the film and the serial, it received very limited rights to the film and often none at all. In case of *With Fire and Sword* TV paid for 25 per cent of production cost which only guaranteed it the right to the serial and no right to the film.[13] In case of another film-serial, *Przedwiośnie (Before Spring Comes)*, it paid for 42.2 per cent of the production and for that got limited income from the film distribution in cinemas in Poland but no right to show it on its own channels.[14] In case of *Before Spring Comes*, the right to the film limited TV's right to TV serial. The serial was going to be shown only within thirty months from the showing of the film in cinemas – and after the film was distributed on video. The film could be shown on cable and Canal+ earlier – within eighteen months of the premier in cinemas.

In fact TV's internal legal advisors pointed out that there were flaws in the co-production contracts regarding serials – clauses which were disadvantageous for television. Krystyna Trzaska, a lawyer working for TV, argues that 'in other TVs films "kill" the serial and the possibilities for its exploitation and reduce financial rewards promised by the serial. (. . .) [the TV serial] has a very small commercial value'.[15] The objection is very important because, unlike in the past, the presence of video in particular changed the opportunities to watch the film. If you do not catch it in cinema, you could get in on tape. This situation works against TV serials. In the same way, being able to watch the film on cable television, just as with video and DVD viewing, can potentially reduce the audience for the serial. This change introduced by new technology transformed the environment in which serials are produced as much as the political and economic transformation did. After over twenty years since the last double production was attempted TV came back to the same formula, which does not work any more because of the changes in technology. TV managers seemed to ignore the changes in the audio-visual ecology, which took place since the mid-1970s.

The production documents show that even though television was such a major co-producer of serials and films it had a very limited input concerning the shape of the film and the serial. It happened quite a few times that according to the contract the producer was to deliver four episodes of the serial but in the course of shooting the director decided to make six episodes.[16] TV agreed to the change and the contract was readjusted accordingly to account for the increase of the episodes and a greater investment on the part of television. In the opinion of a long-standing programme manager for the Polish TV, Carmen Szwec, TV entered these co-productions at a very late stage when the works on the film were advanced and for this reason TV was no longer in the position to suggest too many changes.[17] Szwec is right but she does not answer the question why TV was delaying its decision about engaging in co-production for so long.

These last minute decisions about the engagement in such costly productions could be explained by the internal decision-making problems that Polish TV has been experiencing since its transformation into a partly self-financing institution. At the same time it was also obliged by law to contract 10 per cent of their programming from the outside producers. This meant that the television has to create a new job of a producer who could attract outside projects, select them and then supervise them. In order to really have some impact such producers would need to have access to funds with which they could back their intervention into the making of these outsourced projects. Polish television, like most of the institutions established in the communist era, is very bureaucratic and its main feature is a lack of flexibility and reluctance to let any one individual make decisions about large amounts of the company's money. The lack of dynamism, trust and flexibility within the TV internal structures could be seen as at least partly responsible for slow and often plainly bad decision making when it came to the production of serials and cinema films in the 1990s.

Independent film production companies appeared in Poland only after 1989. They had little of their own capital and lacked their own production and post-production facilities. Polish TV was a very desirable partner for any of their projects because it had both money and infrastructure. In fact, the contracts regulating the production of the film and TV serial stipulate what percentage of TV investment is money and which percentage is material. The material contribution gave independent producers access to the TV production facilities. Moreover, TV was not a very difficult partner to attract because it was under the legal obligation to outsource 10 per cent of TV programming to the independent producers.[18] As we also already know as a result of these co-productions TV had a secured right to the serial but limited rights to the film. This means that a serial was means for co-producers to get TV on board for the production of the film. The co-producers were primarily interested in the making of the film. The serial was a way of attracting TV to the project and thus of gaining access to the TV production facilities and funds.

The institution of a film producer is deeply implicated in the past structures of film production. It is due to the fact that when it comes to cinema production, it is still very important in Poland to be able to secure initial funding from the state. This funding usually is a fraction of the whole film budget, but it is necessary to obtain bank credits and apply for the funding from the European Union. Among producers there are some for whom it is easier to secure this funding than for others. It is due to the fact that these producers were TV production executives or production heads of the film units in the past and they are very well connected which gives them advantage in the competition for state funding. Even after the initial state funding is secured, the producers still have to obtain the rest. It turns out that some headway may be done thanks to some past advantages.[19] This is clearly visible on the example of film units and the biggest Polish production company Heritage Films.

Not only public television but also private one such as Canal+ is under obligation to invest in Polish cinema. Since the mid-1990s film funding coming from the television source in Poland has been interlocked with the operation of a private film company, Heritage Films, established in 1991. The owner of the company, Lew Rywin, became the biggest and most important film producer in Poland. Polish media imply that the fruitful cooperation between public TV and Heritage Films had to do with Rywin's pre-1989 employment in POLTEL – the film production arm of the Polish public television. While the owner of the Heritage Films, Rywin also had a special relationship with Canal+ where he was a member of the Board of Directors between 1997 and 2000. Partly as a result of this relationship out of thirty-five films made by Canal+ nearly half was co-produced by Heritage Films.

The private producers and the film units producers not only share some advantages from their past position but are also united in promoting the same type of cinema in Poland which is that of literary adaptations. The older and established film-makers often associated with film units are well-known to the audiences and to the producers. As a result it is easier for them to attract the attention of the producers for whom when it comes to the financial success of the film the older film-makers are less of a liability than young and unknown directors. This is the reason why it is so difficult for young film-makers in Poland to make a debut and even more difficult to make the second feature.

Nobody can argue with the fact that public TV is drawing privileges from being the only TV station whose existence extends from socialist to post-socialist times. However, if we consider the monopoly of public television in relation to cinema, it looks less convincing. The main reason might be that Polish cinematography itself used to be a huge integrated block. It was founded and developed in this way from the end of World War II. As we have seen in the past, it was TV that needed cinema more than cinema needed television. The growing strength of TV position resulted from its privileges in regard to the government. Nowadays, TV has the money that cinema needs. But cinema has a product of which it is very protective and offers TV only an offspring of this product, that is, TV serials.

The comparison of the dynamics of the TV–cinema interface at the turn of the 1970s and in the 1990s reveals some important differences. In the past television had to rely on the film units because it lacked its own production facilities. Nowadays independent producers want to attract television for their projects in order to gain access to TV production and post-production infrastructure. Another important difference has to do with the fact that the simultaneous production of serials and films is no longer part of the political game where TV and cinema were competing for the scarce funds and recognition towards the socialist government. Nowadays TV needs this particular type of serials in order to fulfil its obligations as a public broadcaster and to attract advertisers. On their part cinema producers offer the making of the serials as a way to attract TV as a co-producer. The two periods in question also show one striking parallel; it is a continuous interest of television in serials only and its indifference towards films on which they are based. This attitude may be an indication that at least from the aesthetic point of view serials are regarded as a more televisual form and thus naturally more desirable from the TV perspective.

Notes

1. *Hrabina Cosel/Countess Cosel* (Jerzy Antczak, film 1968, TV serial 1968); *Pan Wołodyjowski/Sir Wołodyjowski* (Jerzy Hoffman, film 1969) and *Przygody Pana Michała/Sir Michael's Adventures* (Paweł Komorowski, TV serial 1969);

Kopernik/Copernicus (Ewa Petelska and Czesław Petelski, film 1972, TV serial 1972); *Ziemia obiecana/The Promised Land* (Andrzej Wajda, film 1974, TV serial 1975); *Noce i dnie/Nights and Days* (Jerzy Antczak, film 1975, TV serial 1977); *Pierścień i róża/The Rose and the Ring* (Jerzy Gruza, film 1986, TV serial 1986).

2. 'Uwagi Komitetu do Spraw Radia i Telewizji do materiałów przedstawionych na Sejmową Komisję Kultury i Sztuki, p.t. "Analiza sytuacji w kinematografii polskiej – kwiecień 1973" 12/02/74' (1974), *Archiwum Telewizji Polskiej SA*, 1716/68, Volume 1.
3. Antczak also filmed his earlier film *Countess Cosel* in the same way.
4. Anon. (1997: 3). 'Uwagi o adaptacji *Ogniem i mieczem* 11/5/97'.
5. Bossak (1987: 1).
6. Andrzej Wajda, interview, *Dziennik Wieczorny* 110, 17 May 1978.
7. Stempel (1974: 1).
8. Zajicek (1994b: 78).
9. 'Misja Telewizji Publicznej SA Jako Nadawcy Publicznego 06/94' (1994).
10. Unpublished report, 'Kultura polska 1989–1997' (1997: 197).
11. 'Letter to the Principal Accountant of TVP SA from Telewizja Polska SA dotyczący umowy kooprodukcyjnej na realizację filmu i serialu TV *Quo Vadis* 05/05/00', Agencja Telewizji Polskiej SA *Quo Vadis* TIF. 0001375-1379.
12. 'Umowa kooprodukcyjna na realizację filmu i serialu TV *Quo Vadis* 20/6/00' (2000).
13. 'Umowa kooprodukcyjna na realizację filmu i serialu TV *Ogniem i mieczem* 4/8/97' (1997).
14. 'Umowa kooprodukcyjna na realizację filmu i serialu TV *Przedwiośnie* 05/07/00' (2000).
15. Trzaska (2002).
16. 'Umowa kooprodukcyjna na realizację filmu i serialu TV *Przedwiośnie* 05/07/00' (2000).
17. Interview with Carmen Szwec, Dorota Ostrowska, April 2004 (unpublished).
18. 'II Okrągły Stół Medialny March 1996. Znaczenie niezależnej produkcji audiowizualnej w Polsce', *Archiwum Telewizji Polskiej SA*, 2607/8, Volume 1.
19. At this stage it might be important to mention the controversy surrounding the film units, which after 1989 were also accused of unfair advantages. Most of them were dissolved after 1989 because they were not economically viable. The ones which survived hold rights to the films they produced prior to 1989 and profit from broadcasting them. These film units have been reproached by independent producers who do not have a similar source of income. The producers regard the profits drawn by the studios from the older films as a form of a hidden state subsidy that gives the units an unfair advantage on the Polish market. Those who are connected to either private or public television also are more competitive when it comes to producing films in Poland.

9. AUDIO-VISUAL PRODUCTION CULTURES: CONVERGENCE AND RESISTANCE

'Cinema' (writing in movement) can be seen as the result of a history of technological developments aimed at capturing visual reality – or the appearance of such (verisimilitude). Developments within the audio-visual arts and industries, including the introduction of sound and colour, can be seen in the same terms. All the historical developments involving cinema have to be seen in their economic context. To put it bluntly – somebody (person or institution) has to take the risk and pay for the expensive processes of technological development and bear the costs of the actual production and distribution. The history of cinema could be seen as a continuous process of consolidating and controlling film-making in order to increase, or at least secure some return on a usually very high investment. Codifying films into genres, focusing publicity on stardom and celebrity or targeting particular segments of the audience, families, women or in more recent times adolescent males have all been part of the efforts to find a magic economic formula which will turn cinema's alchemy into science and shadows and sounds into gold. This story of convergence of technology, economics and creative talent has been interrupted at regular intervals by pockets of resistance associated with artistic, technological and often funding innovation usually labelled as waves, given a prefix new, national, or even avant-garde or described with some more timely cultural and local-specific term.

Since both cinema and television are audio-visual mediums, it is not surprising that technology offers the most natural basis for comparison between the two. Indeed it is unarguable that the technological similarities between the two audio-visual mediums are at the centre of economic and cultural tensions between the two. The economic and cultural relationship of TV to cinema was introduced at the beginning of this volume and has been a central theme of the national chapters, which outlined the history of the cinema–television interactions. The latter part of this chapter will focus on the way in which the relationship between cinema and television has been affected more recently by the advent of digital technology. The new technology brings with it the possibilities for low-cost filming, intimate and almost artisan production mode and a democratisation of use. Nonetheless the digital film-making 'revolution' would not have been possible without the already established television-bound culture of consuming and producing audio-visual material. Television has allowed more and more people a virtually unrestricted access to images and thus democratised image consumption and raised the issue of the equality-quality of audio-visual material (the fact that televisual and cinematic material is audio-visual, consisting of images and sounds often produced in the same way and by the same individuals, does not mean that the televisual and cinematic material is of the same quality or equality). Digital technology (allied to the possibilities of the internet) has extended the audio-visual democracy of exhibition to all other aspects of film-making: pre-production, production, post-production and finally distribution, and as a result intensified the process of the film-making community (including people working in all parts of the film industry) finding themselves losing control over the cinematic realm. Thus it is unlikely that the digital turn will result in a new consolidation of the film-making industry. Rather, what we are observing is an evolutionary transformation of this industry for which the last thirty to forty years (dominated by the debates about television) was just a stepping stone to a very new world. In this chapter, we will look at the technological history of cinema and television which paved the way for the digital turn. The process of technological innovation was aimed at optimising the audio-visual production by making it cheaper and more accessible while at the same time striving to meet distinct and often conflicting demands (of the popular and art-house audiences to mention just the two most distinctive ones).

THE TECHNOLOGICAL ANCESTRY OF CINEMA AND TELEVISION

Photography (writing in light) was the first visual art to be produced and distributed on a mass scale and manufactured in an industrial manner. This industrial manufacture presupposes the making of articles on *a large scale* (at least potentially) using machinery. Photography is a mechanical process with the potential for large scale distribution – which is not the case with paintings. It was a new form of producing images bringing with it new ways of seeing and doing predicated upon its reproducibility.[1]

Photography began as a scientific experiment but *its primary aim* was to capture reality.[2] The question remained how to keep it and by extension to sell it. Two thousand years of striving to copy reality more accurately and efficiently led to Johann Schulze – in 1727 – discovering that silver nitrate darkens when exposed to light. Joseph Niepce created the first negative (to strike a positive) in 1827. By 1871 Richard Maddox developed a process whereby sensitising chemicals could be coated on a glass plate in a gelatine emulsion to retain the images. Within a decade the emulsion would be coated on celluloid roll film – the state of the art in terms of the 'capture' of images until the introduction of video technology.

Building on the work of Eadward Muybridge, who took the leap to capturing movement with a series of photographs, Thomas Edison developed a machine for 'flicking' pictures to produce a continuous image. The machine utilised 35mm cards with four perforations thus would have worked perfectly well with a modern (pre-digital) camera. The problem with the Edison system was that the 'show' had a maximum length of twenty seconds and you could not project the image (thus restricting the audience at any one time to one viewer). This was the problem exercising Louis Le Prince, who shot a 'film' in Leeds in 1888. In October 1888, a series of pictures was taken by Le Prince in the garden of his father-in-law, Joseph Whitley.[3]

In the autumn of 1894, Antoine Lumière, a successful manufacturer of photographic plates, asked his sons to work on the problem of animated images which had so far stumped such great inventors as Edison and others. This paternal push in the right direction resulted in the invention of the Lumière 'Cinematograph': *Leaving the Lumière Factory*, the first film using the Cinematograph, was thus the first time human beings filmed each other. Cinematography – writing in movement – was born. 'Film' had started with documentary – allowing audiences to 'be' where they could not be . . . and to watch.[4] Innovations in nature of content and aesthetics followed. The move to greater and greater spectator engagement required technological daring in a push towards greater and greater verisimilitude and quality of image. We should note that this engagement was achieved through more sophisticated film-making techniques, such as close-ups, filming in different locations, editing and through the increase in the length of the films which emphasised the narrative rather than just spectacular/attraction aspect of early cinema. Nonetheless, these innovations were in themselves predicated upon technological developments. Further technological revolutions were required to culminate in the ultimate verisimilitude: talking pictures (in realistic colour).

A NEW MEDIUM FOR NEW TIMES – TELEVISION

In the post-war period the cinematic world came under attack from a new technology, television, whose impact proved to be even more pervasive than that of sound or colour in that it involved changing people's viewing habits the first time since the growth of theatrical presentation. In industrialised nation states the post-war 'baby boom' tended to keep people at home. The increasingly prosperous citizens of the developed world turned to the radio and soon after to television for their entertainment. Thus in the post-war period the issue of verisimilitude (largely satisfied) was superseded by the increasingly important issue of ease of delivery. As soon as cinema ceased to be 'a new medium' it had to learn how best to react to and/or exploit the new audio-visual media as they appeared. As we have seen in the nationally focused chapters in this book, television emerged as a competitor to cinema but eventually became a (more or less problematic) funder, supporter, even crutch.

Television – literally 'sight at a distance' – was the 'new medium' of the post-war era, although it had existed as a technology for rather a long time before. Broadcast television is a direct descendant of the telegraph, first proposed by Charles Morrison in 1753 and brought to functional success by Samuel Morse in 1836. TV became a practical technology on 25 June 1923 when John Logie Baird took out the patent on 'seeing by wireless'. This patent itself gives a strong clue to the technological linkage to radio. In March 1925 Baird displayed his equipment at Selfridges store in London going on to form 'Television Ltd.' and – in October 1925 – 'televised' his assistant William Taynton. On 30 September 1929 the Baird Television Company began regular transmission, although they could not transmit sound and pictures at same time. On 2 November 1936 BBC TV (using EMI's 405-lines) was officially launched by the Postmaster General. German state television had been launched in March 1935.

The difference in television's post-war status can be illuminated by consideration of the use of the words 'technology' and 'medium'. The very word medium focuses attention on the issue of delivery, transmission, communication and flow with which television has been equated during its fairly brief history. Technology on the other hand brings to mind the question of production, the knowledge of making, manufacturing i.e. a sense of a process which could be broken into segments in order to be completed. In this sense, television has first been a medium which has gradually become a technology. Digital seems to encompass and express both ideas, that of technology and medium, simultaneously. Arguably, it is thanks to the evolution undergone by television that digital could become that inclusive. While cinema was focusing on telling stories and producing images, TV was about transmitting them. Following this logic, if television had remained only a transmitting medium, but never a producing one – we would have never had the tension between TV and cinema as we have seen in the last forty years. In the digital world the difference which is so apparent between cinema and television is not there any more.

Television was, at least from the mid-1930s, something more than an interesting technological breakthrough. It became a means of communication, as with radio, designed to defeat the natural limits of time and space. What TV shares with radio is a sense of intimacy or at least the ability to give us at least a sense of intimacy. Thus the medium became 'personality' driven not star driven like cinema. In the post-war period the film industries (nationally, regionally or globally) did not abandon the theatrical exhibition option. Indeed, realising that the audience now had many options for its entertainment dollar, pound, lira and so on the major companies focused on film-going as an event. Mainstream US films got bigger and bigger and the theatrical event became a more comfortable experience involving catering and access to other leisure activities.

In Europe the film industries (still relatively starved of capital for investment) seemed liable to simply surrender to the American zeitgeist. France – for clearly articulated *cultural* reasons – made the most concerted effort to 'defend' her film industry. Whilst in Italy there was clearly a surge in cinema building[5] (and therefore increased exhibition) it should be noted that (only) 'about one third of the screenings were from national origin' (see Italy chapter, p. 42). The UK's industry, finding it harder and harder to find distribution space, was in no position to compete with US high-tech blockbuster fare. The fact that many of these films were actually shot in the UK, utilising world-class post-production facilities, made the situation that much more frustrating. When the US-based conglomerates began to roll-out their multiplex solution to (re) attracting audiences back to the cinema the indigenous industries of the European nation states were in no position to supply product or to compete in distributive strategies.

The technological imperative within this 'bigger and better' strategy is to require more and more sophisticated equipment. This cost inflation was exponentially driven by the further drive of the star system – put bluntly films are expensive to make and the only reasonably certain way to recoup the astronomical costs is to market the product via popular stars. The hegemonic model of the (capital-rich) Hollywood domination of the global film market was bound to continue. However history tells us that one effect of increasing access to new technologies (in our case the most pertinent example would be television receivers), especially if linked to mass production, is to drive down costs – as we shall see in the last section of this chapter which investigates the (digital) convergence of the audio-visual media. First however we must look at how the two media developed as *different* technologies.

(see Italy chapter, p. 42)

VIDEOTAPE 'WARS'

Cinema is (or at least was) a celluloid based medium. Once broadcasters realised there were sound reasons for recording their output they naturally turned to film too. How else could they capture, keep and thus resell their product: 'For the first two decades of regular, scheduled transmissions there was no effective means of achieving this electronically, because of the volume of "bandwidth" (analogue signal information) consumed by a broadcast television signal was very much greater than with audio' (Enticknap 2005: 174). Thus 'telecine' and 'telerecording' technology (a rather cumbersome method to convert one medium to another) was born. Within the hybrid technology was the beginnings of video technology.

Sound recording to tape has a history of nearly eighty years.[6] But recording pictures presented far greater problems because the amount of information to be collected is far greater. It took until the 1950s to squeeze the bandwidth of video onto tape. In 1951 an Ampex Corporation team led by Charles Ginsburg began work on a video tape recorder (VTR). The VRX 1000 was launched in March 1956. On 30 November 1956 CBS broadcast the first network television show using videotape, *Douglas Edwards and the News*. Television slowly became a video medium. Early 'video' was a time-shifting rather than recording technology (i.e. for copying whole shows for later retransmission) not least because the nature of the magnetic tape did not allow for re-recording. This issue – and the high-cost implications of early videotape – were dealt with by technological developments including the 'helical scan' which reduced the number of recording heads from four to one in the early 1960s and the introduction of (U-matic) cassettes in 1970.

Stephen Lax has noted that: 'Videotape offered new opportunities in making programmes' (Lax 2006: 29) relating this truth particularly to news and current affairs. But shooting TV on video offered huge advantages over film camera in almost all productions. There was and remains a caveat over 'quality' of the image replaced but that issue in itself is an issue of what we mean by 'quality'. What is certainly true is that without the need for processing, rushes could be viewed instantly. There was the possibility – due to relative speed and reduction of cost – of serial re-takes. In reality, due to the time constraints of most TV production, it was the producers' need for speed rather than the questionable needs of the crafts (actorly or technically) to hone performance.

Editing could be done simply by 'crashing' shots together into a sequence. As the technology developed in more and more sophisticated and stylistically various ways the possibilities were almost unlimited – or at least as wide and various as those offered to a film editor. This is not to suggest that tape empowers the 'video' editor any more than the traditional Steenbeck operator, rather that it allows for a quicker, cleaner process that has ramifications on the cost and speed of production and certainly empowers other members of the creative team (from producer to director) to influence the 'final cut' more directly.

Two basic advantages of video cameras i.e. size/weight and duration of tapes (as opposed to film reels) fundamentally affected the type of programme and nature of material that could be broadcast. This 'revolution' was a more extreme version of the 'evolution' that had taken place with the introduction of lighter film cameras and faster film stocks in the post World War II period.[7] The 'video' revolution was slow to come to film production. 'Films' continued to be shot on 'film'. Indeed 'quality' TV drama and flagship documentary also continued to be shot on film.

The reason for the continued use of film was clearly not economic but rather both aesthetic and cultural. With analogue tape there was never any possibility that the picture quality could approach the richness of film. In this sense the digital is clearly different for both spectacular digital blockbusters and low-budget artisan films are made using digital technology. This supports the hypothesis that television first and later on TV combined with video paved the way for the digital turn allowing the digital technology to affect all aspects of film-making *simultaneously*. Although perfectly acceptable on the standard television receiver of the mid-to-late twentieth century the picture quality of video would not stand up to theatrical viewing. 'Movies' were of course made on video but largely by students and those film-makers who felt themselves wedded to the avant-garde. Paradoxically, nowadays some avant-garde film-makers, such as those working for a video cooperative 'Re-voir' continue releasing their experimental films on video arguing that the same audio-visual effect cannot be achieved directly using the digital technology. In their case the process of making, associated with touching, a sensuous aspect of the video is crucial.[8]

The resistance to 'video' remained as the quality of the image continued to develop and even in the face of the exponential leap offered by digital video tape. Professional 'resistance' continues as the image (e)quality issue becomes spurious. It is arguable that the 'filmic' nature of cinema is being preserved for cultural reasons. These cultural reasons are predicated upon a *habitus* amongst the 'film production' class. Thus *Projections 12: Film-makers on Film Schools*[9] unwittingly exposes a good deal of pretension (not least in the interviewers) but also reveals some very enlightening insights into a 'craft' habitus; including the use of film. Roger Crittenden (Director of curriculum at the UK's National Film and TV School) exhibits a profound worry about digital editing: 'The problem is that technology actually might get in the way of thinking . . . because somehow the machine is telling you not to worry because *it* can do it' (Boorman et al. 2002: 15). The interviewer (Fraser MacDonald, the director of such cutting edge TV as episodes of *Holby City* and *Mayo*) cannot resist joining in: 'on film, there is a real decision to be made there, and a real discussion about what that cut means'. Presumably we are being asked to believe this cutting is more 'real' because the film has a physical reality.

The issue of 'discipline' becomes even more clear when the 'film-maker' priesthood discuss actual shooting. Damien O'Donnell, director of *East is East* (1999), writes thus: 'the access to this cheap medium means that an awful lot of shit will get made . . . there will still be the craftsmen . . . the one thing that film has over digital is that it imposes a discipline on the film-maker' (Boorman et al. 2002: 33). One is left wondering why anybody would choose to watch the 'disciplined' *East is East* as opposed to say Kiarostami's *10* (2002) or Sokurov's *Russian Ark* (*Russkii kovcheg*, 2002) – but as O'Donnell puts it himself: 'you can have too much choice' (Boorman et al. 2002: 35). In any event digital production is now a reality and in its own way brings cinema and TV production much closer together.

THE AUDIO-VISUAL HABITUS OF FILM PRACTITIONERS

Underlying the faintly condescending attitude to television is a habitual concern about 'film' and its relationship to television which parallels the concerns of critics and commentators (e.g. the Susans Sontag and Hayward). However the main driver of concern here in this volume has been economic as much as aesthetic – in brutal terms there would be little or no European film industries without the active involvement of global Hollywood and domestic national television, which were first to embrace and implement technological innovations such as the use of the videotape. It is probably not controversial to suggest that the existence of a global hegemony for 'Hollywood' has not been beneficial to European cinema production. However the role of television is more ambivalent as cost and benefit. The financial relationship has been to a very large extent beneficial (if not problematic); the increasing piquancy of the patronage relationship may be seen as less so. At the extremes of the European ambit of this volume, i.e. Poland and the UK we have two extremes of the ambiguous benefit–threat relationship between Cinema and Television.

In socialist Poland, state run television lacked its own production resources (at least for full-scale fiction projects) and relied on the cinema studios, equipment and talent. This particular state of reliance ended in the second half of the 1970s when television finally developed its own infrastructure with POLTEL (as well as a training school in Katowice) to produce films. According to Zajicek, until the mid-1970s there was practically a civil war raging with TV managers in Poland trying to hijack cinematic production and seize control over cinema by lobbying the government in various ways.[10] In a process which echoes (in a rather more directive and premeditated manner) more recent events in the UK[11] TV managers (like the UK's Skillset) tried to use scriptwriting as a way to gain some control over the product created by film-makers. In Poland with the political support of the Party and ambitious plans for future development, TV managed to work out an agreement, which coordinated the workings of TV and cinema by virtually subordinating cinema to television (Zajicek 1992: 78). In a situation of material scarcity television managers contributed to the development of the atmosphere of competition in which television and cinema practitioners were trying to win favours from the government. Ostrowska (in this volume) has pointed to the transformations linked to the end of communist rule. Economic factors came to prevail over political (or even public) concerns. Even publicly owned television turned to cinema production both for the income derived from TV subscription and to gain government funding. When independent production companies appeared in post-communist Poland their only access to capital and facilities was via television. TV was, in any event, under the legal obligation to outsource 10 per cent of TV programming to the independent producers. Independent producers need this TV link to gain support from the state and (inevitably the most significant in terms of value) bank credits and funding from the European Union (via the MEDIA scheme).

In the UK (as a Western democracy not experiencing the necessary pains of 'transition') the discourse is rather more collegial (even if as businesslike in reality). Within this less 'competitive' relationship there was a perceived difference between the two key sponsors i.e. Film Four and the BBC in the kind of support offered to film-making, described thus by Sue Clayton (a British film-maker beneficiary of both):

> For the BBC the first commitment was still to the license fee payer, therefore although they released some of their dramas theatrically, this was only done after broadcast. Film Four was far more autonomous and certainly in my case did not appear to consider either the aesthetic or practical aspects of TV broadcast while developing the film – it was always a feature film which would later be shown and repeated on television. The Film Four Channel obviously increased Channel Four's branding of 'its' films, but again the branding was to do with cinema films, not TV drama which might later be distributed.[12]

Film Four had a working rule of thumb that if it made eight or ten films every year, at least four or five or these would get a theatrical release in the UK (an achievement in itself given the collapse of the art-house cinemas in the 1990s). At least one or two would do extremely well at box office. Thus profits from *Trainspotting* (Boyle, UK, 1996) and *Secrets and Lies* (Leigh, UK, 1996) would cover the costs for releasing other films which, while they might be critical successes, may for a number of reasons (e.g. lack of stars or innovatory form) have had limited box-office appeal. It was a system that worked both economically and creatively. During the life of Film Four, executives went on to make about one in three of everything they developed whereas in the same period at the BBC only one in eight or ten went forward to be made. Thus at Film Four, development funding was a more sure guarantee of progress, and the relationship was that much more secure. The collapse of Film Four (2001) led to a generation of film-makers who were working without the level of state support they would have had in Italy, Germany or Scandinavia. Those for whom Film Four had been a 'home' were left high and dry:

> The specific mode of Film Four's development, its informality, approachability and human scale, as well as its status internationally for attracting co-finance and distribution deals, was something of great value which was always going to be hard to replace.[13]

Frédéric Bourboulon (a key and consummate example of the 'independent French producer') portrays a less cosy (but equally 'swings and roundabouts') world operating across the Channel. His thoughts have to be seen in relation to how difficult it now is to make films in Europe without any involvement from television. As such they chime exactly with the anglophone 'hard to replace' opinion:

> They [the major companies] . . . understood that the same film, made within the studio was much more expensive than the same film made by

an independent producer with whom one was going to tighten the screw: 'You propose a film to us, we finance it for you, but attention! It must not cost more than . . .' and me I am obliged to them and I must deliver.[14]

This somewhat unequal relationship between studio and independent producer has been ameliorated since Canal+ television become one of the main sources of financing and exhibiting French cinema, obliged as it is to invest 9 per cent of its budget in production. This guaranteed finance does not guarantee quality. Indeed in this volume[15] Dorota Ostrowska has argued that this situation encouraged budget inflation and the entry of incompetent 'one-off' producers to chance their arm (and fail) in film production. In Denmark Henning Camre (Head of the Danish Film Institute) agrees: 'The Media and television agreement stipulates how much TV station must spend for films. . . . The subsidy system results in films that people do not want to see. It is too easy to find money to make a film.'[16]

Nonetheless in the case of France Ostrowska goes on to point out to 'the commitment of the channel [Canal+] to produce films which have a cinema release before they are broadcast on TV. Canal+ was thus a realisation of the film-makers' dream . . .'

Frédéric Bourboulon continues:

> One survives anyway, with our small films, our independent films, as the English cinema which sometimes survives with three comedies. Who will have bet on certain English comedies which were colossal successes like *Four Weddings and a Funeral* which certainly was made with very little money. [Unlike in the old days of domination by the 'halls'] the majority money, it is the money of television. However television imposes its law, it says, here now, my public it wants that.

Vibeke Windelov, until recently the producer of Lars von Trier's films, shares Bourboulon's concerns:

> I can only judge from my own experience. When it comes to the people, their talents, and the way they are collaborating, I can only be extremely optimistic. But when it comes to financing, I am not sure. It is tough to finance movies. And when you're starting a project, you don't know how easy or difficult it is going to be. And I suspect it is going to be tougher for me with Lars in the near future.[17]

Not only Windelov is determined to carry on. Bourboulon is not about to give up either:

> After what do I run? I had my name on many films, I had success, I had failures, I knew both. I am 53 years old. What do I make? I continue,

why? . . . It is not a goal for me, the money. Why? It is to make extraordinary things, to give birth to a director, to prove it.[18]

It is arguable that without television there would not even be that little amount of money (however hard to secure) that would allow producers like Bourboulon and his ilk (such as Viebke Windelov in Denmark) to continue to produce what Bourboulon calls 'extraordinary things'. Television as financial provider and guaranteed outlet is essential to European cinema(s). We have seen that this is the case across Europe. In Italy, as an example, by the 1960s two thirds of the Italian movies were never released (many more had only a limited run). This was a recipe for terminal decline. Yet in the television of the late 1950s and early 1960s they adopted techniques inspired by the cinema. A more cinematic language of TV was made easier by the opening of a second channel (Raidue, more oriented towards experimentation). Film directors and operators were invited to work for television (Caldiron 1976), thus allowing an audio-visual production culture to survive (if not thrive). Cinema production kept on: 'above all because television, especially the RAI, came to the rescue'.[19]

In Spain we have seen in this volume how politicians in charge of audio-visual policy exerted pressure so that TVE would support different projects to revitalise the film industry.[20] If TVE was a reluctant cooperator Valeria Camporesi has shown how private production companies slipped into a practice where an intensive elision between the different audio-visual media simply became viewed as normal if 'uncertain and intermittent'.[21] As a concomitant to this, in Spain and indeed all of our national studies, cinema technicians and professionals would be bound to spend some of their working lives with television companies. In the 1980s legal changes broke the RTVE monopoly in Spanish broadcast television. The beneficiaries were local governments (since 1982), or of private enterprises (beginning in 1988) and so television became an increasingly major source of finance for Spanish cinema (in terms of revenue 30 per cent in 1997 rising to 45 per cent by 1999).

In Germany as is well accepted and understood: 'German independent film-making [. . .] is unthinkable without television' (Elsaesser 1999: 202). As Margit Grieb and Will Lehman have shown,[22] this relationship was a late developer as 'many within the film industry blamed the dramatic decrease in cinema spectatorship on the emergence of television, tainting the reputation of the latter. The then popular slogan, 'not a meter of film for television' (Seidl 1987: 40), aptly describes the antagonistic attitude prevalent at the time.[23]

In Denmark it is clear that our case study of Dogme95 could not have even occurred without television as: 'the Danish Film Institute was not willing to dispense from its usual procedures . . . This financial dilemma was finally solved in 1997 when Bjørn Erichsen, then director of DR TV, offered a financial support of 15 million Kroner (£1.4 million) (Schepelern 1997: 227). It was the success of Dogme productions (*Festen* and *The Idiots*) that allowed Henning Camre to re-negotiate the Film and Media Agreement with Danish television stations, which legally obliged them to partake in the production of Danish films.[24]

Camilla Hammerich (a producer in the drama department of TV2 in Denmark) notes that:

> From the point of view of TV2 – the obligation to spend 35 mln on feature films is too much. It is because making feature films is so expensive and the air time these feature film takes is so much shorter than what you would get with a TV series.

But she also admits that the cinema cachet brings cultural and monetary capital in its wake: 'But then when they [TV] are getting a good Danish film, which did well in cinema, it is almost certain it will do well on TV as well.'[25]

Hammerich is convinced that the success of Danish film continues to hang on von Trier and to some extent was predicated upon his involvement with TV: 'He is the engine. Hence, whatever he was doing in television, he was clearing some new paths . . . Lars von Trier bridged the worlds of cinema and television with *The Kingdom*.'[26]

Henning Camre concurs:

> Cinema and TV were two separate worlds. The real change was brought in the '90s by the work of von Trier, such as *Kingdom*. *Kingdom* was new in itself. But what was also new was the fact that television was seeking out film people to contribute to television programming . . . The worlds of TV and cinema were not interacting but co-existing in such a small country as Denmark, which was very curious.[27]

Hammerich identifies von Trier's contribution to both mediums: 'He was trying to do a popular programme and reach out into the audience. He also used very popular actors, etc. . . . Among directors before that there was a low-level of audience awareness.'[28] Here Hammerich is making a serious point in suggesting that it was television which made the directors aware of the needs of audiences and by extension made cinema in Denmark more interesting as well.

In the French case Bourboulon realises that there are significant overlaps in production between cinema and TV – even for his beloved auteurs – but remains ambivalent about working in both media:

> There are people who are happy making television and cinema. But sometimes television is a ghetto . . . For example, when you make téléfims it will be difficult for you to return in the cinema . . . A telefilm can be noble, there are very beautiful telefilms, there are very beautiful series which one can make with television. There should not be ostracism between the two. But that exists. On the other hand, there are young people who start with

television, it is a start . . . But there is a risk of ghettoïsation for certain people who remain too much with television. I speak about the directors. The technicians, that goes. . . . There is an ostracism on the operators chiefs, yes . . . Not, the editors it is much simpler. They are called assemblers in France, they assemble films or telefilms, it is similar . . . There is a risk of ghettoïsation for the directors. I believe that there always were footbridges . . . I believe that it was always like that. Bertrand [Tavernier] makes the documentaries for television. He did not make telefilms but there are some who do.[29]

The result of the model of economic hegemony, a combination of Hollywood and domestic TV, is that national TV industries are treated with the same mixture of condescension, irritation and fear (admittedly on a less virulent scale) as the all-consuming Hollywood Babylon. A question hangs over this attitude in terms of its justness and indeed the continued veracity of its basis as we move towards a 'digital' age.

THE DIGITAL TURN

Scriptwriting is the single and perhaps the most important area of film-making which has been affected by the combined impact of the digital technology and internet. As it has been demonstrated repeatedly in the national chapters, scriptwriting plays a pivotal role in the television-making as well. The production process begins with the development of a script. The World Wide Web is becoming an essential tool for everybody writing or seeking a story. Scriptwriting programmes are available to buy or are distributed free online. An entire script can be sent around the world within seconds. The internet has spawned discussion groups and global 'communities' that enable scriptwriters to swap ideas and make contacts.

Other film professionals have seized the communication potential of the Web rather more tentatively than writers. Nonetheless there is now a burgeoning sector of film-makers networks. An exceptionally useful site is 'Shooting People'.[30] The facility to discuss and publicise projects with like-minded practitioners is crucial in the fast-changing field of low budget (almost certainly digital) production.

As a medium with a long-standing tradition of innovation and utilisation of new technologies, the actual process of capturing images (at least in mainstream cinema) remained an area of rigid resistance. However there is now no good reason for shooting on 35mm film. Roberto Rodriguez stated baldly: 'Film-makers used 35mm cameras because that was all they had . . .' (*The Guardian*, 23/09/2003). As Wim Wenders has put it: 'In the long run, there is no question that DV will replace film. It gives you a more complex and satisfying control over the image than you ever had before' (interview with Sheila Johnston, the *Daily Telegraph*, 10 November 2000).

DV has already come to replace 16mm as the preferred low-budget alternative to 35mm film: at the 1999 Los Angeles Film Festival, 10 per cent of submissions were on DV. By 2000 it was 30 per cent; in 2001 it was 60 per cent. At the top end of the market, George Lucas shot the final parts of his 'Star Wars' saga entirely on CineAlta digital cameras. Lucas has gone so far as to state that 'I can safely say that I'll never ever shoot another film on film' (one of the reasons he gave was the savings to be made in production insurance) (Roberts 2004: 109–10).

Two of the key established British directors championing DV are Mike Figgis and Bernard Rose. Figgis made *Time Code* (2000). Bernard Rose, who directed *Ivansxtc* (2000), set up the provocatively named website www.filmisdead.com. Danny Boyle and producer Andrew MacDonald (who gave us Brit-hits *Shallow Grave* and *Trainspotting*) made *28 Days Later* (2002) entirely on DV. Boyle's attitude is less evangelical than Rose or Figgis. His reasons for using DV are linked to the material more than the allure of the technology: '. . . you have to have an organic reason to use it. There has to be something in the script that says this story belongs in the digital world' (Floyd 2002: 19) but as digital technology has developed even this attitude seems rather dated. We no longer look for DV to give us a 'documentary' – or even 'televisual' feel. Not only is digital reaching filmic quality – domestic DV is catching up fast too.

In pure monetary/quality terms the Sony HDR-FX1 camcorder (with a falling cost in the region of £3,000) gives a domestic consumer 1,440 pixels × 1,080 lines; whilst the £75,000 Sony CineAlta gives the cinematographer 1,920 pixels × 1080 lines.

On the website dedicated to the Sony HD cameras we can read:

> With the advent of HD camcorders at consumer price levels, Sony *et al* are betting there is a market for amateur cinematographers. This is a good thing. By making high-end technology available at low-end prices, we've taken equipment and acquisition barriers out of the creative process. Who knows but that the next Frank Coppola or George Lucas isn't some high school kid from the poorer side of the tracks somewhere?[31]

A ninety-minute feature with a 7:1 shooting ratio (i.e. 630 minutes of shot material) on 35mm (at $83.64/minute) would cost $52,693. On HD ($2.52/minute) the same amount of shot material would cost $1,587.[32] This substantial factoring down in cost does not even take into account the savings in lighting, transport and personnel (all with addition cost benefits in terms of insurance). Non-linear time-code based digital video editing is good news for small part players. It has reclaimed the creative flexibility of film-editing that was lost in the era of tape-to-tape dubbing based video editing. It is also much more effective than film-editing. It is useful to actually see and hear the material as it is being produced. A single computer inputs, displays, handles and outputs dealing with picture and sound editing, colour correction, light correction, motion graphics, effects, graphics, dubbing and mixing.

As well as being able to shoot high quality pictures and sounds for a fraction of film production costs it is possible to produce an off-line edit for cinema (traditional, digital or online) or straight to DVD.

If production is slowly but surely becoming digital, editing already is. For non-linear editing, film sequences are first converted to video using a telecine film scanner or DV footage downloaded through a 'fire-wire' (which connects the recording technology direct to hard disc). All the material can be stored on a computer hard-drive (the rapid fall in the price of disc space and memory has allowed this technology to be utilised by low or no-budget productions). Every frame can be accessed instantly and sequences can be assembled in an infinite number of ways with no risk of destroying your original rushes. A vociferous apostle in the use of computer editing – with the Avid editing system (now industry standard) – was Thelma Schoonmaker after 'cutting' Martin Scorsese's *Casino*: 'It was a revelation, because I had resisted using it for quite a long time . . . it's just easier to do it faster and without worry; it frees you up.' It is worth noting that – as with any powerful tool – there are dangers: 'The danger of it for an inexperienced director would be to find yourself with sixteen different versions . . . Marty is a very decisive director . . . you have to use the system with discipline: you have to think carefully about your options, make sure they are valid . . .'[33]

The authors of this book tend to agree with the *Screen International* editors who assessing the condition of cinema in the digital era stated (perhaps over-exuberantly): 'the widely reported death throes of cinema have actually been growing pains' (*Screen International*, 17 March 2006: 2).

More than a decade ago James Cameron noted that: 'We're on the threshold of a moment in cinematic history that is unparalleled. Anything you can imagine can be done' (*Wired*, 12/1995). It is a rather bracing lesson to remember that what Cameron achieved when he crossed this threshold with *Titanic* (1997) was a (enormously successful) Hollywood blockbuster with the classic boys meets girl, boy loses girl structure (admittedly with the twist that they both meet an iceberg).

Keith Griffiths has written with great excitement about 'the manipulated image' noting that its possibilities go well beyond Cameron's live-action cartoons or even Dogme's amalgam of 'new wave' and 'direct cinema'. He cites in particular Agnès Varda's 'wandering-road-documentary' *The Gleaners and I* (*Les Glaneurs et la Glaneuse*, 2000) utilising a mass-market DV camera as a tool for a first person authored documentary (Varda the film-maker actually acts as a 'gleaner' of visual material). Griffiths notes that: 'most of the film-makers who have followed this path have discovered that these small domestic digital cameras can be used as both a very sophisticated vacuum cleaner and as a filmic pen' (Griffiths 2003: 21). Or to quote Rossellini's view of the relationship between the camera and the world, which refers to the most enduring concept of cinema as a medium reflecting reality rather than merely representing it: 'things are there; why manipulate them?' (Griffiths 2003: 21).

The powerful allure of the comfort of 'craft norms' continues to rein in a good deal of European (as well as Hollywood) production. This is less the case in other geographical areas: West and North Africa, Southern India and so on. It is arguable (see throughout this volume and particularly in the UK chapter) that TV craft norms rein in creativity the most. However the quest for spectacle which remains at the heart of a good deal of cinematic spectatorship, whilst potentially leading to bigger and bigger (digital) bangs also allows for visionary film-makers to make visually exciting movies that are 'spectacular' (in its several senses).

Peter Greenaway's *Prospero's Books* (1991) actually used HDTV technology as well as digital imaging software known as an 'electronic paintbox' which allowed the British auteur to fill the screen with an intricate series of intertextual multiple exposures and overlays. In 1995 after a series of successful TV documentaries he directed *The Pillow Book* again utilising the 'electronic paintbox'. In a 1997 interview Greenway was asked: What are your feelings about the state of contemporary film?

> In a sense I think it's already too late: Cinema is an old technology. I think we've seen an incredibly moribund cinema in the last 30 years. In a sense Godard destroyed everything – a great, great director, but in a sense he rang the death knell, because he broke cinema all apart, fragmented it, made it very, very self-conscious. Like all the aesthetic movements, it's basically lasted about 100 years, with the three generations: the grandfather who organised everything, the father who basically consolidated it and the young guy who chucks it all away. It's just a human pattern.[34]
>
> Thinking of cinema being a dinosaur, you know what they say about dinosaurs: the brain dies but it takes maybe several weeks before that message gets to the tail. So if we're lucky, maybe, the notion of conventional celluloid cinema has perhaps one or two generations to run. But then I'm sure, quite happily, we'll see the end of it. I would cry no tears for it because I'm quite convinced, and there's no reason not to think this, that all the new languages will certainly be soon giving us, I won't say cinema because I think we have to find a new name for it, but cinematic experiences, which is going to make Star Wars look like an early sixteenth century lantern-slide lecture.[35]

Post his own involvement in digital film-making, British director Mike Figgis has intervened in the developing history of audio-visual distribution via his own production company 'Red Mullet'. They have made strenuous efforts to promote Dubplate Drama,[36] claimed to be 'the world's first interactive TV drama' . . . 'a six part interactive urban music drama premiering on PSP Handheld, Channel 4, 3 Mobile, MTV UK, MTV BASE & E4'.[37] At the same Figgis is personally involved in developing production equipment to enhance digital technology's ease of use:

Red Mullet and Mike Figgis are extremely pleased to announce the launch of the FIGRIG. Working in partnership with both Ben Wilson and Italian Tripod manufacturer Manfrotto the FIGRIG was launched at NAB, Las Vegas in April 2005. It is now commercially available through local stockists worldwide.[38]

In a (suitably) online interview on the BBC's film website he was asked: 'If I wanted to be a film director how and what would I do about it, when I am 14?' Figgis replied: 'Are you lying about your age already? Buy, borrow or steal a digi camera, and get on with it.'[39]

In another place Figgis has stated:

> Now there is no reason to prevent anybody from making a film. The technology exists, the equipment is much cheaper than it was, the post-production facilities are on a laptop computer, the entire equipment to make a film can go in a couple of cases and be carried as hand luggage on a plane. There is nothing to stop people making films.[40]

In *Timecode* (2000) Mike Figgis utilised digital technology's ability to get up close and personal with improvising actors rather than make 'pretty' pictures. Incidentally (contra O'Donnell and MacIntosh) he was disciplined enough to shoot in real time. Of course this type of film-making may be a little too challenging for some spectatators. As one 'Amazon customer review' put it: 'I rented this movie based on the positive reviews, however I found this movie annoying and unwatchable. I couldn't concentrate, and I didn't find the split screen clever at all.'[41]

In the hands of Abbas Kiarostami, Michael Winterbottom, Eric Rohmer, even Ingmar Bergman and perhaps most extraordinarily Aleksandr Sokurov, digital film-making can produce spectacular films but also film production which specifically could only be achieved digitally. What digital will not do, however, is to replace the cornerstones of good film-making: talent, inspiration, knowledge, expertise and skills. Neither will digital technology render a script, i.e. an orderly plan for the narrative, or indeed a rigorous and workable shooting schedule obsolete.

'Web' discourse has the potential to change the way stories are told and consumed. But at the end of the day – whether written on a PC, filmed on DV or streamed on the web – the future of film is entertaining and engaging narratives. As Alfred Hitchcock reputedly once said: 'You need three things to make a good film: a great script, a great script and a great script.'

Digital is already changing production and transforming distribution and exhibition even more. What the prophets of a brave new interactive future fail to recognise is that people like to lean back, be drawn into the film world *and be entertained*. Moving, but not necessarily interactive, pictures still continue to move us. In *Cinema Paradiso* (Tornatore, Italy, 1989) the old 'flea pit' cinema is gone . . . but the small child in all of us still wants to be carried away . . . the jaded director remembers what it was that made him love the movies in the first place: *magic*. Digital technology (and media) is simply yet another way of turning the cinematic golden dust into golden nuggets.

NOTES

1. Thus we can agree with Walter Benjamin *The Work of Art in the Age of Mechanical Reproduction* (first published in 1936) that: 'for the first time in world history, mechanical reproduction emancipates the work of art from its parasitical dependence on ritual. To an ever greater degree the work of art reproduced becomes the work of art designed for reproducibility' without necessarily subscribing to his view that: 'The situations into which the product of mechanical reproduction can be brought may not touch the actual work of art, yet the quality of its presence is always depreciated.'
2. Thus Henry Fox Talbot entitled his 1844 book (the first to be illustrated with photographs) 'The Pencil of Nature.'
3. A general biographical overview of Le Prince can be found at: www.victorian-cinema.net/index with a more detailed account of his technological breakthrough at www.nmsi.ac.uk/nmpft/insight/info/5.3.39.pdf
4. Early responses to the cinematograph from Proust to Gorkii and Einstein dwell on the nature of space-time. Freud noted the obvious connection to dreams and memories (see Stephen Heath, 'Cinema and psychoanalysis: parallel histories', in Bergstom 1999).
5. See the 'Italy' chapter in this volume.
6. In 1928 Dr Fritz Pfleumer applied for a patent in Germany for the application of magnetic powders to strip of paper or film. In 1932 BASF joined with AEG to develop magnetic tape recording. By 1934, BASF was able to manufacture reels of plastic-based tape. See www.history.acusd.edu/gen/recording/notes
7. See Roberts and Wallis 2002: 90–8.
8. We would like to thank Martine Beugnet (University of Edinburgh) for the insights and information about the 'Re-voir' project.
9. Boorman et al. (2002).
10. See Chapter 8, p. 113.
11. 'UK' chapter: pp. 14–21.
12. Sue Clayton in interview with Heather Wallis 3/6/2006.
13. Sue Clayton in interview with Heather Wallis 5/6/2006.
14. Interview with Graham Roberts, Dorota Ostrowska and Stephen Hay, February 2005.
15. See 'France' chapter in this volume.
16. Interview with Dorota Ostrowska, June 2004.
17. Interview with Dorota Ostrowska, June 2004.
18. Interview with Roberts, Ostrowska, Hay.
19. 'Italy' chapter: p. 52.
20. 'Spain' chapter: p. 57.
21. 'Spain' chapter: p. 58.
22. See 'Germany' chapter.
23. 'Keinen Meter Film für das Fernsehen.' See Hickethier (1989).
24. 'Denmark' chapter: p. 100.
25. Interview with Dorota Ostrowska, June 2004.
26. Interview with Dorota Ostrowska.
27. Interview with Dorota Ostrowska, June 2004.
28. Interview with Dorota Ostrowska.

29. Interview with Roberts, Ostrowska, Hay.
30. www.shootingpeople.org
31. www.sonyhdvinfo.com
32. www.24p.bz/digital_cinema_24p
33. Thelma Schoonmaker interviewed by Nicolas Saada in Boorman and Donahue (1997: 27)
34. Salon interview with Peter Greenaway www.salon.com/june97/greenaway2970606
35. http://petergreenaway.co.uk/quotes.htm
36. www.dubplatedrama.tv
37. www.red-mullet.com/home
38. www.red-mullet.com/home
39. www.bbc.co.uk/films/2000/09/01/mike_figgis_chat_transcript_article
40. http://pro.imdb.com/name/nm0001214/quotes
41. www.amazon.co.uk/gp/product

10. *KINESTHETICS:* CINEMATIC FORMS IN THE AGE OF TELEVISION

Where can we identify the fault line between cinema and television in Europe in the last half century? Is there even such a thing? In absolute terms (as seen in every national chapter of this book) we cannot even point to economic barriers as the dividing line. Instead of separation between the two mediums we should perhaps talk about connectivity through at most a very porous barrier indeed. The question of who benefits from this permeable membrane (and how) is carried throughout this volume. The *osmotic* relationship between the two mediums is problematic and not easy to reduce to simple (or reproducible) patterns. This is not least the case in terms of the aesthetic impact and influence the ostensibly independent mediums may have on each other. In order to simplify the process of analysis we have here utilised the work and career of a film-maker, Pawel Pawlikowski who through his creative and ambiguous relationship to both mediums serves as a case study for illustrating the fluidity and connectivity central to the relationship between cinema and television in Europe over the past few decades. Pawlikowski is a suitable case for treatment as an exemplar of a whole range of film-makers in the UK (along with Pawlikowski) from Ken Russell to Michael Winterbottom. Across Europe we see examples of the same experience including Ingmar Bergman, Roberto Rossellini, Wim Wenders, Krzysztof Kieslowski, Lars von Trier and Andrei Sokurov. Beyond Europe we could point to further examples from Hitchcock and Welles to David Lynch.

In the course of this chapter we will contrast the case of Pawlikowski, which highlights the authorship aspect of audio-visual production, with examples of more genre-driven dynamics evident in particular in historical costume drama. This genre when considered from the perspective of television is truly a transnational one whose examples can be found centrally placed in the schedules of public broadcasters across Europe. The reason for drawing a distinction between these two approaches to audio-visual production, authorship and genre, is that the first one demonstrates an osmotic interface between the two mediums whilst the latter points to a much more tense hybridisation.

Pawel Pawlikowski is worthy of analysis as an interesting and original creative talent whose work has 'straddled' both media. In his different original and naturalised nationalities (Polish and British) he also neatly straddles the geographical spread of this volume. He is not an entirely untypical character and could claim iconic status in the story of 'European cinemas in the television age' – transnational in his background whilst clearly shaped by pan-European cultural and production imperatives and able to operate in fiction and non-fiction, cinema and television as evidenced in his television documentaries and feature films.

Last Resort (2000) was a TV production for BBC Films, with which Pawlikowski managed to cross the TV–cinema boundaries and enter cinema distribution networks. The film won the Edinburgh Film Festival award for the Best New British Feature and a year later the BAFTA Award for the 'Most Promising Newcomer'. This prize rather avoided the fact that Pawlikowski was nearly forty years of age, with a fifteen years long experience of making documentaries and dramas for the BBC. Since *Last Resort* Pawlikowski has completed *My Summer of Love* (2004), a cinematic work in terms of funding and distribution.[1] The bulk of Pawlikowski's works were made for television and most of them were documentaries yet in interviews with Pawlikowski we get an overwhelming sense of listening to a cineaste rather than to a TV director[2] (Tobin 2005: 114–19). In his view 'it is necessary to open up to the cinematographic experience . . . [rather than treat] . . . the image as an ornament which does not really penetrate down to the very core of things' (Tobin 2005: 116).

It is important to realise that the issue of cine–TV dynamics could be approached in another, possibly less positive way than that suggested in our analysis of Pawlikowski – via a concentration on genre rather than auteur which could be labelled as 'hybrid' rather than 'osmotic'. There is one type of film which seems to be able to reconcile the worlds of cinema and television and that's the genre of costume and heritage drama. The impact of television aesthetics contributed to the development of the heritage and costume drama for example in 1980s France into a cine-televisual genre. It was important for the homogenisation of popular cinema in France as the same film had to appeal to not only cinematic but also television audiences. Claude Berri's *Jean de Florette* (1986) and *Manon de sources* (1986) are examples of the genre production, which by and large embraces television aesthetics. These films consciously adjust their visuals and their narrative to suit the needs of television and thus to appeal to the tastes and expectations of the television audiences. At the same time they have some stylistic characteristics, which make them attractive to the cinema audiences as well.

The enthusiasm with which French television embraced costume and heritage drama[3] is associated with the fact that television drama shares some important features with costume and heritage drama. The 1950s *tradition de qualité* successfully revived in the films produced in the 1980s was criticised for being a cinema of scriptwriters rather than of film-makers for whom scripts and dialogues were more important than the visuals. It is enough to mention François Truffaut's attack on the 'cinéma du papa' in 'A certain tendency in French Cinema'. The genre was also reproached for its reliance on studio sets, heavy cameras and artificial lighting. Interestingly enough, all these undesirable elements of the *tradition de qualité* were traditionally associated with the production of television dramas and plays whose theatre roots led to the critics' emphasis on the TV script and their praise of scriptwriters rather than directors. The heritage and costume dramas of the 1980s favoured clear plot developments, strong characterisation and dialogues, which could be seen as a legacy of both the *tradition de qualité* and television aesthetics.

In *Jean de Florette* we have very few full shots of Jean; most of the time he is shown in a close-up or a medium close-up typical of television aesthetics which privilege facial expressions as a vehicle for a drama. Numerous conversations between Ugolin and his uncle are filmed in the same surroundings, usually at a dinner table in the evening, in a very repetitive manner with individual shots of the two men alternating with a shot showing both of them. Because the visual representation is uninteresting the spectator focuses on the dialogue instead which carries the story forward. The question is how this film's cinematic identity is maintained in spite of its clearly televisual aesthetics. It is the presence of cinematic tropes (e.g. landscape as *mise en scène*, gaze out of the frame and consistent continuity editing) within the stylistically televisual film which makes *Jean de Florette* such an example of the cine-televisual genre of the costume and heritage drama.

Jean de Florette, shot on location in Provence, would appear as a cinematic rather than téléfilm. But this Provencal location is not just a beautiful backdrop to the film's story but the vehicle for this story and the central character of the film's plot as well. It is important to point out that it is a feature of television drama to create narratives around sets. In television sets are not purpose-built to represent the pre-existing story but the stories are developed in response to the existing sets (Butler 2002: 98). The film's few panoramic shots of the landscape, which are cinematic rather than televisual in nature, are taken from the inside. They are point of view shots of the characters looking out of the windows or doors at the surrounding countryside. The existence of the internal frame created by the windows and doorways seems like a *mise en abyme* of the boundaries of the televisual representation of the landscape contained in *Jean de Florette*. The fact that the shots of the outdoors are point of view shots also suggests that the representation of the landscape is filtered through the minds of the characters. The landscape exists as a figment of their imagination, a mirage or a fantasy, which has only subjective but no objective existence. This subjective representation of the landscape tames it and limits it. This might be the reason why throughout the film the true identity of the land, the information about the water source on Jean's farm, is not disclosed until the end of the film and even then it has no impact on the plot development. The land is enigmatic, mysterious and hidden. The knowledge regarding the true identity of the land is repressed in the same way that the film's cinematic subtext is pushed under the layers of televisual aesthetics and meanings they generate.

According to André Bazin the principal characteristic of cinematic realism is deep focus photography allowing the spectators to explore freely the depth of field of a given shot.[4] He contrasted the effect of this kind of shots to montage editing, which he believed limited the freedom of the spectators imposing the meaning on them rather than allowing them to find it out themselves. Jeremy Butler points out that Bazinian principles had only a limited application for television:

> the smaller size of the television screen is a major impediment to deep focus staging of action. The background/objects can become so small as to have negligible impact on the shot's meaning. (Butler 2002: 122)

Such assessment of televisual limitations would just seem common sense and quite obvious if it did not conflict with another typically televisual characteristic, namely the importance of depth. Critics such as Zettl argue that depth is the only dimension which television can freely explore given the restrictions imposed by the small TV size on the horizontal and vertical camera movements (Zettl 1999: 171). The television camera favours the staging of the action in depth rather than horizontally. Paradoxically, even though depth is the only dimension opened to the television camera, its exploration is restricted due to the small size of the television screen.

The ways used in television to compensate for the limitations of the small TV screen result themselves in manipulating the visual information and directing the spectators' attention. This is the major way in which television aesthetics depart from those of cinema imposed by the concept of Bazinian realism. In *Jean de Florette* a shallow depth of field is captured by using a narrow-angle lens, which shortens the distance between the background and the foreground. Information is not considered of equal importance because at different times either the foreground or the background is brought in and out of focus through zooming rather than the movement of the camera. When Ugolin's uncle is writing a letter, we see him in an extreme close-up. At the same time, Ugolin is in the background but his image is kept out of focus. In the similar way in the café conversation after Jean's funeral, the café owner who is in the foreground and closest to us is out of focus, while other participants are in the background and in focus. The distribution of the characters along the z-axis [depth] is also reminiscent of multi-camera shooting used in television, which restricts the movements of the characters and attempts to block them in order to allow for easy shooting from different stationary cameras (Zettl 1999: 176, 198). Racking the focus in these representations of the depth of field shows that televisual cinematography directs and controls the spectators in the way, which is questionable from the perspective of realism principles in cinema expressed by Bazin.

Central to the visual style of the 'Florette' films is their cinematographer, Bruno Nuytten, who worked with such established auteurs as Jean-Luc Godard, Alain Resnais and André Téchiné. Nuytten cannot stand accused of not having the awareness and experience of cinematographic techniques associated with cinema but it is the source of Nuytten's knowledge of television that is particularly interesting. Nuytten worked as a cinematographer of a series of Marguerite Duras' films, *La Femme du Gange* (1972), *India Song* (1975), *Son nom de Venise dans Calcutta désert* (1976), *Le Camion* (1977). His cinematic collaborations with Duras could be seen as a source of his experience in techniques which evoke televisual focus on scriptwriting because of the literary nature of Duras' works. These films point out to the importance of scripts, the literary source, for television which is greater than in cinema.

In contrast Pawlikowski's journey towards a cinematic–televisual relationship (as opposed to hybridisation) began from a position exploiting rather than re-presenting the literary. Because Pawlikowski is a film-maker the script or text material is a contributory factor rather than the end in itself often suggested in the adaptations of literary classics made for TV. Ryszard Lenczewski, Pawlikowski's cinematographer, points out that Pawliowski's method of developing dramas and film features was rooted in his documentary experience and conflicted with the BBC focus on script development:

> Pawel doesn't write a typical script. He writes a few sentences about each scene, but he doesn't want to write dialogue, so the actors mostly improvise. That's great, because it gives them the opportunity to give such natural performances. (Calhoun 2005: 14)

As we have seen, in the UK chapter of this volume, the problem of 'development' is more widespread than merely in the nation's public service broadcaster. The role of government agencies and an unreflective reliance on faux-Hollywood models is at the heart of the malaise in British cinema production.

It is Pawlikowski's background in photography rather than in television making which 'gave him a sense of drama contained in the real' (Tobin 2005: 116). The aim as stated is to capture the essence of a particular experience, such as war 'in one image' as he claims to be doing in *Serbian Epics* (BBC Bookmark series, 1992). Lenczewski suggests that it is their shared experience of documentary film-making which allows them to communicate so successfully on the set and realise Pawlikowski's vision for the film.[5] It is so because of Pawlikowski's visual sense which we would call 'cinematic' that enthuses his documentary work with a unique kinesthetic quality.

We should not forget that this 'unique' authorial voice was developed within the corporate structure of a national Public Service Broadcaster. Pawlikowski himself does mention the role of BBC as the source of funding, creative ideas and as a distribution platform for his documentaries. In his account the BBC in the 1980s appears as a generous producer who is willing to take risks with a maverick young director who travels to Eastern Europe, still in the communist grip, to bring back the most unusual images and stories e.g. a documentary about the life of Vaclav Havel (*Vaclav Havel: A Czech Drama* [BBC Bookmark series, 1989]), or the Russian writer, Yerofeyev (*From Moscow to Pietushki* [BBC Bookmark series, 1990]). Would it be right to simply think about Pawlikowski as a film director for whom work in television documentary and fiction making was just a build-up to his career in cinema?[6] It is surely not justified in this age and time when directors, such as Pawlikowski, pass a greater part of their career working for television, or like von Trier, Sokurov, Rossellini, Bergman, Kieslowski and Wenders, move between the worlds of cinema and television, and have their cinema films funded by television, to disregard the significance of work they do there and the impact television has on their cinematic works. If we decide instead to examine closely the contemporary film-makers' work in television, we must establish the terms in which the TV experience should be considered and accounted for.

There are continuities and parallels between Pawlikowski's work in television documentaries, TV dramas and film features, which can be viewed as the basis of new types of aesthetics, which are neither purely cinematic nor televisual. The conditions in which the contemporary film-makers such as Pawlikowski work, especially the multifaceted impact of television on their creative output, result in a new type of audio-visual forms which could be best described as kinesthetics. This new aesthetic is about a process of transformation of televisual forms into cinematic ones and the process of what some might call 'contamination'[7] of cinematic forms by the televisual ones. For example Dudley Andrew writes:

> Among other factors, the incessant flow of televisual images has eroded the stability of texts and seeped like an acid to break up the last signs of their authors as authorities who hover over the experience of their work and exert a moral pressure on its interpretation. . . . Cinema is part of the media economy that has reduced the auteur to a sign indeed precisely to a signature. But cinema is also a victim of this economy, its carefully painted images losing out on (and to) the electronic pictures flowing like tap water or sewage down twelve or thirty-four or a hundred channels around the globe. Looked from the perspective of Tokyo, literature and cinema have in common the futile and pathetic struggle to preserve the value of thought, of feeling, of art, in a world that decreasingly cares about such things.[8]

It is more accurate to state that it is because of these processes, akin to osmosis (not hybridisation – a phenomenon more likely to occur in generic products such as costume dramas) – that Pawlikowski's works, amongst others, are *kinesthetic* in nature. They do not seem to belong exclusively to either cinema or television but to both at the same time or even to a new realm which is still in development. His features and dramas are informed by his work in television documentaries not only thematically but also formally. The formal nature of the television works is a reflection of Pawlikowski's mixed origins in cinema and television and a reflection of his authorial imprint.

It is worth noting that Pawlikowski's position within a sphere that is both between and simultaneously bestriding different cultures parallels his – and kinesthetics – position with reference to the two different media. His efforts to forge some presence for his culture of origin in the place which became his home may well be part of the strength of the impact of the kinesthetic forms created in his cinematic works. There are clearly parallels here with the European film-makers who have made such an impact on Hollywood cinema at various stages of its development from Chaplin through Lang to Hitchcock and beyond.

The match between kinesthetics and intercultural identity of film-makers such as Pawlikowski is not just a fortunate coincidence. It indicates that the future of media convergence and globalised interchange will by necessity bring to the fore issues of not of hybridisation (to use a most crude formulation of what may well be an infinitely bifurcating as well as conglomerating impetus) but of osmosis. In the world of media convergence and meetings of cultures we need new ways to talk about film-makers and their works. Strangely it has taken more than forty years since, in 1963, Roberto Rossellini publicly declared that he was abandoning cinema to devote his energies to a pedagogical audio-visual project conceived for television. Historically, as we have seen at various points in this volume, the familial relationship between the two mediums is constantly (and fascinatingly) problematic and loaded with tensions and issues of political economy (as we shall see in the next chapter). It would be a mistake to follow Dudley Andrew's position and fail to note the richness of actual and possible results of the two medium's coupling (utilising whichever of many value-laden metaphors others may prefer).

The invigorating, problematic possibilities of a relationship between cinema and television have been illustrated powerfully within this volume. In Denmark Dogme95 recaptured the youthfulness of cinema. But they did this by reference to the excitement of the emergence of TV, the only new medium invented in their lifetime. In Spain the situation seems to be a mirror image in that the energy came from cinema *to* TV. This may be a function of the polar opposite in political terms too i.e. the nature of TV in Denmark was the result of a Social Democratic libertarianism whilst in Spain – at least in a widespread perception – TV was the tool of a traditionalist-right paternalism. In Germany a film-maker like Wenders could – with a straight face – label TV as 'purely fascist'.[9] In Italy the cine–TV relationship was blessed by the pro-television intervention of such a major 'cinema' figure' as Rossellini. From such auspicious beginnings the Italian experience has been highlighted as one of 'Dilettante films . . . manu-factured in order to be "consumed" and then thrown away'.[10] In France films financed by television channels such as Canal+ are indubitably made as 'cinema' but their primary platform of distribution is television. They have to be both televisual and cinematic. Most of the times this is an impossible mar-riage and that may be why so many of films disappoint on both fronts (as fran-cophone versions of the 'dilettante' film).

In Germany the derogatory label 'Pantoffelkino' (slipper cinema) gave way to Rohrbach's 'amphibious film'. Once again we see the difficulty of coining an adequate metaphor for any production that bridged the gap between tele-vision and the cinema. At least in Germany we find: 'film-makers, subsidy offi-cials, and audiences have ceased to see film as antagonistic (aesthetically, technically, and politically) to television'.[11] Although surely few (on either side of the membrane) would go as far as Rohrbach: 'If the contemporary German feature film is nothing other than nicely made-up television, then we should stand by it and abolish the superficial distinction between cinema production and television production' (2001). Far better to celebrate a reality and aspira-tion summed up nicely in the title of the Spanish chapter in this volume: 'Bipolar visions, unified realities'.

Kinesthetics is our attempt to address the presence of television in the works of contemporary film-makers. Television is upon us; it is part of the contempor-ary visual matrix whose role in shaping contemporary cinema and biographies of two generations of film-makers should be finally recognised and accounted for in more positive terms. Pawlikowski's works feed off each other and are in a kind of a dialogue and exchange with each other. There is a natural circulation between his works because his television documentaries and dramas constantly gesture towards cinematic tradition as though trying to overcome limitations imposed by the televisual frame revealing Pawlikowski's cinematic sensibility which found its spiritual home in *My Summer of Love*. Pawlikowski's position is rather more ambiguous and engaged than that taken by Wim Wenders. Wenders deliberately utilises an (over) abundance of long shots and film formats that exceed the size of traditional 35mm film stock, for example in *End of Violence* (1997) and *The Million Dollar Hotel* (2000). On his part in his docu-mentary works Pawlikowski wants to reach beyond the television screen. Thus he often zooms out of close-ups and breaks the linearity and literariness of television narratives. He obstructs the televisual flow with subtitles, still frames, photographs, archival images, graphs, newsreel footage, excerpts from filmed theatre productions, maps, samizdat video recordings and layers it with a sound-track consisting of foreign poetry and prose, which not only acts as a counter-point to the images but also strengthens the overall effect of this televisual sound-image while intensifying the *unheimlich* of television for Pawlikowski. His use of voice-over, complex layering of image and sound creates an audio-visual structure whose overall effect exceeds the demands of television and is a display of Pawlikowski's cinematic ambitions. His documentaries are audio-visual

Surrealist collages, compilations of found objects brought together in a way which emphasises the differences in texture of the audio-visual material included. As such he is as much the progeny of Dziga Vertov and Chris Marker as he is of British TV.

A key element in Pawlikowski's aesthetics is to impose distance between sound and image, and between various visual elements, and to emphasise differences between them. These effects allow him to create a new dimension, a new sphere in his documentaries and dramas, which is uniquely his and which also is that of new type of cine-televisual aesthetics – kinesthetics. The linguistic element of his films is one of the main loci of this distancing effect. In the documentary, *The Life of Vladimir Voinovich* (BBC Bookmark series, 1989), a polished voice-over reads fragments of Voinovich's novel in English. The Russian language and occasionally German (and if spoken by Russian émigrés German is heavily accented) dominate the documentary. The documentary is subtitled in English throughout which emphasises the spectators' inability to understand the languages which are being spoken and the difficulty of following the image (because of the focus on subtitles). Subtitles add another graphic layer to the visual imagery of Pawlikowski making foreign language visible, doubly intrusive (visually and aurally) and contaminating both audio and visual sphere of the film. This kind of effect appears in every one of Pawlikowski's documentaries. It echoes in *Last Resort* where Atriom takes lessons of English from Alfie and when Atriom and Katya teach each other English at the airport, and languishes in the different accents of the characters of *My Summer of Love*. Pawlikowski's documentaries, TV dramas and his feature films are works of ideas conveyed through audio-visual means which also allow him to bridge visibly televisual and cinematic forms.

Pawlikowski's creative roots can be found in modernism of various European 'waves', British, Polish, Czech and most of all French to which he gives an open homage in the dancing scene of *My Summer Love* where two girls swirl around the room to the rhythm of Rivgauche's 'La Foule' sung by Edith Piaf. The light-heartedness of this sequence, sheer joy and exuberance of pure movement, brings to mind sweeping camera work of Truffaut's *Jules et Jim*, especially the scene when Thérèse paces Jules' room blowing the smoke off her cigarette and pretending 'faire la locomotive' (to play a steam engine).

Pawlikowski uses his documentaries to take lessons in the creative origins of the Czech New Wave (*Kids from FAMU*, 1990) with which he shares the interest in the mystery contained in the real, Surrealist desire for the marvellous locked in the everyday.[12] Pawlikowski's affinity to the European new waves[13] allows him to problematise his relationship with TV in creative and productive ways. This is evident through the presence of TV sets in his dramas and documentaries, becoming a character of the drama. In Pawlikowski's films TV sets are traded, discarded and ignored. But they can also serve as transmitters of forbidden and forgotten images, which is the case in *Havel: A Czech Drama*. Pawlikowski's conflicted, ambiguous and sometimes openly critical attitude towards television and media is a reflection of his cinematic ambitions, which until *My Summer of Love* had to be contained in the television context. In his documentaries there seems to be a lack of resolution regarding television.

Historical examples from across our study show a rather more resolved and negative regard, for example in *Meet Mr Lucifer* (Pelissier, UK 1953) where the devil himself: 'comes up with the most hellish device of all: his weapon of choice is Television'[14] and *Un, dos, tres, al escondite inglés* (*One, Two, Three, Let's Play*, Zulueta, 1969): 'built upon a drastic reprobation of the small screen, depicted as the repository of the most sinister traditionalist conceptions of popular culture'.[15] In Italy television was presented in a sarcastic way as *L'oppio dei popoli* (People's Opium) in *I mostri* (The Monsters, 1963), and *La domenica è sempre la domenica* (Sunday is Always Sunday, 1958) attacked the popular TV quiz show *Lascia o raddoppia?* These are far from isolated examples. Pawlikowski suspends his judgement and this hesitation is most productive because it results in osmotic works, which belong to the realm of kinesthetics. One of the most creative and interesting explorations of the role of television and video takes place in *Havel: A Czech Drama*. The documentary opens with the images of a little baby filmed in black and white in the pre-war period which looks like a more polished version of the Brothers Lumières' *Repas de bébé/Baby's Meal* (1895). The camera draws back and we realise that this early family film has been transferred onto a videotape which smiling Havel is watching on his Sony TV. The images of the baby are inter-cut with those of Havel. These images of baby-Havel survived and their status as home movies is maintained because of video technology. Video appears on two other occasions. First when Havel, whose plays are banned in Czechoslovakia, watches a video recording of a British production of one of his plays by the Royal Shakespeare Theatre Company. The second video is used to record a home production of one of Havel's plays performed in his flat by his family members and friends. TV sets compatible with video technology allow viewing of travelling images, which originated in other countries and screening of illegal material. Television and video technology function as a kind of printing press of the second half of the twentieth century. Video recordings are subversive of the state's effort to regulate the media and infuse television (and radio) with propaganda. Illegal video recordings play the same role as banned books, periodicals and journal publications. They are visual samizdat. The images of tapes lined up on a shelf like books in Havel's flat emphasise how little difference there may really be between videotapes and books.

Blurring of the boundary between television and cinema is a common practice in Pawlikowski's documentaries. In the documentary *Palace Life* (BBC Bookmark series, 1988), we see a film adaptation of one of Konwicki's novels being broadcast on television. Gradually, the frame of the television screen coincides with that of the documentary we are watching and as a result we find ourselves watching the film on our television screens. This framing and reframing is something very important to Pawlikowski and intensifies the ambiguity of the images he creates in his television and also cinematic works. For this reason at least some of Pawlikowski's TV dramas could be regarded as cinematic works rather than televisual. This is particularly true in the case of *Last Resort* which was successfully recuperated in the cinematic circuit. Moreover Pawlikowski's work in television broadly belongs to the area of documentary, while that of cinema is fictional. In this sense any desire to fictionalise, which is an important feature of some of his documentaries, *Dostoyevsky's Travels* (BBC Bookmark series, 1991) in particular, could be regarded as a cinematic sign.

Pawlikowski himself seems to see it as a gesture towards cinema and recalls the reaction of critics in response to *Dostoyevsky's Travels*. For many this documentary seemed too fictionalised to be regarded as a documentary (Roberts 2002: 92–3). *Dostoyevsky's Travels* is a story of raise to fame and wealth of a great-grandson of Dostoyevsky. He had been a humble tram driver in St Petersburg before a German Society of Dostoyevsky contacted him inviting him to deliver a series of lectures about the writings of his illustrious ancestor. Dostoyevsky agrees to what was to become his first ever trip to the West because he wants to realise his greatest dream – to buy a Mercedes. Pawlikowski weaves anecdotes of Dostoyevsky's travelogue into a narrative with an authentic dramatic drive underpinned by Dostoyevsky's desire for the car, which makes us simply forget at time the film's documentary origins. In *Dostoyevsky's Travels* Pawlikowski's talent as a story-teller is given almost a free rein as we find ourselves catapulted into a Godardian world where documentary is a representation of life which imitates fiction. Godard himself has been much more timid in his relationship to television. As Forbes has commented: 'Godard . . . responded to May 1968 and its aftermath by distancing himself . . . from conventional film making . . . He experimented with the different medium of video and with different forms of distribution including television' (Forbes 1992: 114–15).

Forbes claims that Godard was in the process of: 'suggesting not only the considerable social and aesthetic significance of television, but ultimately how two warring media and their respective industries, once described as "Cain and Abel", could be reconciled in such a way that the creative possibilities of television could feed back into the cinema' (Forbes 1992: 116). However she herself notes that *Numéro Deux* (1975) (a key post-*nouvelle vague* work of Godard's): 'mixes and juxtaposes images of technologically different status and apparently different genres. It will not settle down either to one medium (film or television) or to one genre (documentary, fiction, sex film, soap opera)' (Forbes 1992: 117). In other words this is typical Godardian playfulness and intellectual montage in a *film* (questioning the value of all media and genre) not a development bringing together of the mediums to create something new. Godard certainly engaged with television as a medium in two series *Six fois deux/Sur et sous la communication* (1976) and *France/Tour/Detour/Deux enfants* (1978) (under the auspices of INA).[16] Nonetheless at the heart of these two series is a view that television mediates and interferes – in the avant et après segment of the first series: there are 'three of us': the speaker, the received but also (crucially) the TV set (Forbes 1992: 119). With both of his TV series one cannot help but feel that Godard is presenting a thesis about television rather than making it. With *Sauve qui peut (la vie)* (1979) Godard returned to cinema with his 'second first film'. Godard rather than continuing to work in or with televisual language instead flirted (on a regular basis) with various video technologies as means of production rather than as a medium alternative or complementary to film. Where Godard is an occasional tourist in TV Pawlikowski is a traveller through both mediums.

Themes of travel, exile and foreignness feature in many of Pawlikowski's works as they do in the oeuvres of, amongst others, Wenders (from *Kings of the Road* (1976) and *The American Friend* (1977) through *Paris, Texas* (1984) to *Until the End of the World* (1991), *Faraway So Close* (1993) and *Beyond the Clouds* (1995)) and Herzog (from *Fitzcarraldo* (1982) to *Invincible* (2001)). For Wenders travels to the East or his own travels to the West are forms of escape and a sense of closure. For Herzog the journey serves as symbolic of the existential struggle within (thus with little hope of closure). On a rather more complex (and ultimately more positive) note, crossing the boundaries and blurring differences between cultures or different historical moments, but also the impossibility of movement and journey seem to be Pawlikowski's central interest. The story he seems to be telling over and over again is that of return home, a desire to find out about one's origins which makes it necessary to question the limits of one's cultural, national and personal identities. His films seem to be emotional maps of his movements between his different places of belonging. The impulse to travel seems to have its origins in Pawlikowski's mixed identities, Polish and British. The constant travelling from the West to the East and back, desire to be on the move might grow out of a need to redefine his identity, to redraw it, reframe it over and over again. His cultural identity is blurred in the same way that his creative identity is uncertain filling the unnamed space between television and cinema and making it his own.

The theme of journey and travelling could be seen as a cinematic trope in Pawlikowski's television work. Critics of early cinema, such as Thomas Gunning, have pointed out that travel genre, prototyped in a travelogue and developed into road movie genre later on, is a cinematic genre par excellence.[17] The thematic presence of journeys in Pawlikowski's documentaries and dramas might be an expression of his desire to get back to cinema and an indication that there is another, cinematic, layer in his televisual productions. Only two of Pawlikowski's productions up to date do not feature journeys – *My Summer of Love* and *Palace Life*. The fact that both of them relate to what Pawlikowski could describe as home, England and Poland respectively, supports the existence of a strong connection between the film-maker's creative choices and solutions and his mixed cultural identity. *My Summer of Love* has its focus in mysterious mansion where Tamsin lives. This place, just like Warsaw's Palace of Science of Culture featuring in *Palace Life*, is space the living share with the dead. The images of lush blossoming summer countryside in *My Summer of Love* and those of Polish youth performing folk dances are counter-pointed with the threat contained in the walls of Tamsin's mansion and the Palace of Science and Culture. Tamsin's and Mona's spiritist séances and Konwicki's reading of his own novel about the Palace in effect are moments of summoning the ghosts of the past and communion with them. For Pawlikowski there are some ghosts from the past associated with both Poland and England, which fix him to the place and prevent him from journeying. As he says in one of his interviews both places intimidate him and inhibit him (Roberts 2002: 96; Tobin 2005: 119). He is much more comfortable travelling and moving. If he stops, he becomes haunted by the ghosts of the past.

Because of Pawlikowski's movement between cinema and television he is a kineaste and his are not cine- or televisual aesthetics but kinesthetics – this new type of form which can only exist when a kineaste is entrenched in both worlds and is constantly moving between the two. Kinesthetics are aesthetics of motion and transition, movement, reframing and refocusing, rejuvenation and regeneration. Many of the film-makers have crossed into television in order to renew public interest in their film-making, in order to reach a wider audience and to find ways of starting to make films again. In the case of Pawlikowski his kinesthetics grow out of the longing for cinema. He is fully in control of the televisual and cinematic language and fuses the two into new aesthetic forms, the same way in which many film-makers who are crossing between television and cinema are versed in both formal languages. They mould the formal language of television and cinema into a new one. Kinesthetics is a new dialect of visual artists today. They are an unacknowledged diaspora which is growing bigger. Thus kinesthetics explore an ignored, neglected and misunderstood feature of post-war cinema-television.

Television is not the other of cinema, but rather the *unheimlich* of the kineaste (and even more so of many critics), to which they are forced to return and to pass through. In order to return home, to cinema, they must by definition leave it. For many the work in television is a journey towards cinema. In some countries, like Britain, kinema is linked to mixed cultural identities of film-makers. However, not for all, which also makes kinesthetic a wider concept, which addresses first and foremost the materiality of cinema and television and conjoining of the two. Kinesthetics is not a hybridisation of cinema and television, based on the implicit desire to keep the two worlds apart. It is a dynamic structure, where osmosis of televisual and cinematic elements take place.

In formal and aesthetic terms cinema is a dominant element in the kinesthetic equation but television is an indispensable one. When we detect elements of televisual feature film-making in cinema, there is an uproar regarding the collapse of cinema.[18] This is so to such an extent that risible pieces of overblown nonsense (on TV) can be sold as, if nothing else, 'cinematic' as with for example the BBC's *Rome* advertised as being made on the 'largest standing film set in the world'.

Our national chapters have stressed the financial base which television offers to cinema. In a way then television is a foundation and home for many film-makers. The presence of cinema in this televisual framework transforms television into something else. Because of its historical entrenchment in visual arts: photography, painting and also in literature, it is cinema which has an advantage of cultural capital over television. It is also has an advantage of age and the understanding of its own identity, of its core. Hence, there is a limited part of television, which is shaped by cinema into kinema. It is in cinema where the contamination is much more visible and detectable.

The recognition of the cinematic potential of the work is in itself a sign that we are dealing with a kinematic work. This is what makes Pawlikowski's *Last Resort* a kinematic work par excellence. The images of *Last Resort* are not televisual but they are not cinematic either. They are erring images, looking for a new home [cinema] the same way Tanya and Artiom are longing for the end of their journey and maybe finally heading home in the closing images of the film. Pawlikowski is a kind of film-maker, a cineaste par excellence, which we did not have a term to describe until now.

This and other problems of definition and valuation are a function of our ignorance or inexperience. We have not yet learned how to think clearly about the result of media convergence. We are on the cusp of a paradigm shift to a (post) cinema (post) television age. Faltering steps in how to discuss and make sense of such an age are contained in our final chapter.

NOTES

1. In 2004 *My Summer of Love* was awarded an award for Best New British Feature. In 2005 the film won BAFTA Alexander Korda Award for Best British Film.
2. See also Królikowska-Avis (2005) and Roberts (2002).
3. As indeed across Europe; see examples in the UK, Italy and Poland chapters of this volume.
4. This is the core belief which informs all of Bazin's theoretical work best collected (at present) in *What is Cinema?* 1992.
5. Ryszard Lenczewski quoted in Calhoun (2005: 14).
6. Sinclair (2004: 18).
7. See 'Spain' chapter, p. 56.
8. Andrew (2000: 23–5).
9. See Chapter 6, p. 72.
10. See Chapter 4, p. 53.
11. See Chapter 6.
12. See G. Roberts (2006a).
13. Pawlikowski belongs to the family of writers cum film-makers. His creative origins are found in his interest in literature (he began a thesis in Oxford on an Austrian writer Georg Trakl and confesses his great interest in literature). It was in Oxford that he got involved with the student film-making society and began writing for a small film magazine, *Stills*. In the period 1982–3 he managed to get a pass to Cannes, Berlin and Venice. This allowed him to conduct interviews with Wenders and Fassbinder and also discover Polish cinema of the 1950s and 'see eight films a day' (Tobin 2005: 114; Królikowska-Avis 2005). Later on he started making

documentary films for the BBC. These origins in literature, film criticism and documentary film-making echo experiences of New Wave film-makers both in France and in the UK.

14. See Chapter 2, p. 7.
15. See Chapter 5, pp. 60–1.
16. For the role of INA in French audio-visual production see Chapter 7.
17. See for example (amongst a major body of work) Gunning (1989).
18. As we have seen in critical responses throughout this book.

11. REPRODUCTION: RE-CREATION OF CINEMA VIA THE DOMESTIC SCREEN

For most of its parts this book proposes a revisionist account of the history of the cinema–television relationship. Television has been presented as new means of funding and distributing cinema. In reality it has also done a great deal to change our way of thinking about cinema but this transformation was usually coded in catastrophic terms or simply ignored for the sake of saving and preserving what was believed to be the true value of cinema. Throughout much of its history television has been treated by cultural critics (and the film studies academy) as at best an unwanted growth on a healthy cultural body whose visual part was dominated by cinema.[1]

We are all familiar with the audio-visual lore of our culture. Cinema had been around for nearly fifty years, had been through sound and colour revolutions and matured as an art, as an industry and the critical object. Then television appeared (nobody quite knows what for although there is a faint whiff of a conspiracy to utilise 'the goggle box' as a domestic soporific) threatening the very livelihood of cinema. Within a period of the introduction of television in the various nation states of Europe cinema spectators were abandoning movie theatres, although it must be noted that several of the national chapters in this volume point out that the latter phenomenon was not directly or singularly caused by the former. Over a period of slow decline the picture palaces were reduced in number and confined to city centres as their mass audience moved to the suburbs, cinema's 'natural' (and much taken for granted) audience preferring to spend time in front of their TV screens. That much is true. Added to the fact comes a mythology of a generation (which had been flocking to the cinema) and following generations turning more or less slowly from more or less refined cinema goers to domesticated, indolent consumers of images with apparently so little understanding and appreciation of what they were watching that one simply wonders what kept them in front of their TV screens for an average four hours a day.[2]

The outcry against television, the echoes of which can be heard loud and clear, even today, has been deepening the critical difference between cinema and television while the two media were actually growing closer together in terms of production, funding and aesthetic values. The lore teaches us nowadays that the difference between television and cinema is almost nil and (national) art cinemas are the only remaining temples of the cinematic art which itself is clearly withering away crushed by the avalanche of visual images which rarely add up to a sequence that any true cineaste would bother to watch. At least one of the reasons for the anxiety caused by television among critics has been some striking similarities between the two media. Television was a new screen-based medium. In time the small screen came to resemble the silver screen and some would say the silver screen lost its lustre as its creative potential was dwarfed to accommodate the needs of the small screen. Such is the story of the triumph of the small screen and steady decline of the cinematic art, which some have proclaimed as dead quite a few times by now.[3] In short (and in caricature) from the time of the 'New Waves' in the 1960s cinema has been in decline with the monster of television breathing on its back.

There is no denying that the cultural, social and economic role of television in relation to cinema has been significant and indeed growing through the time-span of this volume. We have described this role as part of the changing 'ecology of audio-visual industries' in our introductory chapter. Since the advent of photography, which threatened originality and creativity of visual arts with its potential for reproduction,[4] there was no technological invention which would seem so superfluous and unnecessary as television was once it was born into the cinema-dominated culture of moving images. The cultural impact that the growth of television has had could not have been repeated nowadays because the acceleration in the introduction of technological innovation makes it very difficult to grasp the cultural transformations they bring with them. It is the advent and the combined and multifaceted impact of the digital technology which can serve as a good starting point to re-examine the cine-televisual tragic lore, which has been so pervasive and remains so very present in our culture and our cultural memory. Digital technology has been erasing very effectively the difference between cinema and television, thus continuing the process which started with the invention of the VHS tape.

The rise of video and its digital progeny have illuminated, replicated even heightened another important aspect of the cinema–television relationship. Namely, television has practically since its inception acted as a cinema's lifeline. As an institution television has been providing funding for the making of new films and employment for growing numbers of film industry practitioners. As important was TV's role in the re-creation of films through televisual distribution and exhibition:

The existence of cinematic films is prolonged thanks to audiovisual media while cinematic exhibition does something opposite. The length of the life of films in cinemas is reduced all the time. (Créton 2003: 32)

From its very beginning the sustaining role of television was tightly linked to its role as a public broadcaster obliged to preserve cinematic heritage (and defend some vestige of 'national' cinema traditions) through televisual exhibition.

Thus rather than extinguishing cinema, television became (perhaps inadvertently) the keeper (even reviver) of the flame. This is a phenomenon that can be seen occurring across the continent during our period of study. The one exception to this observable fact was perhaps Poland where particular circumstances of competition for direct funding affected the relationship between the two media. In Italy RAI had during its first decade simply consumed movies of previous vintage to fill its schedule. Then: 'At the end of the 1960s it adopted a radically different scheme. Television grasping at a "public service" mission to retain state support did what it was already doing for literature that is to say introduce its audience to its cinematic heritage.'[5] This was achieved through such series as 'Italiacia, amore mio' (Small Italy, my love), Storia di un Italiano (History of an Italian). In France a similar story unfolded due to the RTF being instituted intentionally as a diffuser of correct French culture (with its director reporting directly to the Minister of the Interior) which regularly showed 'classic French films' that tied in with the official cultural policy of a 'tradition of quality'. When TV2 started in 1967 one of its methods of brand differentiation was to show different types of French films – but films nonetheless. In the UK – a nation-state often accused of ignoring its own cinematic heritage and always that much closer to its American cultural cousins – the state broadcaster was content to produce its own high-quality drama whilst its commercial rivals seemed intent (and content) to concentrate on broadcasting on US product of certain audience appeal and cheaper per-broadcast cost (when bought as a package from the 'majors'). Nonetheless throughout the 1960s and 1970s British (but precious few continental) movies were screened (particularly on weekend afternoons) and thus reached an audience who would not have seen them otherwise. In the UK of the 1980s the symbiotic relationship between cinema and TV as distributive mechanism continued with 'increasing integration of independent cinema and public service television' (Barr 1986: 201). In more recent years what little exposure British-made cinema has to an audience of any significant size is supplied via channels linked to BBC (particularly BBC4) and Film Four. Meanwhile in France, with the advent of Canal+, French television became the main source of financing and exhibiting French cinema. As noted in our French chapter: 'Canal+ . . . was to change what cinema was in France, the ways in which it was made and consumed.' In a 'post public service broadcasting' world, perhaps surprisingly, the situation of TV's dependence on cinema has not changed. Through a combination of, admittedly loosening, legislation but equally the perceived audience demand for and cachet attached to cinema, 'TV' in its now multifarious forms wants and need to supply movies for home consumption. This goes beyond 'art house' channels such as Film Four in the UK to as mainstream an organ of distribution as SKY TV – itself linked to a Hollywood major studio – appears only too happy to screen films of European origin (as well as of an earlier vintage) on its 'Cinema 1' and 'Cinema 2' channels.

Canal+ learned a lesson from its predecessor in support for domestic cinema (INA) that television could and should act as a distribution platform which can complement theatrical distribution. Thus accompanying TV distribution with the theatrical release (with its 'cinema' cachet) was central to the business strategy of Canal+. As noted by Dorota Ostrowska in this volume: 'Canal+ was to become a new way of producing and distributing films in France. Between the two distribution was more important than production.'[6] Laurent Créton has suggested that 'by broadcasting cinematic films, television attempts to appropriate for itself the symbolic value of the cinematographic work as well as the special relationship cinema has with the spectators' (Créton 1994: 71).

In Italy 'public service television' retained the biggest audience share, with a decreasing share, until 2003 when Mediaset, the television division of the Fininvest Group, took the lead due in no small part to its use of sport (especially Seria A football) and pay-per-view movies. The two national networks, with three channels each, are operating with and in competition to many regional stations. Even these small channels utilise cinema to keep their foothold in the ratings. Within Mediaset there is Rete 4, a channel specialised in the transmission of films. As the authors of our Italian chapter (which in general has a rather less positive response to twenty-first-century mass media than much of this volume) state that:

> It must be admitted that the transmission of so many films had a positive effect. Up to the 1980s, after a few weeks of exclusive showing in smart cinema, films were screened for months in smaller theatres. Such long-lasting exploitation was suppressed in the last decade of the 20th century, the films were screened during a few weeks, then definitely taken off: television was their only chance to survive.[7]

The advent of the VCR (with a significance as *player* which ultimately far outweighed its threat as a *recorder*) and the development of the variety of distribution platforms made available thanks to digital technologies makes the role of television as a 're-creator' of cinema directly linked to the development of new technologies. Television as both medium and technology does not 'kill' cinematic films but rather infuses them with new life by offering itself as a platform of cinematic film's redistribution and home-based exhibition. If we rethink the relationship between cinema and television employing this idea of re-creation we can trace how the process whereby the difference between the two has been gradually erased: not in the way which resulted in the death of cinema but in its digitally enhanced rebirth.

Before we can talk about the erasure of the differences between cinema and television accelerated by the introduction of digital technology, and already implied in the impact of the VHS tape, it is necessary to explain what differences we have in mind. It might seem strange at this time and age to refer to an old-fashioned distinction between form and content but I think it might be quite useful to explain the difference between television and cinema. In the same way the designation between small and silver screen to distinguish between the two will also prove very handy. This distinction emphasises cinema's and television's function as vehicles of film exhibition in particular. There may have a difference in size (small versus big), quality (silver screen versus 'goggle-box') and location (private versus public sphere) but in both cases we are watching images projected (or broadcast) on screen.

The distinction between the televisual and cinematic screens could be seen as formal while the films themselves can be viewed as content whose format has been changing over the history of television and cinema. While cinematic films have been screened in 35mm format for most of their history, the material broadcast on television had to be transferred to the magnetic tape. This process has caused a certain amount of grief to cineastes due to material being (mis)shaped through censorship, bowdlerisation not to mention panning and scanning to adjust to the academy ratio in order to 'fit' the needs of television. The transformation that the films were undergoing to be broadcast on television was seen as so detrimental to the quality of the films that even television's commitment and role in preserving and promoting cinematic heritage and fostering new cinematic production could not redeem this medium in the eyes of film and cultural critics. Thus: 'The most provocative formal issue amongst film connoisseurs, though, is usually the changing aspect ratios when a film is translated to TV . . . anathema to serious film enthusiasts . . .' (Howells 2003: 216–17). The fact that the alternative for 'connoisseurs' may well be watching their beloved 'films' on damaged prints projected on redundant screens in appalling conditions is conveniently elided here as is the difficulty of those outside the metropolitan elites in seeing any films beyond standard Hollywood fare without recourse to TV.

We must not forget that from early in its history the role of television as exhibitor of cinematic production powered by the consumer's choice introduced a new quality into the cinema–television relationship. Thus as seminal figure as Martin Scorsese can find himself regularly bemoaning the damage caused by fitting movies on to a TV screen *and* nostalgically praising the seminal effects of watching foreign films (naturally panned and scanned) on *TV* in the 1940s and 1950s in the 'to camera' introduction to his own documentary (shown on PBS television) *My Voyage to Italy* (*Mio viaggio in Italia*, 1999).

TV screens could not match cinematic screens in size, thus the small–silver screen dichotomy was preserved, but TV could become a vehicle for transmitting films, which people could watch in a way which allowed for the development of the notion of a (potential) home cinema available on your TV. Video allowed the viewer to consume movies independently from and freed from all the negative connotations which TV had as a cultural institution. VCR technology encouraged people to purchase TV sets (BARB statistics from the UK[8] tend to confirm this phenomenon with a more rapid increase in TV ownership than in domestic households in the mid-1970s) and put them in their homes not to watch broadcast TV but films (and programmes) they recorded from TV or rented from their local 'video' shop.

Tape technology developed into a domestic incarnation as the home video cassette recorder (VCR) became a standard piece of household equipment. In 1963 Sony marketed the first home Video Tape Recorder (VTR) priced at $995. The VTR utilised an open reel 1/2-inch helical scan deck. The quality was superb – the usability minimal. In 1969 Sony introduced the first video cassette, the 3/4-inch U-Matic one-hour tape, available in the US by 1971. Sony allowed other manufacturers to sell machines that could play the cassette, and thus succeeded in establishing a world standard for the 3/4-inch video cassette. In 1975 Sony introduced the more compact Betamax consumer VCRs with one-hour 1/2-inch tape cassettes selling for under $20. Sony sought to create a standardised format by getting other companies to agree to produce machines that would play the Beta cassettes. TV joined with the VCR offered a format which freed spectators from the network scheduling while offering them a choice of films on tapes. The link between TV content and TV form was severed and new possibilities and challenges arose linked to the question of control over content. Upon the introduction of the videotape, MCA/Universal and Disney filed lawsuits against Sony to protect their broadcast product, which was shown on TV and then could be stored by the spectators on videotapes. Sony had introduced its Betamax VCR deck for $1,300 with an aggressive advertising campaign claiming that you 'can actually videotape something off one channel while you're watching another channel' (Universal had several of its shows airing simultaneously on different channels) and 'build a library of your favorite shows'. JVC's victory with the VHS cassette in the 'format wars' was in no small way due to the fact that: 'it was far less resilient and the picture quality was a lot lower than that of betamax' (Enticknap 2005: 181). Beta was taken up in its natural home i.e. TV (and low-budget cinema) *production* rather than distribution. Sony may have lost the 'format battle' but won for all forms of 're-creation' (in a 1984 Supreme Court decision against MCA) the final victory of the 'home taping' war (Harris, *Variety*, 18 June 1984).

From the very beginnings of VCR issue the major studios had been in an ambivalent position re: the new technology e.g. MCA's aversion to Betamax was linked to its parent company, MCA, introducing the 'DiscoVision' laserdisc system. In addition, whilst campaigning against Sony's threatening 'time-shift' technology, the major Hollywood studios had been exploring various business models for 'sell-thru' i.e. releasing back and current catalogue on tape for commercial hire or sale. The settling on one ubiquitous cassette format was a major step in the new form of distribution. Initially the major studios believed that the only logical way to market videocassettes was through direct sales allowing consumers to buy cassettes and create 'libraries'. In the case of the (in hindsight) rather bulky and poor quality VHS tapes customers actually preferred renting to buying. The business strategy of *selling* to consumers was rather more tenable in the case of 'cult', foreign language and 'art house' movies of all kinds and thus became the favoured strategy of such European companies as Palace (UK) and MK2 (France).

What the VCR certainly did *not* do then was open up a brave new world of consumer controlled television thus putting a (new) nail in the coffin of cinema. Whilst staying at home in increasing numbers the consumers of audio-visual product watched *more* and a wider variety of films. As Stephen Lax has noted: 'we use it for something the industry never anticipated: to substitute for scheduled programming. We go to the video rental shop or the library and borrow a film for a night (now more often on DVD rather than tape)' (Lax 2006: 29). Note well the use of the terms 'substitute' and 'film'. Videotape may have made TV production easier and cheaper (in its Beta formats) but its more vital contribution to the history of the audio-visual industries (in its VHS format) was to give 'films' (literally) a new lease of life. This creation of another lifeline for films was accompanied by an increasing viewers' choice in terms of the films themselves, times and forms of watching them, which usually was confined to the private space.[9] The invention of the VCR also initiated a process of a separation between the content of the material viewed on television screen and the institution of television itself. As indeed – and even more so – did the move to digital technology for, from its triumph of the early 1980s, the videocassette as alpha home-viewing technology had less than twenty years to live.[10] Thus with the videotape three important elements were introduced to the cinema–TV relationship, which were further emphasised with the advent of digital technology: re-creation (of the films' life), variation (of consumer choice), and separation (of form and content, or the dependence of hardware and software). All these aspects of the cinema–television relationship transform the process of film distribution and arguably it is this part of the film-making process which has been most affected by the technological changes in the television age.

The technological evolution which started with the videotape to a large degree has also freed distribution of films from its dependence on the institution of television which resulted in the situation whereby increasingly films are screened rather than broadcast on television. It is thanks to technological advances that the small screen was becoming more like a silver screen, especially in terms of the quality of the images and sound, which were transmitted resulting in a paradoxical situation whereby a digitally remastered print of an old classic film available on a DVD would provide a more pleasurable and authentic experience than seeing an almost certainly well-used copy of the same film on a small screen in an art cinema. Although faced with an almost impossible choice even hardcore cinephiles might opt for individual home-viewing forfeiting the (limited) collective experience of seeing the film in the cinema.

To focus on distribution in the examination of the changes introduced into the cinema–television relationship by technology does not mean that film production itself was not affected by the technological evolution. In our production chapter we have already dwelt on the actuality of and potential for ways in which the film-making and television-making process came to resemble each other when the video and now digital cameras have become available. Our focus here on distribution allows us to speak about not only new films but also old film classics made at the time when television was just taking off or when there was no such thing as television yet. It is in the case of such classics that the question of re-creation offered by new technology is becoming most poignant and apparent. It is also ironic that it was exactly in relation to these (often canonical) films that many of the negative arguments against television were formulated.

The 'digital' age of DVD and Web-distribution naturally provides the focus for a discussion regarding cinematic heritage. DVD has offered an improvement on the video technology while developing some very distinct features, which were not available before the digital and the advent of a new distribution platform: the internet. The internet provides new ways of DVD delivery (online DVD rental shops, such as Netflix or LoveFilm, the latter armed with powerful market penetration due to its links with AOL) and film selection tools (websites containing film reviews and lists of best films to watch in a given category) which replace a traditional rental shop increasing greatly a variety of films available to the viewers living away from urban centres with art cinemas offering a repertory programming, and, more importantly, for the purposes of our discussion, dismiss public television as a platform for conveying and preserving the canon of cinema. On the internet the reviews generated by members of the public are as important as voices of established film critics and academics. The internet also possesses the potential for becoming a new platform of distributing films via both downloading and streaming. This development can now challenge significantly the growth of the DVD market and finally put a limit to the exponential growth of DVD consumption.

The phenomenon of the DVD can be explained in the context of the recreation–separation–variation triad, which determines the dynamics of the cinema–television relationship. For the last decade old and new films have been released on digital versatile disks with accompanying bonus material. Originally, Hollywood studios became interested in the DVD technology because of its commercial value. They discovered that it could be profitable to re-release titles to which they hold rights. Their main target were people with collections of films on VHS tapes whose sales were slowing down. Distribution companies throughout the world quickly realised that these people would be willing to exchange fragile VHS tapes, whose picture was often full of dusty specks and imperfections, for slick light long-lasting discs, which offered incomparable improvements in the quality of picture and sound. After a brief period of hesitation the movie companies came together in their time honoured fashion of 'organised competition' because they saw DVD as a way of stimulating the video market, producing better quality sound and pictures on a disc that, not least, costs considerably less to produce than a VHS tape. The picture quality of the DVD was as at least as good as TV and the disc could carry multi-channel digital sound. DVD encapsulates in a small shiny disc the historical drive of audio-visual industries to supply better and better quality images (verisimilitude) in ever more convenient and/or comfortable form. These consumer friendly shiny discs had some additional features. They had the potential to allow a consumer to choose from up to eight different dubbed languages and from thirty-two different sets of subtitles (all at the press of the remote control button). Finally, if that were not enough, DVDs supported multiple aspect ratios from the 'movie' experience of 16:9 widescreen formats to the more conventional 'TV' of 4:3. In short this was a technology perfect for the multimedia and/or home cinema world of the twenty-first century. The DVD also benefited from both high capacity and compact size. The studio predictions regarding the sales of the DVDs were right. Already in 2001 DVDs accounted for over a third of the studio's revenues. At the end of 2004 *Screen Digest* research indicated that: 'DVD video player/recorder penetration had reached 50.5 per cent of TV households in Western Europe' (*Screen Digest* 1/2005: 11).

The Digital Video Disc's high quality of video and audio, easy access to selected parts of the disc and sheer ease of use, storage and transport has helped DVD to replace VHS for pre-recorded titles in less than a decade. If we think about DVD in terms of the re-creation of a film's life then improvements in comparison with VHS really have to do with the outstanding quality of the digital transfer and the greater longevity of the digital disk. Another and perhaps the greatest change that DVDs instituted was the inclusion of the supplementary bonus material. In the cases of many old films both the digital transfer and the presence of the bonus material helped studios to persuade the consumers to buy a DVD version of the film they had already owned on a VHS. In the cases of many films the bonus material is interesting because it allows for the re-creation of the critical and production context of the film and sometimes even reveals an additional creative dimension by including extra footage, voice-over commentary by the film-maker, etc. The decision as to what extra material is to be included is often an ad hoc decision of a DVD editor whose name is not even listed on the cover of the DVD. At this stage few conventions, which are loosely followed in the design of the DVD bonus material, are just one of many possibilities that the DVD offers and they are not very formalised. However, even these few conventions allow us to make some suggestions regarding the relationship between the films and the bonus material. There are at least three different ways in which they can be related: stylistic, content-based and historical.

The style of the DVD menu and the manner in which the material is presented are derived from the style of the film – the graphics of the credits or commercial spots. Even though the DVD extras have a potential to transform the film in the most fundamental ways, at the same time the style of these extras is determined by the film itself. The objective of the designers is to connect the film and the content of the DVD extras through the menu design, which is inspired and derived from the stylistic features of the film. In turn there is a number of ways in which the DVD extra material can potentially transform the film itself through *fragmentation, expansion, interactivity* and a *fetishistic intimacy.*

Fragmentation is linked to the division of films into chapters. The interviews and documentaries in the extras expose us to the fragmented nature of the film-making process by presenting it as a creative and collective effort of various individuals.

Expansion of the films is visual, sonic and conceptual due to the advanced audio-visual features and the inclusion of deleted scenes, alternative endings, director's commentary over the deleted scenes or the whole film. The extras show the film-making as a process extending beyond the director's artistic vision by familiarising us with the working methods of composers, editors, actors, producers and other members of the cast.

Interactivity comes with the possibility of manipulating images, sounds and the language of the film. This 'hands-on' approach is enhanced by the extras, which cater to the tastes and specific requirements of the viewers in different countries as the content of the extras differ from region to region.

Fetishistic intimacy with the film medium is created through exposure to the oversized screen and surrounding sound, which incorporates spectators into films. In the interviews the cast members comment on the atmosphere during the shoot and the human relationships which were developed.

The examination of these types of bonus material and its relationship to the feature film reveal its hardly realised potential of becoming a future new critical language to accompany films released on DVD. It has to be noted that much of the material packed on to commercial DVDs is largely rehashed from the 'Electronic Press Kit' so beloved of lazy journalists and has very little educational value beyond the study of current press and publicity discourse. Nonetheless the potential is there (not least for portmanteau compilations of films from new directors). A DVD including a film and the extras could become a new art form in itself leading to not just a re-creation but an effective mutation of the film itself. We could think about a film, which is after all the core feature of any DVD, as a genetic code of the DVD. The bonus material is a way of introducing a variation into the film's DNA and thus creating something quite new. DVD thus has a potential to go beyond simple 'repackaging' of back catalogue to break the habitus that movies have to last two hours or that programming has to fit regular formats. This habitus was very little affected by the VHS in spite of the technology's overall revolutionary impact.[11]

Re-creation of the film in DVD form, especially if it relates to an older film or one with limited previous theatrical release, raises important issues regarding the authorship and ownership of such transformed film. If the DVD extras can actually transform the film to a substantial and substantive extent then the anonymous editor of the DVD authors it and by extension partakes in the authorship of the film itself. But for our purposes more important than the questions of the DVD authorship is its spectatorship in the context of cinema–television relationship. In a similar but rather more user-friendly way to the VHS DVD liberates spectators from the TV network schedules giving them a new level of independence regarding their choice of films. The digital technology enhances the spectators' freedom by allowing them to choose not only what they are going to watch but also how they are going to do it. In answering the question of the ways in which the film can be accessed, the issue of DVD menus and their design determined by TV or computer desktop becomes central.

At present most DVDs have standard menus, which enable the spectators to understand the navigation of the disc easily and quickly. These standard elements of the DVD are 'Play movie', 'Main Menu', 'Scene Access', 'Special Features' and 'Audio Setup'. The consistency across different menus is supposed to make it easy and smooth to use any DVD. Hence, this standardisation of the DVD menus makes predictability and convenience central to the spectators' experience of the DVD. This familiarity with the menus is connected to another feature of the menu design – flow and continuity. The objective of the designers is to connect the film and the content of the DVD extras through the menu design, which is inspired and derived from the stylistic features of the film. This could be seen as an effort to extend the film by making the DVD menu its integral part. Most of the DVD menus are designed for viewing the DVD on the TV-connected machine rather than on the computer desktop. In designing the interface the designers must remember that the four buttons on the remote control will not create the same possibilities as clicking on the mouse does. Hence, due to its hardware limitations the DVD format remains closely related to television and VCR viewing. It is interesting to note that the remote control/mouse difference has implications for the DVD public. DVD comes to be associated with the lazy comfort of television and consequently is less challenging than surfing the Web or learning the rules of a new computer game.

The menus are the interface between the spectator and different elements of the DVD, which allow the spectator to access various parts of the DVD, to interact with the film and to connect different elements of the bonus material and the film. The short examination of the menus shows that the use of the menus is supposed to be a predictable, painless and easy experience, which raises a question as to how much a spectator can really do with the bonus material when the spectator's actions are limited to the operations allowed by the menus. We would suggest the variety and richness of this experience is less than one would expect. Even if we as spectators have some sense of re-shaping the film in our own mode and creating our own movie-experience, we are doing it according to the existing map. The spectators are not the auteurs of the DVD. The menu designers, along with the DVD editor and those who research and put together the bonus material of the film, are the anonymous and rarely credited but true creators of the DVD. This fact should not allow us to underestimate the role of the spectator. Despite its obvious limitations DVD spectatorship is a new, valuable and unique learning process, which takes the understanding of the film beyond the story and the spectacle. At the core of the DVD spectatorship is thus the process of demystifying the magic of the film which at least as far as menu design is concerned is driven by the televisual ethos associated with the hardware (TV remote control) which is used.

As a historically centred volume (which after all is discussing cinema in a particular, presumably finite, age) we wish to avoid futurology (however tempting). Nonetheless as this volume came together technological change continued at pace leaving us having to confront a changing ecology of audio-visual production and consumption which was already a reality (admittedly with uncertain further potentialities). We are forced to ask whether the internet will be able to introduce a greater separation between the downloaded or streamlined films and the platform on which the films are going to be viewed. Exciting as the introduction of DVD has been we must face up to the fact that DVD technology will become obsolete, possibly as a result of the internet becomes new means of transferring films. This would clearly further impact on the cinema–television relationship; possibly making the terms irrelevant.

In the twenty-first century 'films' (although less and less 'film' is involved) are being created for and re-created in, through or on an interactive medium: the internet. With this 'new' new/old media relationship we are presented with intriguing problems as well as infinite possibilities. The most obvious problem with the deliverability of moving images over the web is one of whether it can be done at all in any way acceptable to consumers. Along with issues of compression this problem is almost entirely one of bandwidth and reliability. With a suitably fast broadband connection it should be possible to download a full-length movie in less than its running time. European states have seized broadband at different rates. By 2000 40 per cent of German households had broadband connections, Scandinavian nations even higher, with the UK well behind. The UK's problem was almost entirely predicated upon the fact that BT's Broadband infrastructure could only reach 60 per cent of the country – but the cable companies moved into the vacuum. In October 2002 over one million internet users had subscribed to a broadband service – the figure had trebled in nine months. By September 2004 'UK broadband take-up tops five million' (still only 20 per cent of households).

> The Telecom Markets' Broadband Subscriber Database predicts that the figure will rise to eight million by the end of 2005, or 32 per cent of UK homes . . . around 50,000 new broadband subscribers are being added every week. . . . Analyst Gareth Willmer predicted: 'In the next year or so subscriptions will rise rapidly owing to falling prices, VoIP [Voice over Internet Protocol] launches and increasing competition from alternative broadband carriers.'[12]

The time/space problems with downloading moving images are *beginning* to be addressed via streaming i.e. the real time distribution of audio, video and multimedia by the continuous transmission of the digital media data. With a broadband connection, the image and audio is approaching (or exceeding, with the fastest connections) television quality. Five of the major studios – Warner, Paramount, MGM, Universal and Sony – have launched a joint venture for a 'Video on Demand' (VOD) service. Disney and Fox confirmed a second, similar venture to be offered via Disney's www.movies.com website. As of 2006 the latter still only offers: 'movie trailers, movie clips, and special bonus footage online.' VOD systems allow users to select and watch content over a network as part of a television system. The first commercial VOD service took place in Hong Kong in the 1990s but as VCDs were so much cheaper and pay TV a new concept Hong Kong Telecom lost a large amount of money and the service was shut down in 2000. Video on Demand is for the foreseeable future the preserve of cable companies e.g. Time Warner Cable has a video-on-demand service in the US and Canalplay provides a video-on-demand service in France. In the UK Homechoice offers VOD, sixty digital TV channels and up to 8Mb broadband but in London only. NTL in the UK has a Video on Demand service on digital cable in their Glasgow, Swansea, Cardiff, Luton and Nottingham franchise areas.

As with much 'visual' technological advance the potential can be seen in the history of 'audio' especially music. The rise of the DVD (including its rich repackaging and reselling potential as well as its gain in reproduction quality and ease of use) could have been predicted on the success of the audio CD. Digital copying of movies is in essence a development of the current MP3 phenomenon – as is the industry's panic about 'peer-to-peer' sharing. A less threatening and rather heartening phenomenon for the future access to a (potentially) wider range of audio-visual material e.g. via such engines as www.archive.org a digital library of internet sites and other cultural artifacts in digital form ('30,798 movies'): 'Like a paper library, we provide free access to researchers, historians, scholars, and the general public.'

The twin questions hanging over the brave new world of movies on the Web are lack of high speed access in the home and resistance to watching films on a PC. These questions will be answered by broadband to TV. The new digital TV set-top boxes and receivers will increasingly be designed in such a way that internet services are integrated seamlessly into the package. In fact, the latest digital TV set-top boxes are really computers in disguise. They already include computer-type hard disks and ever-larger measures of processing power. While the PC space has been a notoriously difficult arena in which to make paying services work, viewers of movies on TV are used to paying for movie channels via subscriptions or on a pay-per-view basis. For this reason it is easier to make a pay-per-view or subscription model for delivering movies over the internet work.

In what we may choose to call a 'post-television age' we must be careful not to fall into earlier critical discourses in which new media e.g. TV have been treated as 'unwanted growth'. Cinema remains a valuable term of reference to describe audio-visual materials. In historical terms we have not seen, are not seeing and will not see the decline of 'movies'. The period of European Cinemas in the Television Age is part of a seamless continuum of the use and enjoyment of moving images produced, distributed, exhibited and consumed by and in various mediums. LONG MAY IT CONTINUE TO BE SO.

NOTES

1. See Dudley Andrew quoted in Chapter 10, p. 149.
2. Naturally in what is more recently and confidently termed 'television studies' we see a rather more sophisticated engagement with what television viewers actually do with their domestic audio-visual equipment. Such work can be seen displayed in Geraghty and Lusted (1998) and Gauntllett and Hill (1999).
3. For example Susan Sontag 'The Decay of Cinema' www.cinematicthreads.com/sontag1.php, Originally printed 25 February 1996 in *The New York Times*.
4. See as an Ur-text Walter Benjamin's 1936 *The Work of Art in the Age of Mechanical Reproduction*.
5. See Chapter 4, p. 46.
6. See Chapter 3, p. 36.
7. See Chapter 4, p. 51.
8. www.barb.co.uk/TVFACTS
9. Even though in the West VHS is associated with home-viewing it is not necessary the case for the rest of the world. It is enough to mention the recent growth of Nollywood, Nigerian film industry, which for distribution relies exclusively on the VHS. VCRs are installed in the public places, for instance cafés, where people can watch the film for a small fee in the company of the others. See for example 'Welcome to Nollywood', *The Guardian*, Thursday 23 March 2006, www.guardian.co.uk/g2/story/0,,1737225,00.
10. In 1996 DVD players were launched in Japan and in the US a year later. By 2002 annual world production of DVD discs surpassed VHS cassettes (according to International Recording Media Association statistics). DVD sales increased from 1.08 billion in 2001 to 1.74 billion in 2002; VHS declined from 1.53 billion in 2001 to 1.33 billion in 2002. In 2003 DVD rentals increased 51.2 per cent and VHS rentals dropped 29 per cent from the previous year; DVD sales increased 42.2 per cent to $12.1 billion and VHS sales dropped 34.8% to $2.4 billion.
11. We have already noted that DVD has tremendous implications in terms of production. Its ultimate potential may best be seen in terms of distribution as independent content producers (be they small movie companies or community activist groups) engage in *samizdat* (self distribution) activity. DVD is easier to transport and viewable without access to mainstream TV distribution. The 'Extra Features' element of the DVD package may well be the model for future film content. The growth of DVD has itself spurred the flowering of a supporting production sector documenting and celebrating the film-making process with 'the making of' documentaries, director profiles, etc.
12. www.weboptimiser.com/search_engine_marketing_news/6082006

BIBLIOGRAPHY

Abad, I. (2002), 'Il cambiamento nel sistema di produzione', in *Cinema in Spagna oggi. Nuovi autori, nuove tendenze*, Pesaro: Lindau.

Abrams, M. (1956), 'Child audiences for television', *Great Britain Journalism Quarterly*, 33 (1), pp. 35–41.

Agger, G. (2005), 'Summary', in *Dansk tv-drama – arvesølv og underholdning*, Frederiksberg: Samfundslitteratur, pp. 518–22 (in Danish), p. 550 (in English).

Alberoni, F. (ed.) (1968), *Televisione e vita italiana*, Turin: ERI.

Alter, N. (2002), *Projecting History: German Nonfiction Cinema 1967–2000*, Ann Arbor, MI: The University of Michigan Press.

Armiñán, J. de (1970), 'Jaime de Armiñán. Otra vez en TVE', *Teleradio*, 19 January, pp. 20–1.

Anania, F. (1997), *Davanti allo schermo*, Rome: La Nuova Italia.

Andrew, D. (2000), 'The unauthorized author today', in R. Stam and T. Miller (eds), *Film and Theory. An Anthology*, Oxford: Blackwell, pp. 20–30.

Annuario statistico del cinema europeo, www.mediasalles.it

Anon. (1969), 'Pieśń o Małym Rycerzu', *Życie Warszawy*, 310, 30 December.

Anon. (1970a), 'Los hechos de los apostoles', *Teleradio*, 639, pp. 10–11.

Anon. (1970b), 'Cine y tv, colaboración', *Teleradio*, 658, 3–9August, p. 1

Anon. (1975), *La exhibición cinematográfica en España (situación y condicionantes)*, Madrid: Imp. R.C.

Anon. (1983), 'Los que hacen la televisión', *Teleradio*, 1336, 5–11 August, pp. 20–3.

Anon. (1992), 'The visions of Wenders', *Time International*, 11 May, pp. 58–9.

Anon. (1997), 'Uwagi o adaptacji *Ogniem i mieczem* 11/5/97', *Archiwum Telewizji Polskiej 2718/22*, 1, pp. 1–4.

Anon. (2001), 'Himmel, Erde und Rebekuchen', *Der Spiegel*, 26, pp. 194–200.

Anon. (2003), 'German Hero', http://sportsillustrated.cnn.com/soccer/news/2003/08/14/rahn_obit/ (accessed 3 July 2006).

Anon. (2004a), *Public Service redegørelse*, København: DR.

Anon. (2004b), 'ZDF: Das kleine Fernsehspiel', www.zdf.de/ZDFde/inhalt/29/0,1872,1021277,00 (accessed 3 July 2006).

Anon. (2006a), 'Movie capital', *Screen International*, 19 May, p. 1.

Anon. (2006b), 'Welcome to Nollywood', *The Guardian*, 23 March, http://film.guardian.co.uk/features/featurepages/0,,1737425,00.html (accessed 3 July 2006).

Antczak, J. (1968), 'Stenogram z posiedzenia Komisji Kolaudacyjnej 19/4/ 1968', *Filmoteka Narodowa*, A-344, pozyzja 449, pp. 1–20.

Antczak, J. (1975), 'Eksplikacja reżyserska skróconej wersji filmu fabularnego p.t. *Noce i Dnie* Jerzego Antczaka', *Filmoteka Narodowa*, A-344, pozycja 106, pp. 1–3.

Aprà, A. (1997), *Roberto Rossellini, Il mio metodo, Scritti e intervisti*, Venice: Il Marsilio.

Arbeitsgemeinschaft Kino (1987), 'Für eine kulturelle Förderung des Kinos!', in Arbeitsgemeinschaft der Filmjournalisten Hamburger Filmbüro (ed.), *Neue Medien contra Filmkultur?*, Berlin: Wissenschaftsverlag Volker Spiess GmbH, pp. 55–62.

Arocena, C. (1996), *Victor Erice*, Madrid: Cátedra.

Ashby, J. and Higson, A. (eds) (2000), *British Cinema, Past and Present*, London: Routledge.

Baget Herms, J. M. (1993), *Historia de la televisión en España 1956–1975*, Barcelona: Feed-Back Ediciones.

Baier, M. (1996), *Film, Video und HDTV: Die Audiovisionen des Wim Wenders*, Berlin: Kohler Verlag.

Balio, T. (ed.) (1990), *Hollywood in the Age of Television*, London, Unwin.

Ballieu, B. and J. Goodchild (eds) (2002), *The British Film Business*, London, Wiley.

Balling, E. (1980), 'At producere for TV', in E. Trautmann and J. Bang (eds), *Årbog 1980*, København: DR, p. 20.

Barr, C. (ed.) (1986), *All our Yesterdays*, London: BFI.

Bazin, A. (1992), *What is Cinema?* Vols 1 and 2, Berkeley: University of California Press.

Benjamin, W. (1936), *The Work of Art in the Age of Mechanical Reproduction* (reprinted in *Illuminations*, 1999, Pimlico).

Bergstom, J. (ed.) (1999), *Endless Night: Cinema and Psychoanalysis, Parallel Histories*, Berkeley and Los Angeles: University of California Press.

Bettetini, G. and A. Grasso (eds) (1985), *Televisione: la provvisoria identità italiana*, Turin: Fondazione Agnelli.

Bondebjerg, I. and F. Bono (1996), *Television in Scandinavia: History, Politics and Aesthetics*, Luton: Luton University Press.

Bondebjerg, I. and P. Schepelern (eds) (1997), *Dansk film 1972–1997*, København: Munksgaard/Rosinante.

Boorman, J. and W. Donahue (1997), *Projections 7*, London: Faber and Faber.

Boorman, J. F. MacDonald and W. Donahue (eds) (2002), *Projections 12: Film-makers on Film Schools*, London: Faber and Faber.

Borau, J. L. (ed.) (1998), *Dicconario del cine español*, Madrid: Alianza.

Bordwell, D. (2004), 'Strong sense of narrative desire: a decade of Danish film', *Film* (Danish Film Institute), 34, pp. 24–7.

Borish, S. M. (1991), *The Land of the Living*, Nevada City: Blue Dolphin Publishing.

Bossak, J. (1987), 'W związku z serialem *Pierścień i Róża* 5/1/87', *Archiwum Telewizji Polskiej 2110/8*, 1, pp. 1–2.

Bourdieu, P. (1990), *The Logic of Practice*, Stanford: Stanford University Press.

Bourdieu, P. (1993), *The Field of Cultural Production*, Cambridge: Polity.

Bourdieu, P. (1996), *Rules of Art*, Cambridge: Polity.

Bredsdorff, E. (1982), *Revolutionær humanisme*, København: Gyldendal.

Briggs, A. (1995), *The History of Broadcasting in the United Kingdom*, Oxford: Oxford University Press.

Buckingham, D., H. Davies, K. Jones and P. Kelley (1999), *Children's Television in Britain: History, Discourse and Policy*, London: BFI.

Buob, J. and P. Mérigaud (2001), *L'aventure vraie de Canal +*, Paris: Fayard.

Bustamante, E. (2001), 'Creadores de cultura', in *Anuario ATV 2001*, Pozuelo de Alarcón: Academia de las Ciencias y las artes de Televisión, pp. 41–2.

Butler, J. G. (2002), *Television. Critical Methods and Application*, London: Lawrence Erlbaum Associates.

Caldiron, O. (1976), *Il cinema della televisione: dare e avere*, Venice: La Bienale.

Calhoun, J. (2005), '*My Summer of Love* warms the English countryside', *American Cinematographer*, July, pp. 14–16.

Camporesi, V. (1999), 'Imágenes de la televisión en el cine español de los Sesenta', *Archivos de la Filmoteca Valenciana*, 32, June, pp. 148–62.

Camporesi, V. (2000), 'Stereotyping a competitor: images of television in Spanish cinema in the 1960s', in J. Fullerton and A. Söderbergh (eds), *Moving Images: From Edison to the Webcam*, Sidney: John Libbey, pp. 149–58.

Camporesi, V. (2001), 'Dillinger is back, film history and social perception of television', in G. Roberts and P. Taylor (eds), *The Historian, Television and Television History*, Luton: The University of Luton Press, pp. 38–53.

Cerdán, J. (2005), 'Haciendo estudios culturales: Del Nuevo Cine Español a la Televisión Española a través de *Cuadernos para el diálogo*', in 'El cine español durante la Transición democrática (1974–1983)', *Cuadernos de la Academia*, 13/14, March, pp. 219–34.

Cesareo, G. (1979), 'L'avvento della televisione e il cinema negli anni cinquanta', in T. Giorgio (ed.), *Il cinema italiano degli anni cinquanta*, Venice: Il Marsilio.

Christensen, C. L. (2006), 'Børne- og ungdoms-tv's historie', in S. Hjarvard (ed.), *Dansk tv-historie*, Frederiksberg: Samfundslitteratur.

Cobos, J. (1983), 'Los desastres de la guerra', *Teleradio*, 1316, 18–24 March, pp. 6–8.

Cobos, J. and J. Hernández Les (1983), 'Directores de cine en TVE', *Teleradio*, 1332, 5–14 July, pp. 25–9.

Créton, L. (1994), *L'Economie du cinéma. Perspectives stratégique*, Paris: Nathan.

Créton, L. (1997), *Cinéma et marché*, Paris: Armand Colin/Masson.

Créton, L. (2001), *L'Economie du cinéma*, Paris: Nathan.

Créton, L. (2003), *L'Economie du cinéma*, Paris: Nathan.

Cuadra Salcedo, M. (1983), 'Entrevista a Jaime Chávarri', *Teleradio*, 15 April, pp. 10–12.

Curran, J. and V. Porter (eds) (1983), *British Cinema History*, London: Weidenfield.

Curtis, P. (2005), 'Mouse trap: Media studies courses have for years been cruelly mocked by the industry. Can they survive a renewed assault', *Education Guardian*, 26 June.

Danieri, D. (1983), 'Juntos pero no revueltos', *Teleradio*, 1345, 10–16 October, p. 11.

de Grazia, V. (1989), 'Mass culture and sovereignty: the American challenge to European cinemas, 1920–1960', *The Journal of Modern History*, 61, March.

Delmas, B. and E. Mahé (2001), *Western médiatique ou les mésaventures du cinéma au pays de Vivendi*, Paris: Mille et une nuits.

De Mauro, T. (1970), *Storia linguistica dell'Italia unita*, Bari: Laterza.

Dinnesen, N. J. (1980), 'Økonomien bag filmene. Om den danske filmbranche 1945–79', in A. Troelsen (ed.), *Levende billeder af Danmark*, Holte, Medusa, pp. 13–37.

Drotner, K. (1997), 'Filmkultur i børnehøjde - dansk børne- og ungdomsfilm', in I. Bondebjerg, J. Andersen and P. Schepelern (eds), *Dansk film 1972–97*, København: Munksgaard/Rosinante.

'Drugi Okrągły Stół Medialny March 1996. Znaczenie niezależnej produkcji audiowizualnej w Polsce' (1996), *Archiwum Telewizji Polskiej SA 2607/8*, Volume 1.

'Eksplikacja reżyserska skróconej wersji filmu fabularnego p.t. *Noce i Dnie* Jerzego Antczaka' (1975), *Filmoteka Narodowa*, A-344, pozycja 106, pp. 1–3.

Ellis, J. (1992), *Visible Fictions*, London: Routledge.

Elsaesser, T. (1999), *New German Cinema: A History*, New Brunswick, NJ: Rutgers University Press.

Elsaesser, T. (2005), *European Cinema, Face to Face with Hollywood*, Amsterdam: AUP.

Elsey, E. and A. Kelly (2002), *In Short*, London: BFI.

Elsner, M., T. Mueller and P. M. Spangenberg (1990), 'The early history of German television: the slow dvelopment of a fast medium', *The Historical Journal of Film, Radio, and Television*, 10 (2), pp. 193–220.

Emmett, B. P. (1956), 'The television audience in the United Kingdom', *Journal of the Royal Statistical Society*, 119 (3), pp. 284–306.

Enitknap, L. (2005), *Moving Image Technology From Zoetrope to Digital*, London: Wallflower.

Entrevista (1984), 'Entrevista co José Luis Cuerda', *Teleradio*, 1356, 26 December – 1 January 1984 , '*Los santos inocentes*. Gañanes y señoritos', *Fotogramas n 1590*, May, p. 32.

Fact and Figures, Danish Film Insitute: www.dfi.dk/English.

Farchy, J. (1992), *Le cinéma déchaîné. Mutation d'une industrie*, Paris: Presses du CNRS.

Feinstein, J. (2002), *The Triumph of the Ordinary: Depictions of Daily Life in the East German Cinema, 1949–1989*. Chapel Hill, NC: University of North Carolina Press.

Floyd, N. (2002), 'Living dead visit the digital age', *Metro*, 9 October, p. 19.

Foot, J. (1995), 'The family and the economic miracle: social transformation, work, leisure and development at Bovisa and Comasina (Milan)', *Contemporary European History*, IV, 3, November, pp. 251–9.

Forbes, J. (1984), *INA-French for Innovation: the Work of the Institut National de la Communication Audiovisuelle in Cinema and Television*, BFI Dossier, no. 22, London: BFI.

Forbes, J. (1992), *The Cinema in France After the New Wave*, London: MacMillan.

Forgacs, D. (1993), *L'industrializzazione della cultura italiana*, Bologna: Il Mulino.

Gabardos, F. (1969), 'Opus Primum. "Al escondite inglés" de Iván Zulueta', *Pantallas y escenarios*, 91, February.

Galán, D. (1978), 'Memorias del cine español', *Fotogramas*, 11, 18, 25 August and 1, 8, 15 September (unpaginated).

Galán, D. (2005), 'Los Goyas de la "tele"', *El país*, 3 February, p. 50.

García, L. V. (1972), *Chequeo al cine español*, Madrid: Talleres Gráficos Casteló.

Garwood, I. (2002), 'The *Autorenfilm* in Contemporary German Cinema', in T. Bergfelder, E. Carter and D. Göktürk (eds), *The German Cinema Book*, London: British Film Institute, pp. 202–10.

Gauntlett, D. and A. Hill (1999), *TV Living*, London: Routledge.

Geraghty, C. (2000), *British Cinema in the Fifties*, London: Routledge.

Geraghty, C. and D. Lusted (eds) (1998), *The Television Studies Book*, London: Arnold.

Gil, M. (1976a), 'RTVE Directores. La nueva generación (I): Josefina Molina', *Teleradio*, 24 May, pp. 12–13.

Gil, M. (1976b), 'RTVE Directores. La nueva generación (III): Antonio Giménez Rico', *Teleradio*, 963, 7 June, pp. 17–18.

Gil, M. (1976c), 'RTVE Directores. La nueva generación (IV): Emilio Martínez Lázaro', *Teleradio*, 21 June, pp. 12–13.

Gil, M. (1976d), 'RTVE Directores. La nueva generación (V): Ramón Gómez Redondo', *Teleradio*, 966, 28 June, pp. 12–13.

Grasso, A. (1992), *Storia della televisione italiana*, Milan: Bompiani.

Griffiths, K. (2003), 'The manipulated image', *Convergence*, 9 (4), pp. 12–26.

Gunning, T. (1989), 'The cinema of attractions: early film, its spectator and the avant-garde', in T. Elsaesser and A. Barker (eds), *Early Film*, London: British Film Institute.

Hacker, J. and D. Price (1991), *Take 10*, Oxford: Oxford University Press.

Hake, S. (2002), *German National Cinema*, London: Routledge.

Hand, C. (2002), 'Television Ownership in Britain and the Coming of ITV: What do the statistics show?' (unpublished paper), available from www2.rhul.ac.uk/~umwf133.

Harper, G. (2005), 'DVD and the new cinema of complexity in post-punk cinema', in N. Rombes (ed.), *New Punk Cinema*, Edinburgh: Edinburgh University Press, pp. 89–101.

Harris, P. (1984), 'Supreme Court OK's home taping: approve "time shifting" for personal use', *Variety* (Los Angeles), 18 June, p. 1.

Havn, L. (2003), 'Today's children share tomorrow's growth', *Film/Kids* (Danish Film Institute), pp. 20–1.

Hayward, S. (1993), *French National Cinema*, London and New York: Routledge.

Henning Pryds, H. (1991), 'Medea – et tv-æstetisk eksperiment', in *Sekvens*, København: Institut for Film, TV & Kommunikation, pp. 141–56.

Heredero, C. F. (1997), 'El Sur 1983', in J. Pérez Perucha (ed.), *Antología crítica del cine español 1906–1995*, Madrid: Cátedra, pp. 844–6.

Heredero, C. F., 'Iván Zulueta: la mirada poliédrica', in *Tiempos del cine español*, San Sebastian: Ayuntamiento de San sebastián (no date of publication), pp. 25–6.

Hessel, M. A. (1969), 'Mości Panowie – proroctwa mnie wspierają!', *Tygodnik Powszechny*, 20, 18 May.

Hickethier, K. (1980), *Das Fernsehspiel der Bundesrepublik. Themen, Form, Struktur, Theorie und Geschichte 1951–1977*, Stuttgart: Metzler.

Hickethier, K. (1989), 'Vom Ende des Kinos und vom Anfang des Fernsehens. Das Verhältnis von Film und Fernsehen in den fünfziger Jahren', in H. Hoffmann and W. Schobert (eds), *Zwischen Gestern und Morgen. Westdeutscher Nachkriegsfilm 1942–1962*, Frankfurt am Main: Deutsches Filmmuseum, pp. 282–315.

Hickethier, K. (1998), *Geschichte des deutschen Fernsehens*, Stuttgart, Weimar: Metzler.

Hill, J. (1999), *British Cinema in the 1980s*, Oxford: Clarendon.

Hill, J. and M. McLoone (eds) (1996), *Big Picture, Small Screen,* Luton: ULP.

Hjarvard, S. (ed.) (forthcoming 2006), *Dansk tv-historie*, Frederiksberg: Samfundslitteratur.

Hjort, M. and S. Mackenzie (eds) (2000), *Cinema & Nation*, London and New York: Routledge.

Hjort, M. and I. Bondebjerg (eds) (2003), *The Danish Directors. Dialogues on a Contemporary National Cinema*, Bristol: Intellect, pp. 8–22.

Hollender, B. and Z. Turowska (2000), *TOR. Zespół*, Warszawa: Prószyński & S-ka.

Honoré, A. M. (1994), *Filmpolitik midt i en medierevolution*, Århus: Klim.

Howells, R. (2003), *Visual Culture*, Cambridge: Polity.

Interview with Andrzej Wajda (1978), *Dziennik Wieczorny*, 110, 17 May.

Interview with Bodil Cold-Ravnkilde (2004), Dorota Ostrowska, June (unpublished).

Interview with Camilla Hammerich (2004), Dorota Ostrowska, June (unpublished).

Interview with Carmen Szwec (2004), Dorota Ostrowska, April (unpublished).

Interview with Frédéric Bourboulon (2005), Graham Roberts, Stephen Hay, Dorota Ostrowska, March, February (unpublished).

Interview with Henning Camre (2004), Dorota Ostrowska, June (unpublished).

Interview with Ken Loach (1999), Graham Roberts, March (unpublished).

Interview with Kirsten Drotner (2004), Dorota Ostrowska, June (unpublished).

Interview with Mogens Vemmer (2004), Dorota Ostrowska, June (unpublished).

Interview with Per Schultz (2004), Dorota Ostrowska, June (unpublished).

Interview with Peter Greenaway, www.salon.com/june97/greenaway2970606.

Interview with Poul Nesgaard (2004), Dorota Ostrowska, June (unpublished).

Interview with Søren Kragh-Jacobsen (2000), Dorota Ostrowska, June (unpublished).

Interview with Sue Clayton (2006), Heather Wallis, June—July (unpublished).

Interview with Thelma Schoonmaker (1997), N. Saada in J. Boorman and W. Donahue (eds) (2002), *Projections 7*, London: Faber and Faber, pp. 22–8.

Interview with Ulrich Breuning (2004), Dorota Ostrowska, June (unpublished).

Interview with Vibeke Windeløv (2004), Dorota Ostrowska, June (unpublished).

Interview with Wim Wenders (2000), S. Johnston, *The Daily Telegraph*, 10 November.

Iordanova, D. (2003), *Cinema of the Other Europe. The Industry and Artistry of East Central European Film*, London: Wallflower Press.

Jackel, A. (2003), *European Film Industries*, London: BFI.

Jenkins, H. (ed.) (1998), *The Children's Culture Reader*, New York: New York University Press.

Jousse, T. and S. Toubiana (1992), interview with René Bonnel and Pierre Lescure, 'Horizons lointains', *Cahiers du cinema*, 455 (45), May.

Kaes, A. (1992), 'History and film: public memory in the age of electronic dissemination', in B. A. Murray and Christopher J. Wickham (eds), *Framing the Past The Historiography of German Cinema and Television*, Carbondale and Edwardsville: Southern Illinois University Press, pp. 308–23.

Kay, A. (1902), *Barnets Aarhundrede*, København: Gyldendal.

Klein, U. (2000), 'Erfahrungen mit Neuen Medien im Inland', in Arbeitsgemeinschaft der Filmjournalisten Hamburger Filmbüro (ed.), *Neue Medien contra Filmkultur?*, Berlin: Wissenschaftsverlag Volker Spiess GmbH, pp. 38–54.

Kluge, A. (2003), 'Büchner-Preis 2003 Rede', accessed at www.kluge-alexander. de/ presse_dankrede_buechnerpreis-2003.shtml (accessed 3 July 2006).
Kluge, A. (2004), 'Die Fernsehmagazine', accessed at www.kluge-alexander.de/fernsehmagazine (accessed 3 July 2006).
Knudsen, E. (2004), 'The eyes of the beholder', *Journal of Media Practice*, 5 (3), pp. 181–6.
Królikowska-Avis, E. (2005), 'Strasznie nieangielski świat', interview with Pawel Pawlikowski, *Kino*, 455, April, pp. 20–2.
'Kultura polska 1989–1997' (1997), *Archiwum Telewizji Polskiej SA 2614/6*, 1, pp. 184–231, p. 197.
Lamberti, A. (ed.) (1988), *Camorra: analisi e stereotipi,* Turin: ERI.
Lax, S. (2006), 'Television and video technology: from analogue to digital', in D. Gomery, and L. Hockley (eds), *Television Industries*, London: BFI, pp. 28–30.
Lecasble, V. (2001), *Le roman de Canal+*, Paris: Editions Grasset & Fasquelle.
Lequeret, E. (2000), 'Le cinéma enchaîné', *Cahiers du cinéma*, 548, July–August.
'List do głównego księgowego TVP SA od Telewizji Polskiej SA dotyczący umowy koprodukcyjnej na realizację filmu i serialu TV *Quo Vadis* 05/05/00' (2000), Agencja Telewizji Polskiej SA *Quo Vadis* TIF. 0001375-1379.
Low, R. (1949), *The History of British Film 1906–1914*, London: Allen and Unwin.
MacDonald, I. M. (2003), 'Finding the needle: How readers see screen ideas', *Journal of Media Practic*, 4(1), pp. 5–19.
MacDonald, I. M. (2004), 'Manuals are not enough. Relating screenwriting theory to practice to theories', *Journal of British Cinema and Television*, 1(2), pp. 260–74.
McLuhan, M. (1994), *Understanding Media: The Extensions of Man*, Cambridge, MA: The MIT Press.
Marcussen, E. B. (1995), 'The struggle for children's films. The post-war pioneers', in I. Zeruneith (ed.), *Wide-Eyed. Films for Children and Young People in the Nordic Countries 1977–1993*, Copenhagen: Tiderne Skifter, pp. 15–28.
Marías, M. (1992), '*El sol del membrillo* (Victor Erice, 1982)', *Archivos de la Filmoteca Valenciana*, 13 (Fall), pp. 118–31.
Messenger-Davies, M. (2001), 'Studying children's television', in G. Creeber (ed.), *The Television Genre Book*, London: BFI, pp. 96–7.
Michelsen, L. (2003), 'Fantastic Tales', *Film*, Special Issue 'Kids', Danish Film Institute, p. 6.
Miró, P. (1976), 'Los de la Escuela Oficial de Cinematografía', *Teleradio*, special edition: '20 años de TVE, 1956–1976'.
'Misja Telewizji Publicznej SA Jako Nadawcy Publicznego 06/94' (1994), *Archiwum Telewizji Polskiej SA 2804/1*, 6.

Monaco, J. (1981), *How to Read a Film*, Oxford: Oxford University Press.

Monteleone, F. (1992), *Storia della radio e della televisione in Italia. Società, politica, strategie, programmi*, Venice: Il Marsilio.

Morris, T. (2000), *You're Only Young Twice. Children's Literature and Film*, Chicago: University of Illinois Press.

Murphy, R. (ed.) (2000), *British Cinema of the 90s*, London: BFI.

Novrup Redvall, E. (2005), 'Debutanternes indtogsmarch', *Film* (Danish Film Institute), 44, p. 4.

Ortega, M. L. and A. Albertos (eds) (1998), 'La ciencia en Televisión Española: primeros acercamientos a la divulgación', *Secuencias*, April, pp. 61–74.

Ortoleva, P. (1995), *Un ventennio a colori*, Florence: La Nuova Italia.

Ortoleva, P. (1999), 'Cinema e televisione', in G. P. Brunetta (ed.), *Storia del cinema mondiale*, I, 1, *L'Europa. Miti, luoghi, divi*, Turin: Einaudi, pp. 993–1012.

Palacio, M. (1992), *Una historia de la televisión en España. Arqueología y modernidad*, Madrid: Capital Europea de la cultura.

Palacio, M. (1996), *Historia de la televisión*; *Archivos de la Filmoteca Valenciana*, 23/24, June–October.

Palacio, M. (2001), *Historia de la televisión en España*, Barcelona: Gedisa.

Palacio, M. (2002), 'Enseñar deleitando. Las adaptaciones literarias en televisión', in C. F. Heredero (ed.), 'La imprenta dinámica. Literatura española en el cine español', *Cuadernos de la Academia*, 11/12, pp. 519–38.

Palacio, M. and Ibáñez, J. C. (2004), 'Biografía y ficción histórica en la obra del Bardem televisivo (1985–1992)', in J. L. Castro, M. de Paz and J. Pérez Perucha (eds), *El cine a codazos. J. A. Bardem*, Orense: Festival de Cine Independiente, pp. 141–51.

Pérez Ornia, J. R. (1989), 'Peculiaridades de una televisión gubernamental', in J. T. Álvarez (ed.), *Historia de los medios de comunicación en España. Periodismo, imagen y publicidad (1900–1990)*, Barcelona: Ariel, pp. 304–25.

Pérez Pinar, J. A. (1985), 'La colaboración entre cine y TV: una realidad insuficiente', *Cine español 1975–1984*, Murcia: Servicio de Publicaciones de la Universidad, pp. 51–7.

Petelski, C. (1972), 'Stenogram z posiedzenia Komisji Kolaudacyjnej w dn. 28/6/1972', *Filmoteka Narodowa*, A-344, pozycja 62, pp. 1–10.

Pikulski, T. (2002), *Prywatna historia telewizji publicznej*, Warszawa: Muza SA.

Pilati, A. (1987), *Il nuovo sistema dei media*, Milan: Comunità.

Pokorna-Ignatowicz, K. (2003), *Telewizja w systemie politycznym i medialnym PRL. Między polityką a widzem*, Kraków: Wydawnictwo Uniwersytetu Jagiellońskiego.

Powrie, P. (2001), *Jean-Jacques Beineix*, Manchester: Manchester University Press.

Prédal, R. (1991), *Le cinéma français depuis 1945*, Paris: Nathan.

'Produkcja filmów dla programu telewizyjnego' (1963), *Archiwum Telewizji Polskiej SA*, 1445/4, 2.

Pryds, H. (1991), 'Medea – et tv-æstetisk eksperiment', in *Sekvens*, København: Institut for Film, TV & Kommunikation, pp. 141–56.

Puente, C. A. (1994), *Las relaciones entre el cinema y la televisión en España y otros países de Europa*, Madrid: CAM/Egeda.

Puttnam, D. (1997), *Undeclared War: Struggle for Control of the World's Film Industry*, London: HarperCollins.

Quintana, A. (1995), 'El proceso del conocimiento. *Socrate* de Roberto Rossellini', *Archivos de la filmoteca valenciana*, 20, June, pp. 132–45.

Raspiengeas, J.-C. (2001), *Bertrand Tavernier*, Paris: Flammarion.

Rentschler, E. (2000), 'From new German cinema to the post-wall cinema of consensus', in M. Hjort and S. Mackenzie (eds), *Cinema & Nation*, London and New York: Routledge, pp. 260–77.

Rickett, J. (2006), 'Word association', *Screen International*, 2 June, pp. 12–13.

Roberts, G. (2004), 'Movie making in the new media age', in D. Gauntlett and R. Horsley (ed.). *Web.Studies*, London: Hodder Arnold, pp. 103–13.

Roberts, G. (2006a), 'Soluble fish', in G. Harper and R. Stone (eds), *The Unsilvered Screen*, London: Wallflower, pp. 91–102.

Roberts, G. (2006b) 'Television and DVD', in D. Gomery and L. Hockley (eds), *Television Industries*, London: BFI, pp. 31–5.

Roberts, G. and P. M. T. Taylor (eds) (2001), *The Historian, Television and Television History*, Luton: University of Luton Press.

Roberts, G. and H. Wallis (2002), *Introducing Film*, London: Arnold.

Roberts, L. (2002), 'From Sarajevo to Didcot: an interview with Pawel Pawlikowski', *New Cinemas: Journal of Contemporary Film*, 2, pp. 91–7.

Roberts, M. (2003), 'Decoding "D-Day": multi-channel television at the millennium', in M. Hjort and S. MacKenzie, *Purity and Provocation. Dogma 95*, London: BFI.

Rohrbach, G. (2001), 'Günter Rohrbach: Geld regiert das Geschäft', MMA-Seminar Address, 13 November, Munich, www.film20.de/wir/?c = zieleundpositionen&ID = 698 (accessed 3 July 2006).

Romanò, A. (1985), *Televisione. La provisoria identità italiana*, Turin: Fondazione Agnelli.

Rose, J. (1984), *The Case of Peter Pan or the Impossibility of Children's Fiction*, London: Macmillan Press.

RTVE Anuario (1976 to present), Madrid, RTVE.

Sandford, J. (1980), *The New German Cinema*, London: O. Wolff.

Sargeant, A. (2005), *British Cinema*, London: BFI.

Schepelern, P. (1997), *Lars von Triers elementer*, København: Rosinante.

Schepelern, P. (2003), 'Lidelse i et allegorisk univers', *EKKO*, 20, p. 26.

Schulte, C. and W. Siebers (eds) (2002), *Kluges Fernsehen. Alexander Kluges Kulturmagazine*, Frankfurt: Suhrkamp.

Seidl, C. (1987), *Der deutsche Film der fünfziger Jahre*, München: Wilhelm Heyne Verlag.

Sepúlveda, C. R. de (1970), 'Sócrates en Venecia', *Teleradio*, 663, 7 September, p. 9.

Sinclair, I. (2004), 'The cruel seaside', *Sight and Sound*, 10, October, p. 18.

Skotte, K. (2003), 'Filmland for children from "hygge" to humanism', *Film/Kids* (Danish Film Insitute), pp. 14–17.

Smith, A. (ed.) (1995), *Television, an international industry*, Oxford: Oxford University Press.

Smith, P. J. (2003), *Contemporary Spanish Culture. TV, Fashion, Art and Film*, Cambridge: Blackwells.

Soderbergh Widding, A. and J. Fullerton (eds) (2000), *Moving Images from Edison to Webcam*, Eastleigh: John Libbey.

Sontag, S. (1996), 'Decay of Cinema', www.cinematicthreads.com/sontag1.php Originally in *The New York Times*, 25 February.

Søndergaard, H. (1996), 'Fundaments in the history of Danish television', in I. Bondebjerg and F. Bono (eds), *Television in Scandinavia: History, Politics and Aesthetics*, pp. 11–40.

Stachówna, G. (1994), 'Film telewizyjny', in E. Zajicek (ed.), *Encyklopedia Kultury Polskiej XX Wieku*, Warszawa: Instytut Kultury/Komitet Kinematografii, pp. 181–98.

Stempel, W. (1974), 'Notatka w sprawie udziału filmu i materiałów filmowych w programie TVP oraz współpracy telewizji z kinematografią 9/12/74', *Archiwum Telewizji Polskiej 1658/20*, 1, pp. 1–7.

'Stenogram z posiedzenia Komisji Kolaudacyjnej 19/4/1968' (1968), *Filmoteka Narodowa A-344*, pozyzja 449, pp. 1–20.

'Stenogram z posiedzenia Komisji Kolaudacyjnej w dn. 28/6/1972' (1972), *Filmoteka Narodowa A-344*, pozycja 62, pp. 1–10.

Stevenson, J (2002), *Lars Von Trier*, London: BFI Publishing.

Steward, J. (1955), *Theory of Culture Change: the Methodology of Multilinear Evolution*, Urbana: University of Illinois Press.

Street, S. (1997), *British National Cinema*, London: Routledge.

Tobin, Y. (2005), 'Pendant un tournage, je ne dors jamais', interview with Pawel Pawlikowski, *Positif*, 533, July/August, pp. 114–19.

Toeplitz, K. T. (1968), in 'Stenogram z posiedzenia Komisji Kolaudacyjnej 19/4/1968', *Filmoteka Narodowa*, A-344, pozyzja 449, pp. 1–20.

Torreiro, M. (1995), 'Del tardofranquismo a la democracia (1969–1982)', in *Historia del cine español*, Madrid: Cátedra.

Trasatti, S. (1978), *Rossellini e la televisione*, Rome: La Rassegna.

Trautmann, E. and J. Bang (eds) (1980), *Årbog 1980*, København: DR.

Trzaska, K. (2002), 'Uwagi dotyczące umowy kooprodukcyjnej na *Przedwiośnie* z dn. 12/06/02', Agencja Telewizji Polskiej SA *Przedwiośnie* TIF 0001677-1681.

Uecker, M. (2000), *Alexander Kluge*, Marburg: Schüren Verlag.

Ulmer, G. (1989), *Teletheory: Grammatology in the Age of Video*, New York: Routledge.

'Umowa koprodukcyjna na realizację filmu i serialu TV *Ogniem i mieczem* 4/8/97' (1997), Agencja Telewizji Polskiej SA *Ogniem i mieczem* TCX97 10280.

'Umowa koprodukcyjna na realizację filmu i serialu TV *Przedwiośnie* 05/07/00' (2000), Agencja Telewizji Polskiej SA *Przedwiośnie* TIF 0001677-1681.

'Umowa koprodukcyjna na realizację filmu i serialu TV *Quo Vadis* 20/6/00' (2000), Agencja Telewizji Polskiej SA *Quo Vadis* TIF. 0001375-1379.

Uricchio, W. (1992), 'Television as history: representations of German television broadcasting, 1935–44', in B. A. Murray and Christopher J. Wickham (eds), *Framing the Past The Historiography of German Cinema and Television*, Carbondale and Edwardsville, IL: Southern Illinois University Press, pp. 167–96.

Uricchio, W. (1996), 'Envisioning the audience: perceptions of early German television's audiences, 1935–1944', *Aura Filmvetenskaplig Tidskrift*, 2 (4), accessed at www.let.uu.nl/~william.uricchio/personal/SWEDEN1.html (accessed 3 July 2006).

'Uwagi Komitetu do Spraw Radia i Telewizji do materiałów przedstawionych na Sejmową Komisję Kultury i Sztuki, p.t. "Analiza sytuacji w kinematografii polskiej – kwiecień 1973" 12/02/74' (1974), *Archiwum Telewizji Polskiej SA*, 1716/68, 1.

Soto Vázquez, B. (2003), 'El censo, el mapa y el museo (Autocrítica con crisis como excusa)', in Alonso (ed.), *Once miradas sobre la crisis y el cine español*, Madrid: Ocho y medio, pp. 181–92

Vincendeau, G. and R. Dyer (eds) (1992), *Popular European Cinema*, London: Routledge.

Walker, A. (2000), *Icons in the Fire*, Orion: London.

Wenders, W. (2001), *Wim Wenders: On Film*, London: Faber and Faber Limited.

Wertenstein, W. (1974), 'O realizacji filmu *Ziemia obiecana*', *Film*, 70, 2 June, pp. 15–16.

Wetzel, K. (1987), 'Erfahrungen mit neuen Medien im Ausland: Italien, Großbrittannien, Frankreich', in Arbeitsgemeinschaft der Filmjournalisten Hamburger Filmbüro (ed.), *Neue Medien contra Filmkultur?*, Berlin: Wissenschaftsverlag Volker Spiess GmbH, pp. 11–27.

Winston, B. (1996), *Technologies of Seeing*, London: BFI.

Zajicek, E. (1992), *Poza ekranem. Kinematografia polska 1918–1991*, Warszawa: Filmoteka Narodowa/Wydawnictwo Artystyczne i Filmowe.

Zajicek, E. (ed.) (1994a), *Encyklopedia Kultury Polskiej XX Wieku*, Warszawa: Instytut Kultury/Komitet Kinematografii.

Zajicek, E. (1994b), 'Kinematografia', in E. Zajicek (ed.), *Encyklopedia Kultury Polskiej XX Wieku*, Warszawa: Instytut Kultury/Komitet Kinematografii, pp. 35–100.

Zeruneith, I. (1995a), 'Carrots and candyfloss – the diary of a children's film consultant', in I. Zeruneith (ed.), *Wide-Eyed. Films for Children and Young People in the Nordic Countries 1977–1993*, Copenhagen: Tiderne Skifter, pp. 33–48.

Zeruneith, I. (ed.) (1995b), *Wide-Eyed. Films for Children and Young People in the Nordic Countries 1977–1993*, Copenhagen: Tiderne Skifter.

Zettl, H. (1999), *Sight Sound Motion. Applied Media Aesthetics,* Belmont, CA: Wadsworth Publishing Company.

WEBSITES

http://histv2.free.fr/cadrehistory
www.bbc.co.uk/bbcfilms
www.bfi.org.uk
www.cinema.italiano.net
www.dogme95.dk
www.draftzero.co.uk
www.guardian.co.uk
www.history.acusd.edu
www.mediasalles.it
www.nao.org.uk
www.screendaily.com
www.Screenyorkshire.co.uk
www.ukfilmcouncil.org.uk
www.weboptimiser.com
www.dfi.dk/English

INDEX